Northwest
women

Northwest women

An Annotated Bibliography of

Sources on the History

of Oregon and Washington

Women, 1787-1970

Karen J. Blair

WSU PRESS

Washington State University Press
Pullman, Washington

Washington State University Press
PO Box 645910
Pullman, Washington 99164-5910
Phone: 800-354-7360   Fax: 509-335-8568
©1997 by the Board of Regents of Washington State University
All rights reserved
First printing 1997

Cover and title-page photographs courtesy of University of Washington Libraries.

Library of Congress Cataloging-in-Publication Data
Blair, Karen J.
    Northwest women : an annotated bibliography of sources on the history of Oregon and Washington women, 1787-1970 / Karen J. Blair.
      p.   cm.
    Includes index.
    1. Women—Oregon—History—Bibliography. 2. Women—Washington (State)—History—Bibliography. I. Title.
Z7964.U5073 1997
[HQ1438.07
016.3054'09795—dc21   96-52437
                                CIP

To Jesse Blair Smith

Photographer Asahel Curtis captured two steam cooks at work in the Apex Fish Company.
(#27677, Special Collections, University of Washington Libraries)

This float in the Rose Parade, a June ritual in Portland, won the 1936 Sweepstakes for its portrayal of early settlers bound for the Oregon Territory.
(#17205, Special Collections, University of Washington Libraries)

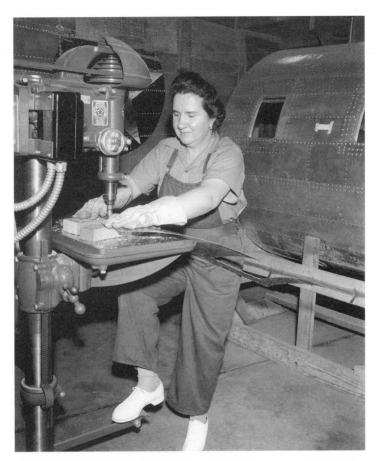

The Northwest defense industry during World War II attracted women to factory work, especially airplane construction, in significant numbers. Karen Tucker Anderson, Karen Beck Skold, and Amy Kesselman are among the historians who have documented this phenomenon in Seattle and Portland. *(#2330, Special Collections, University of Washington Libraries)*

CONTENTS

This yeomanette assisted the U.S. Navy during World War I. War service has provided Northwest women the opportunity to demonstrate patriotism through hard work and sacrifice.
(#17206, Special Collections, University of Washington Libraries)

PREFACE

On Labor Day of 1979, I moved to Seattle to teach women's history at the University of Washington. Anxious to acquaint myself with a region that was totally unfamiliar to me, I immediately began to explore the city's bookstores. I was eager to acquire every volume available on Northwest women's history to fill in the gaps in my knowledge and become familiar with the historical figures my students had grown up with. Puzzled by the absence of titles on the shelves, I first assumed that local enthusiasm for my subject was so great that the citizens had purchased all the works off the stands. I quickly realized that the problem was quite different. The studies were all too scarce, indeed non-existent. There were none to be bought.

In the popular as well as the scholarly literature, the men's contributions loomed multitudinous and colorful. The presence of explorers, frontiersmen, fishermen, and early commercial entrepreneurs was vivid. In modern times, the aviation and lumber industries loomed largest. A reader might infer from the standard histories by Norman Clark, Nard Jones, Bill Speidel, Murray Morgan, and Clifford Drury that women were in as short supply throughout the century as they were in the earliest days of settlement. If women were raising families on farms or in cities and experimental communities; founding churches, charities, and symphonies; working as nurses, waitresses, teachers, journalists, and boarding-house keepers or as aviators and riveters; agitating for suffrage, peace, and civil rights; this did not appear to be documented. That the Japanese-American women had experienced internment during World War II as fully as their husbands, fathers, brothers and sons, that women felt the Great Depression as deeply as their spouses is very likely, yet these tales did not appear in the historical literature.

It became clear that the only way to rectify these omissions was to discover the extent of women's participation and contributions by locating all the relevant historical works, skimpy as they might sometimes be. From such a bibliographic foundation, new efforts could arise to examine neglected topics. With the evidence assembled, better narratives would make possible fuller histories that detailed women's as well as men's contributions.

To that end, I began to assess the collections in major Northwest libraries, including the University of Washington, University of Oregon, and Oregon Historical Society Library. I recorded the title of every published book, scholarly article, and important reference work published before 1995 that addressed women's roles in Washington and Oregon history. The sources I recovered provided documentation about women as early as 1787, when the historical record began to be documented by Euro-American traders of American Indian goods. My study encompasses sources published prior to 1995 that describe women's experiences through 1970. That was the year the citizens of Washington State passed the Equal Rights Amendment. The energy behind that amendment and the consequences of the contemporary women's movement are topics that historians have yet to interpret.

In addition to reading shelves of books and combing Northwest bibliographies, I exhausted the standard reference guides, including *America: History and Life*, Christine Fisher's *Index to Women's Periodicals*, and indices to the *Pacific Historical Review*, *Pacific Northwest Forum*, *Pacific Northwest Quarterly*, *Quarterly of the Oregon Historical Society*, *Washington Historical Quarterly*, *Western Historical Quarterly*, and *Western States Jewish History Journal*. After locating and reading over a thousand historical works, I identified 722 sources with material of value for researchers in women's history. How relieved and excited I was to discover this array of sources in the libraries after my discouraging first search in bookstores. The 722 sources I describe in this volume will not be found in most bookstores, but they can be readily obtained by inter-library loan offices at college and large public libraries. My annotations of the texts listed here will, I hope, provide sufficient specificity to identify the particular people, locales, and subjects illuminated therein. (The spellings of names in my annotations respect the choices of the authors surveyed.) Some summaries are longer than others, reflecting the variety of subject matter included in each work of history.

I have also listed the subjects of the photographs included in these texts, for researchers who seek to study women's history from visual materials. At the back of my book, an index identifies the specific individuals, locales, and subjects to be identified for researchers.

What, then, is contained here for students of Northwest women's history? This record identifies a stunning array of women players from the region's past. Seattle boasts the first woman mayor of a large American city, Bertha Landes (1926-1928). The first woman to conduct a symphony orchestra, Madame Davenport-Engberg, did so in Bellingham, Washington. Seattle native Anna Louise Strong, revered and buried in the People's Republic of China, began her political education at the Everett massacre of 1916. Mary Carr Moore, composer of operas, enjoyed her first hearing in Puget Sound women's clubs during the early part of this century. May Arkwright Hutton, the mining-town cook and boarding-house keeper who invested successfully in silver mines, became Spokane's outrageous millionaire and friend of unions and woman suffrage. In Portland, Abigail Scott Duniway penned eighteen novels while she edited the *New Northwest* and led the Oregon suffrage campaigns. The reader will meet these and many other women in historical studies of their careers.

Besides these distinguished individuals, the sources listed here also will enable researchers to locate the invisible groups of women who founded the Astoria Sanitary Commission during the Civil War, who operated the canneries, who cooked at lumber camps and on salmon trollers, who ran the schools and organized the charities. The available body of historical literature is not balanced, however. While considerable material exists on missionary Narcissa Whitman, the Lewis and Clark expedition guide Sacajawea, and the homesteaders who moved west by overland trail, attention has yet to be bestowed on most other women who helped to build the Pacific Northwest. Much work remains to be done by future scholars of the region.

For all my long effort, readers should not expect to find here a comprehensive guide to Northwest women's history. I have not attempted to include sources in languages other than English. I have not included the growing numbers of unpublished oral history transcriptions by and about women. I have excluded women's memoirs, unless they are complemented by notes from historians or editors. I have not included works of fiction by or about local women, although novelists like Mary McCarthy, Ella Rhoads Higginson, and Abigail Scott Duniway are identified herein through autobiographies or biographies. Finally, I have not incorporated primary sources. Readers can turn to reference works in my text, including Andrea Hinding's *Women's History Sources* and the Washington State Archives Guide, for superb lists of manuscript collections on women. Government documents, newspapers, films, men's overland diaries, and photograph archives will, of course, yield other assistance.

On balance, then, this annotated bibliography provides a keyhole to a large and unexplored history. Its entries identify some crucial published materials for those who care to conduct deeper investigations into women's roles in the development of Washington and Oregon. To the scholars and students, teachers and librarians, journalists and local history enthusiasts, storytellers and feminists, and others who seek material on Northwest women's history, I wish you well. My hope is that you will write the new histories that do justice to all those women who helped build the region. May the near future bring a heavy shelf of historical studies that document women's vast contributions to the Pacific Northwest.

BIBLIOGRAPHY

1. Abbot, Mabel. "The Waitresses of Seattle." *Life and Labor* (February 1914): 48-49. One photograph of Waitresses Recreation Home, Seattle; one of Alice M. Lord, Secretary-Treasurer, Waitresses Union, Local 240.

This article provides a brief history of the Waitresses Union, including its gains in attaining improved wages and hours for members. Its Recreation Home, a community center and retreat, is highlighted. Lists of officers are given.

2. Abdill, George B. "New Odessa: Douglas County's Russian Communal Colony." *Umpqua Trapper* 1, pt. 1 (Winter 1965): 10-14; 2, pt. 2 (Spring 1966): 16-21. One photograph of site of New Odessa communal hall.

This article offers a brief history of New Odessa, a commune in Douglas County, Oregon, which existed from 1882 to 1886. The principal residents were immigrant Russian Jewish men. There is little mention of women, with the exception of the marriage of Annutta Glantz, one of four single women members of the community.

3. Ackerman, Lillian A. "The Effect of Missionary Ideals on Family Structure and Women's Roles in Plateau Indian Culture." *Idaho Yesterdays* 31 (Spring/Summer 1987): 64-73. Notes.

Ackerman explores the issues that created tension between Christian missionaries to the Pacific Northwest and Native Americans: monogamy, patriarchy, farming, permanent dwellings, and divorce.

4. ———. "Sexual Equality on the Colville Indian Reservation in Traditional and Contemporary Contexts." In *Women in Pacific Northwest History: An Anthology*, ed. Karen J. Blair, pp. 152-169. Seattle: University of Washington Press, 1988. Notes. Photograph of Nancy Judge.

The author, an anthropologist, asserts that men were not dominant over females in eleven Plateau Indian groups on the Colville Indian Reservation in Washington state. Between 1979 and 1980, she interviewed forty-five elders, aged sixty to ninety, and collected considerable information about the customs of their youth from 1910 to 1930. She compared her findings to observations by younger informants, describing the contemporary scene. Ackerman looked at men's and women's roles in politics, economy, religion, and domesticity.

5. Adams, Cecelia E.M. "Crossing the Plains in 1852." *Transactions of the Oregon Pioneer Association, 1904*. 32nd annual reunion, pp. 288-329. Portland: Oregon Pioneer Association, 1905.

This is a detailed record of pioneer Cecelia Adams's overland trip from Missouri to Oregon in 1852. She includes details about geography and fauna along the way, and also about the food supply for people and cattle. She provides few references to individuals in her account.

6. Adams, Emma H. *To and Fro, Up and Down in Southern California, Oregon, and Washington Territory, with Sketches in Arizona, New Mexico and British Columbia*. Cincinnati: Cranston and Stowe, 1888. 608 pages. Many drawings of places, not of people.

Nearly half of this long journalistic narrative is devoted to Oregon and Washington. Between 1883 and 1886 Emma Adams traveled throughout the West as a reporter. The book records her impressions of local geographies, population characteristics, economy, and agriculture. Women are mentioned anecdotally throughout. Chap. 37, "A Noble Woman," is about the life of Abigail Scott Duniway. Chap. 61, "A Peculiar Wedding-trip," is an account by Mrs. Tolman of her trip across the plains in 1852. Chap. 27, "Women as Cultivators of the Soil," is a fascinating description of women land owners, speculators, and farmers in Southern California.

7. Adams, Harriet L. *A Woman's Journeyings in the New Northwest*. Cleveland, Ohio: B-P Printing Company, 1892. 180 pages.

This is an account by a woman who came to Washington in the spring of 1890 to establish chapters of the Women's Christian Temperance Union. She provides some strong descriptions of local women and their achievements, such as the woman school superintendent in Lincoln County who won three elections, but was denied office on account of her sex.

8. Additon, Lucia H. Faxon. *Twenty Eventful Years of the Oregon Woman's Christian Temperance Union 1880-1900*. Portland: Gotshall Printing Company, 1904. 112 pages. Twenty-eight photographs of officers, one of Corvallis Headquarters.

As state historian for the Oregon Women's Christian Temperance Union, Additon provides a detailed narrative of the organization's programs, conventions, and officers in its early years. The book is rich in song lyrics, poetry, correspondence, and speeches from the 1891 Pacific Coast Conference in Portland and from annual state conferences, and contains twenty-six biographies of prominent members.

9. Agatz, Cora Wilson. "A Journey Across the Plains in 1866." *Pacific Northwest Quarterly* 27 (April 1936): 170-174.

This reminiscence emphasizes the positive aspects of the journey across the plains which the author took as a seven-year-old girl. She provides details about the outfitting equipment, the women's clothing, and one friendly encounter with Native Americans.

10. Alcorn, Rowena L., and Gordon D. Alcorn. "'Tacoma Seamen's Rest': Waterfront Mission 1897-1903." *Oregon Historical Quarterly* 66 (1965): 101-131. Notes. Pictures of sailing ships, portraits of seamen, one photograph of the Seamen's Rest building, one portrait of Mrs. Birgitte Funnemark and her daughter Christine Funnemark.

This is a detailed account of Seamen's Rest in Tacoma (1897-1903), a non-denominational mission for sailors founded by Birgitte Funnemark and managed by Birgitte and her daughter Christine. Details are provided about the mission's services and the seamen who used the mission. The biography of its founder is provided as well.

11. *All My Somedays.* Tacoma: Tacoma Public Library, 1982. A photograph of each of the subjects is provided in each pamphlet.

Oral histories, conducted under the auspices of the Pierce County Library and Tacoma Public Library in the late 1970s and early 1980s, have been printed in separate, attractive pamphlets, with cover photographs of the subjects. Ninety-three of the 113 edited transcriptions reveal women's life stories, but all make mention of women in Pacific Northwest history.

12. Allen, A.J., comp. *Ten Years in Oregon: Travels and Adventures of Doctor E. White and Lady West of the Rocky Mountains.* Ithaca, New York: Mack, Andrus and Company, 1848. 430 pages.

This book contains a detailed, almost daily, account of the life of Dr. Elijah White and his wife, Methodist missionaries to American Indians during the 1840s in Oregon Territory. The emotions, physical difficulties, and activities of Mrs. White are included throughout. Other female friends and acquaintances of the Whites, Native American and Caucasian, are also described anecdotally.

13. Allen, Barbara. *Homesteading the High Desert.* Salt Lake City: University of Utah Press, 1987. xx, 190 pages. Notes, bibliography, and index. Five photographs of women, including homesteaders; Anna Long and Laura Anderson, Fourth of July celebration; picnic; gathering of Jennie Anderson, Mildred Steinhoff, Anna Long, Bertha Hatch, Ethel Johnson, Anna Steinhoff, and Mary Long.

Allen interviewed twelve women in the Fort Rock–Christmas Lake–Silver Lake area of northern Lake County, eastern Oregon, in 1978. They reported on their homesteading experiences in the 1910s and described their early houses, furnishings, and inventories. Quotations and examples from the oral histories are used throughout the essay. Included is rich detail on women's activities, including chopping wood, grubbing sagebrush, securing supplies, constructing schoolhouses, and initiating church, holiday, and social activities.

14. Allen, Eleanor. *Canvas Caravans.* Portland: Binfords and Mort, 1946. 125 pages.

This book consists largely of quotations from the 1852 overland trail diary of Esther Belle Hanna, supplemented with commentary by the author. Allen provides details about clothing, food, and forts along the way. The diary excerpts are detailed, conveying the emotional as well as the practical side of the overland journey.

15. Allen, Michael. "The Rise and Decline of the Early Rodeo Cowgirl: The Career of Mabel Strickland, 1916-1941." *Pacific Northwest Quarterly* 83 (October 1992): 122-127. Notes. Three photographs of Mabel Strickland in competition at the rodeo and one with a group of six other cowgirls.

This is a biography of Mabel Delong Strickland (1897-1976), who was born in Walla Walla, Washington, and became a world champion relay and trick rider, calf roper, and bronc rider. It catalogues her early life, career highlights, prizes of the 1920s and '30s, and her family life. There is discussion of post-World War II opportunities for cowgirls in rodeo competition.

16. American National CattleWomen, Inc. *Cowbelles/Cattlewomen: American National Cattlewomen, 1977-1986.* Englewood, Colorado: American National CattleWomen, Inc., 1987. vii, 230 pages. Photographs of members.

This is a history of the women's voluntary organization, the American National CattleWomen, which was renamed from Cowbelles in the 1980s. Wives of ranchers formed the group in Arizona in 1939 to promote the cattle industry. The section on Oregon (pp. 165-168) narrates the members' cooperation with the Oregon Beef Council, local businesses, and home economics classes. In Washington (pp. 182-184), members used in-store demonstrations, the Agricultural Exposition in Spokane, and 4-H Club functions. National and state officers are listed.

17. Andersen, Helen McReavy. *How When and Where on Hood Canal.* Everett, Washington: Puget Press, 1960. 83 pages. Photographs of the author, Skokomish women including Phoebe and her granddaughter weaving baskets in 1903, and an 1889 picnic at Hoodsport.

This is an autobiographical account, developed from a paper created for the Hood Canal Woman's Club. The author, born in 1882 in Union City, Washington, describes her teachers, neighbors, and work as a postmaster from 1915-1952. The volume also contains poetry, newspaper clippings, correspondence, and the autobiography of Andersen's mother, Fannie Dow Gove (Mrs. John) McReavy, as reported to the Daughters of the Pioneers of Washington in 1924. This details her 1854 voyage from Boston around Cape Horn via San Francisco, to join her father in Steilacoom, Washington. She became a rancher in Nisqually Valley, and the book describes her social life there.

18. Anderson, Florence Mary (Bennett). *In Memoriam: Ellen Garfield Smith, Librarian of Walla Walla Public Library from 1907-1938.* Cover Title: *The Good Librarian.* Walla Walla, 1939. 15 pages. Photographs of Ellen Garfield Smith.

This very brief essay is concerned mainly with the history of the concept of the library. It was written to be read before members of the Altrusa Club of Walla Walla. It contains little specific information about Ellen Garfield Smith herself, but details the characteristics of a good librarian.

19. Anderson, Irving W. "Probing the Riddle of the Bird Woman." *Montana: The Magazine of Western History* 23 (Fall 1973): 2-17. Notes. Two photographs of Sacajawea statues in Bismarck, North Dakota, and Helena, Montana.

Sacajawea was the only woman who accompanied the Lewis and Clark expedition. This account summarizes the debate over her death date, asserting that she probably died in December of 1812 at Fort Manuel, South Dakota. Anderson provides extensive quotations from Clark's journal and Professor Grace Hebard's history of the exploration.

20. Anderson, Karen. *Wartime Women: Sex Roles, Family Relations, and The Status of Women During World War II.* Westport, Connecticut: Greenwood Press, 1981. 198 pages. Footnotes, bibliography, index.

This examines women in the factory and in the family, as well as their child-care systems in World War II, using evidence from three cities—Baltimore, Detroit, and Seattle—where defense production was significant. Although the author recognizes that important new patterns emerged during the war years, such as better job opportunities, greater numbers of married women working for wages, and increased divorce and mobility, she asserts that wartime changes did not signal a radical revision of conventional ideas regarding women's proper social and economic roles.

21. Anderson, Martha. *Black Pioneers of the Northwest, 1800-1918.* No city: Privately printed, 1980. 228 pages. Bibliography, index. Photographs of Oregon women: Rose and John Jackson's family, slaveholder Nathaniel Ford, Louisa Thatcher Flowers, Lavina Wright, Gwendolyn Eliza Hooker, Sybil Haber, Mrs. Clifford Freeman Dixon, Beatrice Cannady-Taylor (first African American woman lawyer in Oregon), Rosebud Study Club marching in the Rose Festival Parade, officers of the Oregon Association of Colored Women's Clubs, dressmaker Mrs. Julia L. Fuller, suffragist Hattie Redmond, and Portland churches and residences. Photographs of Washington women: teacher Mary Victoria Hinckling Coones and her daughter Audrey, Mrs. Horace Cayton (daughter of U.S. Senator Hiram Revels), Seattle Rescue Mission founders Mr. and Mrs. L. P. Ray, Women's Christian Temperance Union membership, musician Nettie J. Asberry, Tacoma hairdresser Ella Ryan, stewardesses from the African Methodist Episcopal Church in 1917, Rev. J. Logan and Lillian Craw, hotel owner Cleo Jones, Princeton Cafe owner Mabel M. Stanway, grocer Margaret Cogswell, beauty school founder Elizabeth M. De Neal.

Chap. 3 deals with Oregon pioneers and chap. 7 with those from Washington. Anderson discusses schools, churches, politics, publishers, servicemen in World War I, businesses, occupational patterns, neighborhoods, and organizations, and provides thumbnail biographies of early African American settlers in the Pacific Northwest.

22. Andrews, Mildred. *Seattle Women: A Legacy of Community Development, a Pictorial History, 1851-1920.* Seattle: Seattle-King County YWCA, 1984. 64 pages. Notes, bibliography, index. Seventy-nine photographs of individuals: Princess Angeline, Sarah Yesler, Theresa Brown Dixon, Mother Joseph, Mina Eckstein, Esther Levy, Lizzie and Isaac Cooper, Catherine and Rev. David Blaine, Lucy Whipple Carr, Mrs. Reuben Hill, Georgina MacDougall, Nellie Cornish, Nettie J. Asberry, Caroline McGilvra Burke, Louisa Boren, Mary Ann Boren Denny, Hyang Family), buildings (Providence Hospital, YWCA Restaurant at 1909 Fair, Phyllis Wheatley Branch of YWCA, Settlement House, Seattle Children's Home, Florence Crittenton Home, Holy Names Academy, Woman's Building at 1909 Alaska-Yukon-Pacific Exposition); groups of women: Washington Equal Suffrage Association, Frances Harper Women's Christian Temperance Union, Young Women's Christian Association, Seattle Colored Red Cross, Camp Fire Girls, Tanaka Dressmaking School alumnae, Ladies Musical Club string quartet, YWCA Pageant, Madame Nakatani dance program, Chinatown women, Japanese picture brides, Mercer Girls, nurses, and Philippine women.

Here are brief histories of women's involvement with and development of Seattle institutions prior to 1920. The areas explored are health care (Providence Hospital, Children's Orthopedic Hospital); social services (Seattle YWCA, Settlement House, Ladies Relief Society, Mother Ryther Home, Florence Crittendon Home for Unwed Mothers, Seattle Red Cross Society, Camp Fire Girls, Girl Scouts); education (Seattle public schools, Holy Names Academy, University of Washington Young Women's Christian Association, University of Washington Woman's Building, Theta Sigma Phi, Japanese schools); arts (Ladies Musical Club, Cornish School, children's theatre, Japanese dancers), and urban amenities (Seattle Public Library, Museum of History and Industry).

23. ———. *Woman's Place: A Guide to Seattle and King County History.* Seattle: Gemil Press, 1994. xii, 339 pages. Bibliography and index. Photographs of suffragists tacking up posters; defense workers at Boeing in World War II; nuns canvasing miners for donations; Native Americans picking hops; Snoqualmie Mill workers; Woman's Building at Alaska-Yukon-Pacific Exposition of 1909; Vasa Sewing Club float in Swedish parade; daughters of U.S. War Veterans drill team in the 1930s; fund-raisers from the Children's Orthopedic Hospital Guild; YWCA parade in 1913; garment workers in the 1903 Labor Day parade; day care center for Japanese Americans; African American nurses during World War II; Red Cross motor brigade in 1917; Cornish School dancers in 1916; Mayor Bertha Landes; Carrie Shumway, Alice Seaton, and Sadie Holloway, postmistress.

This compendium surveys 262 sites in eleven neighborhoods where women's activities took place through Seattle and King County history. For each, Andrews provides an address and a short description of the building's link to women's history. Among the places included are the estates of founding families, the Girl Scout camp, Red Cross offices, charitable institutions and arts facilities founded by women, Waitresses Union Hall, churches and businesses in which women played prominent roles, YWCAs, dorms at the University of Washington named for trustee Ruth Karr McKee and professor Theresa McMahon, Raitt Hall (the home economics building), Helene Madeson swimming pool, the Woman's Building from the Alaska-Yukon-Pacific Exposition of 1909, girls' academies, and clubhouses.

24. Applegate, Shannon. *Skookum: An Oregon Pioneer Family's History and Lore.* New York: Beech Tree Books, 1988. 464 pages. Bibliography, index. Twelve photographs of women, including Cynthia Parker Applegate, Lucy and Irene Applegate, and Evea Applegate.

The Applegate family crossed the plains from Missouri to Oregon in 1843 and the women members kept extensive records of their experiences, including diaries, letters, published and unpublished memoirs, sketches, and photographs. The documents and the author's narrative describe the journey and the homesteading story. Biographies of five women are provided: Melinda Miller Applegate, Irene Applegate, Lucy, Eva, and Evea Applegate.

25. Appleton, John B., comp. *The Pacific Northwest, A Selected Bibliography, 1930-1939.* Portland: Northwest Regional Council, 1939. 456 pages.

This bibliography covers research in Northwest natural resources and social-economic fields. It treats the period from 1930 to 1939. Section 8, "Human Resources and Problems," contains many citations relevant to women's studies. This section includes studies on population trends, emigration patterns, housing, employment, labor relations, cost of living, and welfare and relief organizations. A large number of the entries are publications of local and regional governmental bodies. Several entries about employment are specifically related to women.

26. Appleton, Marion B. *Index of Pacific Northwest Portraits*. Seattle: University of Washington Press, 1972. 210 pages. Bibliography, index.

This work lists paintings of twelve thousand men and women associated with the history of the Pacific Northwest up through the first quarter of the twentieth century. These likenesses were located in 324 books, listed by author and region. Thousands of women are accessible through the index.

27. Armitage, Susan H. "The Challenge of Women's History." In *Women in Pacific Northwest History: Essays*, ed. Karen J. Blair, pp. 233-245. Seattle: University of Washington Press, 1988. Notes, bibliography. Photographs of harvest cook for crew in eastern Washington wheat fields, and Ella Diedrich Potter, operator in the old Chewelah Telephone Company Exchange.

Armitage asserts that "women's history seeks to explain the significance of the daily lives, activities, and values of ordinary women" and declares that "present Pacific Northwest history is incomplete" without it. Using Gerda Lerner's framework for the development of women's history, Armitage explains the virtues of beginning research with biographies of women worthies who made obvious contributions to the past and then moving on to document the general contributions women have made to families, education, health care, community building, and other arenas where they have been prominent but undervalued. Finally, we will arrive at transitional history, whereby scholars can enrich their view of the past by contrasting the ways men and women viewed their place in Northwest development. The use of women's diaries, letters, and oral histories will produce new issues, evidence, and perspectives about the past.

28. ————. "Everyday Encounters: Indians and the White Woman in the Palouse." *Pacific Northwest Forum* 7 (Summer-Fall, 1982): 27-30.

Drawing on oral histories from the Latah County Historical Society, Whitman County Historical Society, and the Idaho Rural Women's Oral History Project, this describes white contact with Native Americans in the late-nineteenth-century Palouse region of eastern Washington and western Idaho. Expansive quotations describe traders' friendly interactions, along with tense occasions they experienced.

29. Armitage, Susan H., and Deborah Gallacci Wilbert. "Black Women in the Pacific Northwest: A Survey and Research Prospectus." In *Women in Pacific Northwest History: Essays*, ed. Karen J. Blair, pp. 136-151. Seattle: University of Washington Press, 1988. Notes, bibliography. Photographs of Calvary Baptist Church members and Leola Cravens.

Declaring that "the black woman is truly the forgotten person in Pacific Northwest history," the authors urge researchers to investigate demographic and legal sources, to examine mining town histories and records of urban churches and voluntary associations, to use oral histories for the story of work, and to appreciate the value of black newspapers. They provide a selected bibliography of black women in the Pacific Northwest, with categories devoted to background information and statistics, bibliographies and indexes, black women and slavery in the Pacific Northwest, clubs and clubwomen, communities, professional women, work, oral history, and black newspapers.

30. Armitage, Susan, Helen Bannan, Katherine G. Morrissey, and Vicki L. Ruiz. *Women in the West: A Guide to Manuscript Sources*. New York: Garland Publishing, Inc., 1991.

This reference work catalogues the primary sources available at archives throughout the Pacific Northwest. Scholars who push to move beyond the study of secondary works catalogued in this volume will welcome this guide to one-of-a-kind primary materials available in regional repositories.

31. Attwell, Jim. *Early History of Klickitat County*. Skamania, Washington: Tahlkie Books, 1977. 279 pages. Index.

This volume includes an account of the Native American "Sapotiwell," who was friendly to the Joslyn Family; Mrs. E. P. Roberts' story to her daughter Charlotte Roberts about White Salmon block house; and an interview with Mrs. W. D. Bruton about her father's pioneer experiences.

32. Ault, Nelson A. "The Earnest Ladies: The Walla Walla Women's Club and the Equal Suffrage League of 1886-1889." *Pacific Northwest Quarterly* 42 (April 1951): 123-137. Notes.

This article provides a brief history of the women's club and suffrage movements, and of the early legislative and constitutional struggles for suffrage in Washington. The specific activities of the Walla Walla Women's Club and the Equal Suffrage League are discussed in the context of these larger movements. The author draws extensively on minutes of the Walla Walla group.

33. Avery, Mary W. *Washington: A History of the Evergreen State*. Seattle: University of Washington Press, 1961. 362 pages. Notes, bibliography, index. Photographs of women include a painting of a Chinook woman and suffragists hanging political posters in 1910.

This textbook includes a discussion of daily tasks of missionary women Eliza Hart Spalding, Narcissa Prentiss Whitman, and Mary Walker, and briefly mentions the successful campaign of 1910 to win women the vote.

34. Bagley, Clarence B., ed. *Early Catholic Missions in Old Oregon*. 2 vols. Seattle: Lowman and Hanford Company, 1932. 360 pages.

This two-volume set contains early reminiscences and documents of Catholic missionaries in Oregon in the 1830s and 1840s. Vol. 2 contains forty-nine pages of letters written by six Sisters of Notre Dame, established at St. Paul on the Willamette River, to their Mother Superior in Belgium. In the letters they recount their journey to Oregon and their work of establishing and running a school for Native American children.

35. Bagley, Clarence B. *History of King County, Washington*. 4 vols. Chicago-Seattle: The S. J. Clarke Publishing Company, 1929. Index. Vol. 1, 888 pages; vol. 2, 938 pages; vol. 3, 940 pages; vol. 4, 520 pages. Portraits of Susannah Rogers Bagles; Susie Mercer Graham; Alice Mercer Bagles; Indian women; all in vol. 1.

Vol. 1 presents a detailed history of King County, including Seattle, with details of pioneer settlement, relations with Native Americans, industry, public institutions, anti-Chinese agitation, and churches. The book includes a discussion of the Mercer expedition. It also treats the life of Princess Angeline. The biography of Hanna M. Denton includes a long paragraph on the Century Club, of which she was an active member. Also included are Hannah Johnson, M.D.; Elizabeth M. McGilvra, pioneer; Dr. Marmora DeVoe Moody, homeopathic physician; and Mary Brown Winslow, M.D. Portraits and brief biographical sketches of Caroline McGilvra Burke and Mary Boren Denny are included in the biographies of their husbands. Vol. 3 has biographies of Minnie B. Burdon, M.D. and Mabel Seagrave, M.D. Vol. 4 has biographies of Ruth Frances Doherty, dance and drama teacher; Florence Gertrude Douglas, educator; Isabelle Emily Evans, pioneer; Dr. Susie Ethel Frasier, chiropodist; Mary B. Hansen, pioneer; Blanche Livesley Hedman, pioneer; Margarethe S. Raining; and Mary Ann Wells, dance teacher. The biographies include the club memberships, religious and politi-

cal affiliations of the women, as well as their life histories told in one to four pages.

36. ———. *History of Seattle: From the Earliest Settlement to the Present Time*. Chicago: The S.J. Clarke Publishing Company, 1916. Vol. 1: x, 454 pages; vol. 2: vi, 434 pages; vol. 3: 1,157 pages. Index for each volume. Photographs of Angeline, daughter of Chief Seattle, and Mrs. John Webster. A few portraits accompany family biographies.

Vol. 1 is largely concerned with commercial development in the Northwest, but chap. 22 deals with the Mercer expedition, which imported marriageable women to Seattle in the 1860s from the East Coast. Included are the names of all the "Mercer Girls" who married and their children and a 1901 reminiscence of the experience by Asa Mercer. Vol. 2 contains chap. 27 on woman's work, summarizing the contributions of women to Seattle's development, including the fight for woman suffrage and the 1914 Pageant of American Women at Volunteer Park. It surveys many women's organizations, offering their founders, officers, and histories; among them the Ladies Mite Society, Women's Christian Temperance Union, Ladies Relief Society, Equal Rights Association of King County, Woman's Exchange, Library Association, Woman's Home Society for Working Women, Washington Children's Home, Washington State Federation of Women's Clubs, Young Women's Christian Association, Seattle Federation of Women's Clubs, Tuesday Club, Woman's Century Club, and Home Consumer's League. Chap. 36, on philanthropic societies, lists charitable groups of women. Vol. 3, an encyclopedia of biographies, mentions women only as wives and mothers of celebrated male citizens.

37. ———. *In the Beginning: A Sketch of Some Early Events in Western Washington While It Was Still A Part Of 'Old Oregon'*. Seattle: Lowman and Hanford, 1905. 90 pages.

This book offers a brief recounting of Washington history in the 1830s and 1840s, centered primarily around people and events at Fort Nisqually. Women are mentioned only in passing, as brides, wives, and mothers.

38. ———. "The Mercer Immigration: Two Cargoes of Maidens For The Sound Country." *Quarterly of the Oregon Historical Society* 5 (March 1904): 1-24.

This essay compiles in one short space several interesting documents of the Mercer expeditions, including a letter of A. S. Mercer describing the 1866 expedition, the diary of Harriet F. Stevens during the journey of the ship S.S. *Continental* in 1866, a list of "Mercer girls" in both 1864 and 1866, a copy of Mercer's advertisement for the 1866 journey, and other materials. In this narrative, Bagley concentrates on Mercer himself. There is no specific information about the women involved except some marriage announcements.

39. Bailey, Margaret Jewett. *The Grains, or, Passages in the Life of Ruth Rover, with Occasional Pictures of Oregon, Natural and Moral.* Corvallis, Oregon: Oregon State University Press, 1986. Reprint of 1854 edition. Ed. Evelyn Leasher and Robert J. Frank. Notes, bibliography.

In this edition, Edwin R. Bingham has provided a biography of Margaret Jewett Bailey, enumerating the many parallels between the novelist's own life and that of her fictional protagonist. Ruth Rover, *The Grains* heroine, represented a thinly veiled autobiography of Methodist missionary Bailey, whose romantic life inspired controversy in its day. Bailey's poems, diaries, and reviews are quoted in this introduction to the 1854 novel.

40. Baker, Rev. J.C. *Baptist History of the North Pacific Coast with Special Reference to Western Washington, British Columbia, and Alaska.* Philadelphia: American Baptist Publication Society, 1912. xxiii, 472 pages. Most photographs of women are of wives of ministers but also included are Mrs. A.J. Hanford, "Mother of the First Seattle Church"; Mrs. B.S. MacLafferty, Mrs. T.W. Boardman, Mrs. Henry Warren, and Fanny Cheney Bennett, officers in the Woman's Foreign Mission Society of the Pacific Coast; and Mrs. E.T. Tremble, Mrs. A.F. Cruttenden, Mrs. Jennie M. Baker Shank, Mrs. D.A.B. Swansey, faculty of Grace Seminary, Centralia in the 1880s.

Biographies of women include that of Mrs. A. J. Hanford, "Mother of the First Baptist Church in Seattle." Mrs. Elizabeth Holgate, mother of Mrs. A. J. Hanford, donated the land on which the first Seattle Baptist Church was built. Part 5, "Auxiliary Organizations," explores the Women's Foreign Mission Society of the Pacific Coast, organized in 1874. The section is rich with names of women supporters.

41. Bakken, Lavola J. *Lone Rock Free State: A Collection of Historical Adventures and Incidents in Oregon's North Umpqua Valley, 1850 to 1910.* Myrtle Creek, Oregon: The Mail Printers,

1970. 156 pages. Notes, index. Three photographs of women: Elizabeth McReymonds Tipton, Douglas County pioneer Mrs. James Watson, and teacher Lizzie M. (Langworthy) Connine.

Chap. 2 provides an account of Mary Priscilla Avery, who crossed the plains in 1848 and became the bride of Carsena A. Huntley. It provides details about the land, Native Americans, and child-raising.

42. Barchus, Agnes. *Eliza R. Barchus: The Oregon Artist.* Portland: Binfords and Mort, 1974. ix, 168 pages. Photograph of Eliza Barchus and seventeen color photos of her paintings of Crater Lake, Mt. Hood, Three Sisters, Forest Giant, Multnomah Falls, and Mt. Sunset in Oregon.

Written by the painter's daughter, this biography recounts the long life (1857-1959) of the Utah-born Eliza Barchus. The work quotes generously from Eliza Barchus's diaries and letters and examines her hobbies, family life, and career in detail.

43. Barette, Leonore Gale. *Thumb Papers: Sketches of Pioneer Days.* Eugene: Picture Press Printers, 1950. ix, 64 pages. Five photographs of women including Mrs. Sara Ann Moore Gray, Miss Anna Underwood, Miss Elizabeth Gale, Elizabeth Maria Kincaid, and an unidentified Native American woman.

This volume is dedicated to Barette's parents, James Newton Gale and Elizabeth Maria Gale, who were pioneers on the Oregon Trail in 1853. She has collected memories of the pioneer experience, including the early interest in education. Describing the early schools established in Oregon, she pays special attention to Eugene's private and public education, examining acquisition of school lands, buildings, and supplies, the hiring of teachers, and the establishment of curriculum. Barette also provides accounts of her mother's wedding in 1859, the stake and rider fences split by settlers, baskets made by Digger, Klamath, Modoc, and Klickitat women, pioneer shelters, and food.

44. Bargo, Michael. "Women's Occupations in the West in 1870." *Journal of the West* 32 (January 1993): 30-45. Notes, bibliography. Six photographs of western women at work.

Using the 1870 U.S. census, the first to record women's occupations, Bargo examines non-rural work patterns of Oregon and Washington Territory women, with domestic servants, teachers, milliners, dressmakers, and laundresses dominating the picture. Five tables enable researchers to compare Oregon and Washington Territory patterns to those of other western states and territories for female population, divided by age group; females employed by age group; women's population in relation to total population; percentages of women in agriculture, personal and professional service, trade and transportation, and manufacturing, mechanical and mining industries; and rural/urban percentage.

45. Barnhart, Edward N. *Japanese-American Evacuation and Resettlement: Catalog of Material in the General Library.* Berkeley, California: University of California General Library, 1958. 177 pages.

This paper is a catalog of materials at the University of California/Berkeley Library on the Japanese American resettlement during World War II. One of the major resources in the collection is the diaries and recollections of the internees. Many of the diary and eye-witness accounts listed are by women.

46. Barrett, Helen. *Sternwheelers and the Skagit River.* Skagit County Historical Series, No. 1. Mt. Vernon: Skagit County Historical Society, 1971. 22 pages. Bibliography.

This is a history of sternwheeler boats on the Skagit River from 1870 to 1966. Women are mentioned only in the context of families of male settlers, except for Mrs. William Weaver. Her husband was captain of the *Skagit Belle* and she worked as a cook aboard ship for many years.

47. Barrow, Susan H.L. *Green Gold Harvest: A History of Logging and its Products.* Seattle: Craftsman Press, 1969. 78 pages. Bibliography. Many photos: pioneer family and shake cabin in 1906; wood sculpture of Patti Dodd, 1969; oil painting of Emily Carr.

This catalog contains short essays on the settlement of Whatcom County and the development of the logging industry and the history of Puget Sound Pulp and Timber Company. In the chapter entitled "Wood and the Artist," reference is made to women settlers, especially Mrs. Eldridge and Mrs. Charles E. Roberts, early women residents of Whatcom County; Phoebe Judson, first settler of Lynden; Miss Alice Eldridge, first school teacher in Ferndale; and Mrs. Elizabeth Lyle Saxon, early homesteader in Saxon. Two contemporary artists, Patti Dobb of Oregon and Emily Carr of Canada, are also included.

48. ———. *Whatcom Seascapes; The Influence of the Sea on Whatcom County.* Seattle: Craftsman Press, 1970. 78 pages. Bibliography. Etching by Helen A. Loggie of the *Vigilant.*

This museum catalog contains short essays about shipping in Whatcom County, sea life in the waters of Puget Sound, and a "capsule" history of the Port of Bellingham. Women are mentioned in passing as early travelers/pioneers on the ships. Miss Marion A. Wood is mentioned as a part owner and sponsor of the *Vigilant.* Emma Newberry and Doris Young Duponti are mentioned in short paragraphs as early clerical employees of the Port of Bellingham.

49. Barrows, William. *Oregon: The Struggle for Possession.* American Common Wealths series, vol. 2. Cambridge: The Riverside Press, 1884. viii, 368 pages. Notes, index.

This flowery account of the arrival of missionaries Narcissa Whitman and Eliza Spalding uses the women as symbols for the coming of Caucasian family life on the frontier. Barrows views this as an improvement over the partnerships by traders and trappers with "squaws" who produced "half breed children." He reports that the presence of white women had a civilizing effect.

50. Barry, J. Neilson. "Madam Dorion of the Astorians," *Oregon Historical Quarterly* 30 (1929): 272-278. Bibliography.

This is a biography of Madame Pierre Dorion, Jr., Iowa Indian and wife of a Sioux interpreter for the overland expedition to Astoria, Oregon, in 1811.

51. Bartholomae, Annette M. "A Conscientious Objector: Oregon, 1918." *Oregon Historical Quarterly* 71 (September 1970): 213-245. Notes. Illustration of the Multnomah County Library in 1917-18.

Miss M. Louise Hunt, pacifist and assistant librarian of the public library of Portland refused to buy war bonds in April 1918 on the grounds of conscientious objection to war. Here is great detail about the entire case, including the general hysteria about disloyalty among many members of the community.

52. Barton, Clara. *The Red Cross: A History of This Remarkable International Movement in the Interest of Humanity.* Washington, D.C.: The American National Red Cross, 1898. 684 pages. Photographs of volunteers and the Oregon Emergency Corps.

The Oregon chapter narrates the origins of the Red Cross in Portland during the Spanish American War. It lists the officers in the organization who aided Oregon volunteers and their families. It also lists the committees which met weekly and describes their activities. The Washington chapter lists the names of officers in Seattle, Tacoma, Walla Walla, and Spokane.

53. Barton, Lois, ed. *One Woman's West: Recollections of the Oregon Trail and Settling the Northwest Country by Martha Gay Masterson 1838-1916.* Eugene, Oregon: Spencer Butte Press, 1986. xvii, 222 pages. Bibliography. Photographs of the author and her relatives.

Lois Barton, the editor of *Lane County Historian* in Eugene, Oregon, has provided a biography of a Missouri family who came to Oregon in 1851 by overland wagon. Arkansas-born Martha Gay Masterson was thirteen years old during this journey. She married in 1871 and became a frontier wife, following her spouse to gold rush towns, Northern Pacific Railroad construction camps, and homesteads throughout the Pacific Northwest.

54. Bass, Sophie Frye. *Pigtail Days in Old Seattle.* Portland: Metropolitan Press, 1937. 178 pages. Sketches of school girls and American Indian women.

This history of Seattle makes brief mention of pioneer daughters. There is specific discussion of Emma Guttenberg, Miss Bacon, Julia Jones (Jumpin' Julia), Catherine Blaine, Caroline Parsons, Susan B. Anthony, Bridal Row, and Rosamond Densmore.

55. ———. *When Seattle Was a Village.* Seattle: Lowman and Hanford Company, 1947. 209 pages.

This is a personal memoir by a resident who spent her girlhood in pioneer Seattle. In an anecdotal style she recalls Native American women, early churches in Seattle, pioneer housekeeping, and gives one-to-three-page vignettes of early prominent Seattle families. While women are included throughout the book, Sophie Bass chronicles the growth of Seattle through the major activities of pioneer men.

56. Baxandall, Rosalyn Fraad. "Elizabeth Gurley Flynn: The Early Years." *Radical America* 9 (January-February 1975): 97-115. Notes. One photograph of Flynn.

Flynn (1890-1964) was a Socialist orator who, among many of her radical activities, participated in the 1909 Spokane Free Speech Movement. In 1926, she collapsed from the physical exhaustion of a life as an activist and she recuperated at the home of Portland physician Marie Equi, "an avowed lesbian."

57. ———. *Words on Fire: The Life and Writing of Elizabeth Gurley Flynn.* New Brunswick: Rutgers University Press, 1987. xii, 310 pages. Notes and index. Seven photographs of Flynn.

The introduction by Baxandall deals briefly with Flynn's Pacific Northwest activism on behalf of the Industrial Workers of the World. Flynn was pregnant when she was jailed in Seattle for her radicalism and blamed her foul treatment there for her miscarriage.

58. Baxandall, Rosalyn, Linda Gordon, and Susan Reverby, eds. *America's Working Women.* New York: Random House, 1976. xxii, 408, ix pages. Index. No photos of Northwest women, many other photos of American working women.

This collection contains an essay by Amy Kesselman entitled "Women on the Oregon Trail." It draws on unpublished manuscripts held at the Oregon Historical Society and surveys observations about the westward journey by Elizabeth Goltra, Sarah Cranstone, Cecilia McMillen Adams, Agnes Stewart, Mary Warren, Mrs. Haun, and Maria Belshaw. The rest of this book does not deal with Northwest women, but is an excellent overall history of American working-class women.

59. Beard, Geraldine, ed. *A Check List of Washington Imprints, 1853-1876.* Seattle: The Washington Historical Records Survey, 1942. 89 pages. Index.

The compilation was a WPA project in the 1930s, and is preliminary in scope because WPA staff were diverted to war projects in the early 1940s. The book provides valuable references to documents that may relate significantly to women's history, such as church archives. Specifically, however, two women, Mrs. A.H.H. Stuart and Mrs. Elizabeth D. Wilson, are mentioned in the text.

60. Beaton, Welford. *The City That Made Itself; a Literary and Pictorial Record of the Building of Seattle.* Seattle: Terminal Publishing Company, 1914. xiv, 275 pages. Index.

This is a history of physical change and growth in Seattle from its founding until 1914. The activities of women are mentioned in chap. 13, "The Schools of Yesterday and Today" and in chap. 20, "How Women Started the Library."

61. Becker, Ethel Anderson. *Here Comes the Polly.* Seattle: Superior Publishing Company, 1971. 127 pages. Index. Photos: Aleut women, Eskimo women, Eskimo family, Chilkat nation gathering for potlatch, Mrs. Henry Yesler outside her home in Seattle, women on Seattle streets, "squaws" cleaning fish on Puget Sound, Indian

women weaving fishing nets, Indian women hop pickers, Seattle residents in the 1890s, Princess Evangeline.

This book is an impressionistic history of Puget Sound and Alaska as seen through the "eyes" of the tugboat *Politkosky,* which plied the region's waters between the 1860s and 1910s. While women are mentioned only in passing in the text, they are featured in several fine photographs, detailed above.

62. Beckham, Stephen Dow. *The Indians of Western Oregon: This Land Was Theirs.* Coos Bay, Oregon: Arago Books, 1977. vii, 236 pages. Notes, index. This work is rich in photographs of Northwest women: Annie Miner Peterson, Coos teller of the oral tradition; Delia, a Tolowa Indian of 1901; Geneva Mattz; Isty-ilshe in 1906; Eliza, a Kalapuya Indian; Lottie Evanoff; Coos woman in 1900 in fringed cedar-bark skirt and cape; basketmaker, Tsin-is-tum, a Clatsop Indian in 1894; Old Polly, a Tututni; children at the training school in Forest Grove; a family picking hops in Willamette Valley; students at Carlisle Indian School; Ida Bensell of the Sitetz Tribe in 1977; staff of Willow River Indian Benevolent Association on the Coos Reservation.

The narrative includes details about women's clothing, dwellings, diet, child-raising, contact with traders and trappers, missionaries and miners, and reservation life.

63. Bede, Elbert. *The Fabulous Opal Whiteley: From Oregon Logging Camp to Princess in India.* Portland: Binfords and Mort, 1954. 181 pages. Fourteen photographs of Opal and her family.

In 1919, the *Atlantic Monthly* serialized seventy thousand words from the 250,000-word diary believed to have been written by Opal Whiteley thirteen years before, when she was a mere child of seven. She wrote about her unhappy life with her foster parents, the Whiteleys, with whom she moved nineteen times in her youth, from one Oregon logging camp to another. The possibility that the diary was a hoax has never been put to rest.

64. Beeton, Beverly, and G. Thomas Edwards. "Susan B. Anthony's Woman Suffrage Crusade in the American West." *Journal of the West* 21 (April 1982): 5-15. Bibliography. Photographs of Susan B. Anthony, Elizabeth Cady Stanton, Anna Howard Shaw, and Abigail Scott Duniway.

This article is about the journey taken by Susan B. Anthony and Elizabeth Cady Stanton to the western

United States in 1871. Included is a section on Anthony's travels and speeches in the Pacific Northwest, including popular and press response to her message. Anthony was accompanied by Oregonian Abigail Scott Duniway on her tour of Washington and Oregon.

65. Belknap, George N. *Oregon Imprints 1845-1870.* Eugene: University of Oregon, 1968. 305 pages. Notes, bibliography, index.

This bibliography lists Oregon imprints between 1845 and 1870. It supersedes Douglas C. McMurtrie's book of the same title published in 1950. Women are listed frequently in the subject index. Entries include Margaret Bailey, author of Oregon's first novel, and Abigail Scott Duniway, a prolific writer and activist. Women are most frequently listed in reference to their printed marriage announcements or divorce decrees.

66. Belknap, Ketturah. "Ketturah Belknap's Chronicle of the Bellfountain Settlement." Ed. Robert M. Gatke. *Oregon Historical Quarterly* 38 (September 1937): 265-299. Notes.

This chronicle, a group of long letters by Mrs. Ketturah Belknap of Benton County, Oregon, written from 1847-1868, concentrates on church meetings, preachers, Sunday school, and camp meetings. She describes in great detail how the itinerant Methodist ministers operated. There is little detail about non-religious aspects of her life.

67. Bellingham Public Libraries. *A History of Bellingham, Washington: Compiled from Newspaper Articles, City Directories and Books of Local History.* Bellingham: Argonaut Press, 1926. 104 pages.

Included among the materials collected here are: "American Reveille" by Mary B. Haight, an account of Mrs. Lysle, Mrs. Roeder, and their children during the "Indian troubles" of 1855 and 1856; Ella Higginson's story of her first voyage to Bellingham; a biography of Phoebe Judson, "Mother of Lyndon"; and a tribute to Katherine M. Ryan, Bellingham city librarian, by Ella Higginson.

68. Bennion, Sherilyn Cox. "A Working List of Women Editors of the 19th-Century West." *Journalism History* 7, no. 2 (Summer 1980): 60-65. Bibliography. Four photographs of women, including editor Abigail Scott Duniway.

The introduction to this article is a bibliographical essay on the subject. Following that is a useful list of women editors in each of the western states, including full names, the names of the newspapers edited, whether the publication was a weekly or a monthly, the place of publication, the dates of publication, and the current location of old issues. For Oregon, Bennion lists eighteen women; for Washington, fifteen.

69. ———. *Equal to the Occasion: Women Editors of the Nineteenth-Century West.* Reno: University of Nevada Press, 1990. ix, 212 pages. Notes, bibliography, index. Photograph of Abigail Scott Duniway signing Oregon's Equal Suffrage Proclamation in 1912, with Governor Oswald West and Dr. Viola M. Coe.

Sherilyn Cox Bennion, a professor of journalism with a doctorate in mass communications, has determined that 1 percent of western editors from 1854-1900 were women. She has traced the private lives and public careers of thirty-five of them, editors of small-town weeklies and publications devoted to women's issues or social reforms. She has also provided a compilation of three hundred women editors whose careers she has researched in archives in Arizona, California, Colorado, Hawaii, Idaho, Nevada, New Mexico, Utah, Wyoming, Oregon, and Washington. Among the editors featured is Abigail Scott Duniway. While Bennion summarizes other scholarship on Duniway's women's rights advocacy in *The New Northwest*, she details new insights about the suffragist's editorship at *Coming Century* and *Pacific Empire* and documents the role of Duniway's sister, Catharine Scott Coburn, in western journalism.

70. ———. "*The New Northwest* and *Woman's Exponent*: Early Voices for Suffrage." *Journalism Quarterly* 54 (Spring 1977): 286-292. Notes.

This essay compares two western periodicals which supported women's right to vote: Oregon's weekly, *New Northwest*, edited by Abigail Scott Duniway, and Utah's bi-monthly *Women's Exponent*, a Mormon publication. Both periodicals dealt with a variety of women's issues, but their perspectives were not the same. Duniway, whose biography and philosophy are examined here, opposed polygamy, which the Mormon periodical endorsed.

71. Berg, Norah. *Lady on the Beach.* New York: Prentice Hall, 1952. 251 pages.

This book is a charming, rambling story of a woman's life as a beachcomber at Ocean City, Washington, in the late 1940s. She begins by telling of her life in Seattle, meeting her husband, and then moving away from the city that suffocates them both. The main part of the book is devoted to anecdotes and observations about the men, women, and land in Ocean City.

72. Bergamini, Sister Rita, S.P. and Netta Wilson. "Bibliography: Mother Joseph of the Sacred Heart: a Sister of Providence." Seattle: Sisters of Providence Archives, 1978. 11 pages.

This bibliography is not annotated, but contains an impressive list of books, periodicals (including thirty-eight chapters by Ann King in *Thrifty Nickel* from Vancouver, Washington), twenty-seven newspapers, and legislative materials pertaining to Mother Joseph and the successful effort to put her statue in Statuary Hall, the Capitol Building, Washington, D.C.

73. Berner, Richard C. *Seattle 1900-1920, from Boomtown, Urban Turbulence, to Restoration.* Vol. 1 of *Seattle in the Twentieth Century.* Seattle: Charles Press, 1991. xviii, 398 pages. Notes, bibliography, index. Photographs.

This survey mentions the early sex ratio of men to women; the Washington State Federation of Women's Clubs' exclusion of African American members in 1901; the disparity between the wages of men and women teachers; the activities of the Ladies Musical Club; the arts program of Nellie Cornish; and Anna Louise Strong's support for the Seattle general strike of 1919. There are several references to women's club support for urban reforms.

74. ———. *Seattle, 1921-1940, from Boom to Bust.* Vol. 2. of *Seattle in the Twentieth Century.* Seattle: Charles Press, 1992. xix, 554 pages. Notes, bibliography, index. Photographs of African American actress Anne Oliver in the WPA Negro Repertory Theater; Washington State Theater cast; Mayor Bertha Landes with Will Rogers.

This survey includes a biography of the first woman mayor of a major city, Bertha Landes, who ran Seattle from 1926-28. The study also includes references to Nellie Cornish's Cornish School, the civic theater of Florence Bean James, the women who helped found the Seattle Symphony Orchestra, and the conservation efforts of the Washington State Federation of Women's Clubs. Chap. 9 deals with women in the work force and contains tables dealing with gainfully employed women in 1920 and 1930 and major occupations of women in Seattle in 1940.

75. Bingham, Robert D. "Swedish-Americans in Washington State: A Bibliography of Publications." *The Swedish Pioneer Historical Quarterly* 25 (April 1974): 133-140. Bibliography.

This is a bibliography of key books, articles, and newspapers devoted to Swedish American history in Washington. Newspaper articles related to women are "Memories of the 'Old Country' Awakened by Seattle's Own Swedish Women's Chorus," "Monroe Farm Wives Bake Their Bread for Winter," and "Widow Recalls Flavor of Old Logging Town." Women are undoubtedly discussed in many of the books and articles listed, including those which are biographical in character.

76. Binheim, Max, ed. *Women of the West: A Series of Biographical Sketches of Living Eminent Women in the Eleven Western States of the United States of America.* Los Angeles: Publishers Press, 1928. 223 pages. Index. Photographs: a collage of seven Washington women and five Oregon women.

This book is divided into eleven chapters, each dealing with one state. Within the chapter on Washington, subdivisions include "Women of Washington," "Activities of Washington Women," and "Women and the Making of the Northwest." Each of these subdivisions was written by a woman. Women of Washington are given good and broad coverage. Included are those involved in politics, charitable work, women's clubs, Lighthouse for the Blind, and authors, musicians, and composers. After the text on Washington is a list of 136 women important to Washington and a short biography on each.

The Oregon section highlights women's articles too. One by Marion Miller, editorial and feature writer of the *Oregonian*, explores women's leadership roles in Oregon. "Pioneer Women of the West," by Sheba Hargreaves, relates the hardships of crossing the Rockies. "The Last Frontier," by Lois Randolph, provides a romantic picture of life in nature. Pages 156-166 include an alphabetical list of Oregon women who have made an impact on public life. Anne Shannon Monroe provides a list of pioneer women in Oregon.

77. Bjoring, Bob, and Susan Cunningham. *Explorers' and Travellers' Journals Documenting Early Contacts with Native Americans in the Pacific Northwest.* Seattle: University of Washington Press, 1982. No pagination.

This is a bibliography with three citations by Oregon women, eight by Washington women, seven by women journeying on the overland trail to the Pacific Northwest, and four in the Pacific Northwest section. It provides references for journals by Theresa Gay, Helen Maria Fiske Hunt Jackson, Sarah Fiducia Hunt Steeves, Emily Fitzgerald, Olive Rand, Susan Margaret Somerset, Carrie Adell Strahorn, Lila Hannah Firth, Emily Inez Denny, Georgianna Mitchel Blankenship, Caroline C. Leighton, Mary Rhodes Carbutt, Eloise McLoughlin Harvey, Phoebe Newton Goodell Judson, Catherine Sager Pringle, Mae Conrad Sickler, Sarah J. Cummins, Emiline L. Fuller, Augusta Dix Gray, Mary Jane Hayden, Elizabeth Laughlin Lord, Polly Jane Claypool Purcell, and Sara White Smith.

78. Björk, Kenneth O. *West of the Great Divide: Norwegian Migration to the Pacific Coast, 1847-1893.* Northfield, Minnesota: Norwegian-American Historical Association, 1958. viii, 671 pages. Footnotes, index.

This history of Scandinavian migration and settlement of the western United States contains very few references to women and their activities. The only exception is the discussion of Mormon polygamy in chap. 6.

79. Blackwell, Ruby Chapin. *A Girl in Washington Territory.* Tacoma: State Historical Society, 1972. 31 pages. Photographs of Blackwell and early Tacoma.

This work is based on Bruce Le Roy's interviews with ninety-six-year-old Ruby Chapin Blackwell, watercolor artist, about her residency in Tacoma from 1891-1923. Blackwell describes early Tacoma from an adolescent's perspective, addressing Chinese household help, friends, family, church, playing, the 1884 opening of the Tacoma Hotel, teaching second grade at Central School in 1884, a local talent show at the YMCA, and the disturbance to exclude Chinese from the city in the 1880s.

80. Blair, Karen J. *All These Things Stayed with Me: Study Guide.* Olympia: Washington Humanities Commission, 1983. 47 pages. Bibliography.

This study guide was designed to assist teachers in providing instruction around four half-hour radio programs produced on KUOW Public Radio Station in Seattle for International Women's Day in March 1983. Mary Molodovsky and Roberta Shorruck prepared the programs, three of which dealt with Northwest women. The first program drew on the diaries and letters of Alice Morrison Clay of Whidbey Island to describe her family life during the Great Depression, when she raised a grandson on her farm. The second program, "Curtain Call Grandmother," used interviews conducted by the Washington Women's Heritage Project in 1981 to narrate the experiences of a wide range of women, including a switchboard operator, boilermaker, and the first woman to climb Mount Rainier. Program three dealt with women's techniques for winning the vote in 1910. Blair's guide provided a summary of each tape, a list of discussion questions, and suggestions for visual aids in the classroom, audio aids, class trips, class activities, documents, and supplementary readings. The tapes and guide have been distributed by the Washington Commission for the Humanities.

81. ———. "AYP Woman's Building Restored to Serve University of Washington Women." *Landmarks* 1 (Summer 1981): 30-31. Photographs of interior and exterior of the building.

Here are outlined the origins of the 1909 Alaska-Yukon-Pacific Exposition building on the University of Washington campus, which displayed Washington women's literary and artistic achievements. After the fair, it was used by women students for seven years, becoming an important social center for women until World War I.

82. ———. "The Limits of Sisterhood: The Woman's Building in Seattle, 1908-1921." *Frontiers* 8 (1984): 45-52. Notes.

In this article, Blair documents an extensive network of women's voluntary associations in Washington State at the turn of the century. She emphasizes their cooperation in recruiting young reformers for their causes, teaching them the skills to make civic change, and winning their support for women's involvement in public life. The article focuses on the Washington State Federation of Women's Clubs, which established a Woman's Building at the Alaska-Yukon-Pacific Exposition in Seattle in the summer of 1909. There, women were provided with day care facilities, lecture rooms, reception centers, resting lounges, a restaurant, and displays of women's artistic achievements. From 1909-1916, the building became a significant meeting place for University of Washington women students. Campus and community women's use of the space to develop themselves and their projects was impressive until World War I. During the war, however, the structure was awarded by the university administrators to the Department of Mining. After the national emergency, women tried and failed to secure another meeting place. The story of their struggle illuminates the limitations of women's networks in the early 1920s.

83. ———. "Seattle Ladies Musical Club." In *Experiences in the Promised Land*, ed. G. Thomas Edwards and Carlos Schwantes, pp. 124-138. Seattle: University of Washington Press, 1986. Notes.

This history of the Seattle Ladies Musical Club begins in 1891 and surveys the biographies of the founders and early members, the subjects of their musical programs, and the goals of developing the musical skills of the club women and bringing classical music to their community.

84. ———. *Women in Pacific Northwest History: An Anthology*. Seattle: University of Washington Press, 1988. xii, 259 pages. Notes, bibliography, index. Photographs of editor Abigail Scott Duniway, suffragist May Arkwright Hutton, Woman's Building at Alaska-Yukon-Pacific Exposition of 1909, Seattle Mayor Bertha Landes, Sona Murphy at Oregon Shipbuilding Corporation, Alberta LeLano and Orrel Weichman at the drill press during World War II, African American Calvary Baptist Church members, Nancy Judge of the Colville Reservation, Professor Blanche Payne, poet Tei Tomita, harvest cook and crew in eastern Washington wheat fields, and telephone operator Ella Diedrich Potter.

This anthology contains twelve essays by historians, anthropologists, communications professors, sociologists, and journalists. Their studies are divided into sections dealing with woman suffrage, work, race and ethnicity, the arts, and new directions for research. See separate entries for: Ruth Barnes Moynihan, "Of Women's Rights and Freedom: Abigail Scott Duniway"; Patricia Voeller Horner, "May Arkwright Hutton: Suffragist and Politician"; Lauren Kessler, "The Fight for Woman Suffrage and the Oregon Press"; Karen J. Blair, "The Limits of Sisterhood: The Woman's Building in Seattle, 1908-1921"; Doris H. Pieroth, "Bertha Knight Landes: The Woman Who Was Mayor"; Karen Beck Skold, "The Job He Left Behind: Women in the Shipyards During World War II"; Susan H. Armitage and Deborah Gallacci Wilbert, "Black Women in the Pacific Northwest: A Survey and Research Prospectus"; Lillian A. Ackerman, "Sexual Equality on the Colville Indian Reservation in Traditional and Contemporary Contexts"; Janice L. Reiff, "Scandinavian Women in Seattle, 1888-1900: Domestication and Americanization"; Diana Ryesky, "Blanche Payne: Scholar of Costume History and University Professor"; Gail M. Nomura, "Tsugiki, a Grafting: A History of a Japanese Pioneer Woman in Washington State"; and Susan H. Armitage, "The Challenge of Women's History."

85. ———. "The Women in Seattle's Past." *Portage* 2 (Fall 1981): 4-9. Photographs of suffragists, Imogene Cunningham, Esther Levy, Mrs. Theresa Dixon, Jeanette Rankin, Bertha Landes, Mother Joseph, cannery workers, and World War I Red Cross volunteers.

Here is a brief survey of prominent women and anonymous volunteers and wage earners in Washington history from the mid-nineteenth to mid-twentieth century. The work of study clubs, the Ladies Musical Club, and 1909 visitors to the Alaska-Yukon-Pacific Exposition like Pauline Steinem and Emmeline Pankhurst are mentioned. So are charity efforts which established the YWCA, House of the

Good Shepherd to Reclaim Fallen Girls, Children's Orthopedic Hospital, the St. Xavier Episcopal Mission, and Ladies Relief Society.

86. Blankenship, Mrs. George E.. comp., ed. *Early History of Thurston County, Washington, Together with Biographies and Reminiscences of Those Identified with Pioneer Days.* Olympia, 1914. Also under *Tillicum Tales of Thurston County.* 392 pages. Drawings of Thurston County scenes and many photographs including Mrs. Amelia Bettman, Mrs. Margaret Chambers, Mrs. Isabel Mills, Mrs. Annie Macleary, Mrs. G.C. Blankenship, and Mrs. Lurana Percival.

Mrs. John G. Parker, Mrs. Jane W. Pattison, Mrs. Jacob Ott, and Mrs. John G. Sparks give anecdotal, down-to-earth accounts of their respective journeys to Thurston County, and problems of adjustment, hardships, relations with the American Indians, and their friends and families.

87. Bledsoe, Lucy Jane. "Adventuresome Women on the Oregon Trail: 1840-1867." *Frontiers* 7, no. 3 (1984): 22-29. Notes.

Between the years 1840 and 1867, more than 350,000 people crossed the plains to the Pacific Coast on the overland trail. This essay refutes assertions that women were reluctant to undertake the journey. Bledsoe collects examples from women's overland diaries that demonstrate their enthusiasm for the trip and their strong contributions in leadership, writing, science, art, and exploration.

88. Blee, Kathleen M. *Women of the Klan: Racism and Gender in the 1920's.* New York: Oxford University Press, 1991. viii, 228 pages. Notes, postscript on sources, index. Photograph of women in Klan parade in Grants Pass, Oregon.

While this history examines the national story of women in the Ku Klux Klan in the 1920s, there is special attention to conflict in the Portland and Oregon organizations between Mae E. Gifford and Lem Dever, the "Mother Counselor."

89. Boas, Franz. *Chinook Texts.* Smithsonian Institution Bureau of Ethnology. Washington, D.C.: U.S. Government Printing Office, 1894. 278 pages.

In 1890 and 1891, Boas studied the Salishan languages of Washington and Oregon in order to learn about Native Americans of the Pacific Northwest. In the Salishan language and also translated into English are accounts of pregnancy and birth, puberty and marriage among the lower Chinook in Clatsop near Seaside, Oregon. In addition, the text offers details about interactions between brothers and sisters, parents and daughters, and husbands and wives.

90. ———. "Notes on the Tillamook." *University of California Publications in American Archaeology and Ethnology* 20 (1923): 3-16. Notes.

Based on two interviews of 1890, this essay describes dwellings, pregnancy, infancy, marriage, and, most extensively, puberty rites for girls among the Tillamook on the Oregon coast between Northern California and the lower Columbia River and into Washington's Puget Sound area.

91. Boas, Franz, and James Teit. *Coeur D'Alene, Flathead and Okanogan Indians.* Fairfield, Washington: Ye Galleon Press, 1985. 22, 384 pages. Notes, bibliography, and index. Thirty-nine illustrations including designs from women's clothing, baskets, and beaded bags.

These anthropologists examine Coeur d'Alene women's clothing, birth experiences, childhoods, tattoos at puberty for girls as well as boys, and women's dances. They describe Okanogan women's clothing, pregnancy, puberty customs including isolation during menstruation, and marriage customs. Flathead women's clothing, birthing, childhood, and round or "squaw" dances are detailed.

92. Bogle, Kathryn Hall. "An American Negro Speaks of Color." *Oregon Historical Quarterly* 89, no. 1 (1988): 70-81. Photographs of the author and Beatrice (Mrs. E.D.) Cannady, first black woman admitted to the Oregon Bar.

This is a reprint of an article published on February 14, 1937 in the *Sunday Oregonian*, set here in context with remarks by *Oregon Historical Quarterly* editor Rick Harmon. It is a memoir of Kathryn Bogle's twelve-year education in eighteen schools in Oregon, Washington, California, Montana, and Minnesota. She recounts both the racism and the fairness she observed and details her efforts to find employment in Portland, Oregon, upon her graduation from high school. She became an employee of Meier and Frank department store.

93. Bogle, Kathryn Hall, with Rich Harmon, interviewer. "Interview: Kathryn Hall Bogle on the Writing of 'An American Negro Speaks of Color.'" *Oregon Historical Quarterly* 89, no. 1 (1988): 82-91. Three photographs of Bogle.

This is the transcript of a portion of a twenty-hour interview with Kathryn Hall Bogle, conducted between 1985 and 1986. It includes details about

Portland's branch of the National Association for the Advancement of Colored People, the Urban League, and the Boys and Girls Aid Society. In this excerpt, Bogle relates the circumstances that led to her being invited to write "An American Negro Speaks of Color" in 1937. Rick Harmon, the interviewer, provides introductory remarks.

94. Bohm, Fred C., and Craig E. Holstine. *The People's History of Stevens County.* Colville, Washington: *Statesman-Examiner,* 1983. xv, 133 pages. Notes, bibliography, index. Photographs of Mrs. John Hofstetter, Mary Walker, woman on a thresher, and women in a quarry.

Chap. 4 examines the history of Stevens County women, using oral histories to explore their hard work at home, bearing children, and wage-earning tasks like packing oranges and working for the lumber company. Chap. 5, on education, names the early woman schoolteachers and draws on the recollections of boys and girls to provide details about the history of the school system.

95. Bonney, William Pierce. *History of Pierce County, Washington,* 3 vols. Chicago: Pioneer Historical Publishing Company, 1927. Vol. 1, 602 pages; vol. 2, 635 pages; vol. 3, 760 pages. Index in vols. 2 and 3. Photographs and drawings include the Annie Wright Seminary, Mrs. Sherwood Bonney, Mrs. M. E. (Bonney) Storey, and Susan Kincaid Thompson.

This is a comprehensive three-volume history of Pierce County. Vol. 1 covers the period from 1841-1916. Vol. 2 deals with the years from 1917-1926 and also includes thirty chapters, each covering a topic such as early marriages, history of the Tacoma Public Library, the Tacoma Goodwill Industries and the Tacoma General Hospital. The final volume is comprised of short biographies of prominent local people, including Dorothy F. Alward, Dr. B. Elizabeth Drake, Nelle E. Guthridge, Genevieve Martin, Mrs. T. C. Sweeney, and Lillian S. Wieland. Women are most prominent in the chapters entitled, "History of the Tacoma Public Library," "History of the President's Club" (includes history of women's clubs in Tacoma), and "A Pioneer Story" by Mrs. M. E. (Bonney) Storey.

96. Bowden, Angie Burt. *Early Schools of Washington Territory.* Seattle: Lowman and Hanford, 1935. 631 pages. Bibliography, index. Photos of Julia H. Bauer, Sarah Jane Gallagher, Lizzie W. Ordway, and Miss Shumway.

This is a comprehensive survey of early territorial schools. Women are featured throughout, although the author gives more attention to men than to women. This book is arranged by county and the author includes character sketches and general history to provide context for the growth of the schools. Women's roles on boards of education and as administrators are also covered.

97. Brightbill, Sandra. "Mamie Sasse Growing Up in Pine Creek, Washington, 1902-1920." *Pacific Northwest Forum* 7 (Summer-Fall 1982): 31-38.

Here are excerpts from a 1980 interview with Mamie Sasse about her early life in Pine Creek, Okanogan County, Washington. Sasse describes their chores, education, delivery of siblings by midwives, disease, fear of Indians, menstruation, and her marriage in 1920 to a Methodist minister.

98. Brimlow, George F. "The Life of Sarah Winnemucca: The Formative Years." *Oregon Historical Quarterly* 53 (1952): 103-134. Notes.

This biography details the life of the Piute interpreter in Oregon. Born in 1844, Sarah Winnemucca grew up in the Sierra Nevada Mountains border between Nevada and California. This essay describes the terrain, her family, the influence of railroads and white settlement of the West, her career as an interpreter, and her marriage. It does not record her entire life, but ends in 1874 when she assisted in the negotiations to establish the Great Piute Reservation in Oregon.

99. Brisley, Melissa Ann. "Cornelia Marvin Pierce: Pioneer in Library Extension." *Library Quarterly* 38 (April 1968): 125-153.

Cornelia Marvin Pierce (1873-1957) served for twenty-four years as the head of the Oregon State Library. She built the Oregon library system into a top facility, establishing innovations in service and democratizing access to information.

100. Bromberg, Erik. *A Bibliography of Theses and Dissertations Concerning the Pacific Northwest and Alaska.* Reprinted from *Pacific Northwest Quarterly* 40 (July 1949): 203-252; *Oregon Historical Quarterly* 59 (March 1958): 27-84; *Pacific Northwest Quarterly* 42 (April 1951): 147-166; *Oregon Historical Quarterly* 65 (December 1964): 362-391. 49 pages. Bibliography.

Works are listed alphabetically by author and divided into general topic headings. Headings include: history, economics, business administration, agricultural economics, sociology, social work, anthropology, political science, geography, education, miscellaneous. Camp Fire Girls, Sisters of St. Mary of Oregon, Abigail Scott Duniway, Edith Green, Marion

E. Hay, marital problems, Catherine May, woman suffrage, divorce, nursing legislation for women, women in literature, girls' employment, widows' pensions, Young Women's Christian Association, women's sports, women in industry in Portland, Prohibition, social welfare, and churches are among the categories illuminated.

101. Brown, D. Alexander. "Brides by the Boatload." *American History* 1 (1966): 40-46. Sketches from *Harper's Weekly* (January 6, 1866), by Alfred R. Waul, of the Mercer girls' trip.

Considerable detail is provided about Asa Mercer's attempts to fund the second boatload of eastern single women heading to Seattle in 1866. Lively portraits of the travelers on board and their flirtations en route appear. Here also is a brief summary of Mercer's later life.

102. Brown, Dee. *Gentle Tamers: Women of the Old Wild West*. New York: Bantam Books, 1974. 295 pages. Notes, index. Photographs of 23 women, but none from Washington or Oregon.

This is a general survey of women in the western half of the U.S. in the nineteenth century, using a thematic approach (westward journey, fashion, social gatherings, entertainers, educators, suffragists, army wives, ladies of easy virtue). Washington and Oregon are poorly represented, but there are references to Narcissa Whitman, Eliza Hart Spalding, and the Mercer girls.

103. Brown, Mrs. Tabitha. "A Brimfield Heroine—Mrs. Tabitha Brown." *Oregon Historical Quarterly* 5 (1904): 199-205. Reprinted from *Congregational Work* (June 1903).

This is a narrative by a pioneer about the hardships of her journey from the eastern United States to western Oregon in 1846. She arrived in the Willamette Valley at age sixty-six with six cents. She worked first as a seamstress, then founded a boarding school that was incorporated as Pacific University at Tualatin Plains in early 1850.

104. Brown, Olympia, ed. *Democratic Ideals: A Memorial Sketch of Clara B. Colby*. Washington, D.C.: Federal Suffrage Association, 1917. 116 pages. Photograph of Colby.

Although Clara Bewick Colby (1846-1916) is not now revered among the pantheon of nineteenth-century American woman suffragists, she was appreciated in her own time for her activism, particularly as a journalist for women's rights. Brown's biography summarizes Colby's management of the

1882 suffrage campaign in Nebraska and her sixteen-year tenure as president of the Nebraska Suffrage Association. From 1883 to 1888, Colby edited the *Woman's Tribune* in Nebraska, providing suffragists with a forum for their opinions. In 1888, she moved the paper to Washington, D.C. and published it there until 1904. Of interest to Pacific Northwest scholars is her move to Portland, Oregon, where she continued to edit the *Woman's Tribune* until March 9, 1909. Brown quotes poetry by Colby, a memorial tribute to her, and a 1915 address she gave at the San Francisco Pan-Pacific International Exposition.

105. Buckham, Sidney H. *A Triumphant Life*. San Mateo: n.p., 1945. 4 pages.

This very brief essay is a transcript of the eulogy read at Margaret Meany Younger's funeral. It is mainly a tribute and contains little information about the woman herself.

106. Budlong, Caroline Gale. *Memories: Pioneer Days in Oregon and Washington Territory*. Eugene: Picture Press Printers, 1949. 45 pages. Photographs of Caroline Gale Budlong.

This brief book of memories is from the early life of teacher and painter Caroline Gale Budlong. Budlong (1856-1939) was born in Eugene, Oregon, where her father was a pioneer newspaper publisher and abolitionist. She describes her family history, her parents' journey from Illinois to Oregon, and Civil War days in Astoria. The activities of the Sanitary Commission in Astoria are discussed. Also included are memories of recreational activities, the Indians, the Chinese, and especially of her family life.

107. Buerge, David M., and Junius Rochester. *The Religious Heritage of Washington State: Roots and Branches*. Seattle: Church Council of Greater Seattle, 1988. xxi, 277 pages. Bibliography, index. Photographs: Anne Marie Pitman, Chloe Aurelia Clark, Narcissa Whitman, Mother Joseph, Catherine Blaine, Agnes Healy Anderson, and Gertrude Apel.

A few women are featured in this account, including missionary wives, Esther Pariseau (Mother Joseph), Aimee Semple McPherson's mother Minnie Kennedy, and philanthropist Agnes Healy Anderson, a Christian Scientist who gave twelve million dollars to the Cornish School, the School of Forestry at the University of Washington, Shelton Public Library, Young Women's Christian Association, Whitman College, and Principia College. There are details about Sister Emma J. Ray, an African American woman who organized the first black Women's

Christian Temperance Union in Seattle, and Gertrude Apel, a Methodist pastor who was a circuit rider in eastern Washington from 1920 to 1929.

108. Burn, June. *Living High; an Unconventional Autobiography.* New York: Duell, Sloan and Pearce, 1941. x, 292 pages.

This dual autobiography of June Burn and her husband, Farrar, describes their colorful, adventurous life homesteading in the San Juan Islands, teaching Eskimo children in the Aleutian Islands, and walking across the country. The Burns eventually published a magazine called *Puget Soundings*.

109. Burton, Katherine. *All the Way is Heaven. The Biography of Mother M. Thomasina, Foundress and first Prioress General of the Dominican Congregation of Saint Thomas Aquinas of Marymount, Tacoma, Washington.* Bronxville, New York: Katherine Burton, 1958. 188 pages. Photos of Mother M. Thomasina, her mother, Sister M. Alorpia, and Mother M. de Chantal.

The Dominican congregation of Saint Thomas Aquinas operates Aquinas Academy in Tacoma, Washington. The founding sisters of the congregation came to Washington in 1887 and operated schools in Pomeroy and Seattle, and settled in Tacoma in 1893. Chronologically, in an anecdotal fashion, this book features the work of Mother Thomasina.

110. Butler, America E.R. "Mrs. Butler's 1853 Diary of the Rogue River Valley." Ed. Oscar Osburn Winther and Rose Dodge Galey. *Oregon Historical Quarterly* 41 (December 1940): 337-366. Notes.

Short diary entries provide intelligent and detailed accounts of domestic activities, including cooking and washing, which the author hated to do. Mrs. Butler comes across as a spirited individual who expresses feelings more openly than many other diarists have. She discusses the family's economic condition, difficult relations between Native Americans and whites, visitors and neighbors, and her role in the farm work.

111. Butrille, Susan G. *Women's Voices From the Oregon Trail: The Times That Tried Women's Souls.* Boise, Idaho: Tamarack Books, 1993. vi, 256 pages. Notes, bibliography, index. Photograph of a Washington pioneer mother, Oregon's Ruth and Ella Lazinko, pioneer woman's grave, and Mother Joseph.

Part 1 quotes poems and diaries by women, written while they undertook the overland journey, and discusses death, storms, river crossings, dust, danger, girls, wives, work, quilt patterns, and recipes. Part 2 enumerates sites pertinent to women's experience, including the site of Narcissa Whitman's home in Walla Walla, and Esther Short Park, named for a pioneer mother in Vancouver, Washington. In Oregon: a marker to Marie Dorion in North Powder; Pendleton Round-up, in which women used to participate as cowgirls; a pioneer woman's grave at Government Camp; and in Portland, the Abigail Scott Duniway Memorial and the Sacajawea Statue in Washington Park.

112. Cain, Mary. "Washington Women's History Preserved in Photographs." *Pacific Northwest Forum* 7 (Summer-Fall, 1982): 10-26. Twenty-one photos of women at work and play.

In this essay are twenty-one photographs of the 300 collected by the Washington Women's Heritage Project, now deposited for use by researchers at the Center for Pacific Northwest Studies at Western Washington University in Bellingham. The photographs in the collection describe family life as well as women in public roles. Many include women engaged in industrial work and political activity.

113. Calhoun, Anne H. *A Seattle Heritage: The Fine Arts Society.* Seattle: Lowman and Hanford Co. 1942. 121 pages. Index.

The author, a charter member of the Fine Arts Society, discusses the origins of the institution. She documents women's efforts in developing a cultural life in the city, 1908 to 1934. In 1908, local women were significant in organizing to exhibit art on loan to the community. Photographer Imogen Cunningham was among them. The text describes the exhibitions sponsored, the growth of the membership, the fund-raising efforts, the spaces inhabited, and the relationship to the Washington State Art Association.

114. Camp, Helen C. *Iron in Her Soul: Elizabeth Gurley Flynn and the American Left.* Pullman: Washington State University Press, 1995. xxi, 396 pages. Notes, bibliography, index. Photographs of Flynn as a child and an adult.

Camp's doctoral dissertation has been recast as a lively biography of the radical activist Elizabeth Gurley Flynn. Although Flynn worked for Socialism and Communism throughout the nation, Camp provides details about her work in the Free Speech Movement of the Industrial Workers of the World in Spokane, Washington, in 1909. Camp also provides the fullest account in print of physician and radical Dr. Marie Equi of Portland, with whom Flynn lived for much of 1926-36.

115. Campbell, D'Ann. "Was the West Different: Values and Attitudes of Young Women in 1943." *Pacific Historical Review* 47 (1978): 453-463. Notes.

The author has quantified results of 2,800 interviews conducted in May 1943 by the fifth Roper Survey of women in the Mountain and Pacific states, including Washington and Oregon women. She has classified their expectations about their future, observing Pacific coast women to be more optimistic than Mountain state women.

116. Campbell, Esther W. *Bagpipes in the Woodwind Section: A History of the Seattle Symphony and Its Women's Association.* Seattle: Seattle Symphony Women's Association, 1978. ix, 309 pages. Photograph of symphony conductor, M. Davenport-Engberg.

Among the women discussed in this history of the symphony are women officers; trustees; board members; soloists like Louise Van Ogle; Mrs. Charles D. Stimson, president in 1907 of the Seattle Symphony Orchestra Society and generous donor; musicians like harpist Eleanor Nordhoff and conductor Madame Davenport-Engberg; orchestra managers Cecilia Augsburger Schultz, Mrs. H.M. Stryker, and Mrs. Lester Turner, Jr.; and Women's Committee members who raised funds and endorsed children's concerts.

117. Canfield, Gae Whitney. *Sarah Winnemucca of the Northern Paiutes.* Norman: University of Oklahoma Press, 1983. xiv, 306 pages. Notes, bibliography, index. Sixteen photographs of Paiute women.

This twenty-four chapter biography recounts the life of Paiute interpreter and U.S. Army scout Sarah Winnemucca. In addition to drawing on Winnemucca's autobiography, the author uses Northwest newspaper accounts, government documents, memoirs, and materials of other historical figures who engaged with her, providing a sound context for the details of her life, which took her to Nevada, California, Oregon, and Washington state.

118. Cannon, Miles. *Waiilatpu, its Rise and Fall, 1836-1847.* 1915. Reprint, Fairfield, Washington: Ye Galleon Press, 1969. ix, 171 pages. Footnotes, bibliography. Photos of Oregon pioneers: Rebecca Hopkins, Eliza Spalding Warren,

Nancy A. Jacobs, Susan M. Wert, and Lorinda Chapman; women survivors of the Whitman massacre; Mrs. Sarah Kimball Munson; Mrs. Gertrude Hall Denny; Mrs. Mima Kimball Negler.

This book is a reprint of a 1915 publication about the Marcus and Narcissa Whitman journey across country, life at the Walla Walla mission, and the massacre in 1847. A new introduction by Thomas E. Jessett quotes a lengthy letter by Reverend W.H.K. Perkins of The Dalles about the life and character of Narcissa Whitman. The book by Cannon is a readable account of the Whitmans based on the materials available at that time. He draws heavily on Narcissa Whitman's journal and letters, and she is the central character of the book. The diaries of other people are also utilized, including that of Mrs. Catherine S. Pringle.

119. Cantwell, Robert. *The Hidden Northwest.* Philadelphia: Lippincott, 1972. 335 pages. Bibliography, index, several maps.

This well written history of Washington and Oregon is not strictly narrative, but tends to focus on the stories of prominent Northwest personalities, such as David Thompson (explorer and cartographer) and Theodore Winthrop (author), and on events such as the Weyerhaeuser kidnapping. Women are mainly mentioned briefly and sporadically as with Mrs. Catherine Maynard (chap. 3); Elizabeth Champney, author (chap. 5); and various women authors, including Margaret Jewett Smith and Mrs. Elizabeth Smith, Oregon pioneer, in chap. 8. There is, however, an extended biographical sketch of Frances Fuller Victor, Northwest historian, in chap. 8.

120. Carey, Charles H. *General History of Oregon.* 2 vols. Portland, Oregon: Metropolitan Press, 1935. Vol. I, 416 pages; vol. 2, 500 pages. Notes, index. Illustration of Sacajawea.

Women are treated only briefly in this study. Mention is made of Sacajawea's contribution to the Lewis and Clark expedition. The wives of missionaries Jason Lee, Marcus Whitman, Henry Spalding, Cushing Eells, A.B. Smith, and Elkanah Walker are catalogued. Towns named for women are enumerated. Early schools are discussed, with names of pioneer teachers, parents who sent their children to school, early Roman Catholic girls' schools, and Normal Schools.

121. Carhart, Edith Beebe. *A History of Bellingham, Washington, Compiled from Newspaper Articles, City Directories, and*

Books of Local History. Bellingham: The Argonaut Press, 1926. 99 pages.

This small work is full of women's history. It is a compilation of articles, mostly from the *American Reveille*. In "A Chapter Never Before Written," Mary B. Haight tells the story of Mrs. Eldridge (first white woman in Bellingham), Phoebe Judson, Elizabeth Austin Roeder, and Mrs. Lysle. Their difficulties as pioneer farmers, wives, and mothers, and relations with American Indians are described. There is an article by Mary B. Haight about the first school in Bellingham, taught by Isabelle Eldridge, daughter of Teresa. This article also discusses Mrs. Nellie Coupe, a dedicated and beloved early school teacher. There is another article by Mary B. Haight devoted to Phoebe Judson, "Mother of Lynden." There are reminiscences of early pioneer life by Ella Higginson, Lottie Roedy Roth, and Theresa Eldridge. There is also a tribute to Mrs. Katherine M. Ryan, founder of the Bellingham Public Library.

122. Carlson, Kathryn "Kate." *Rich Heritage: Summit Valley's Past.* Colville, Washington: *Statesman-Examiner*, Inc., 1979. xii, 273 pages. Photographs of women in their families and of groups of club members.

This history was compiled by members of the Summit Valley Extension Homemaker's Club, between 1970-1976, for the nation's bicentennial celebration. Chap. 10, on schools, includes the names of many women teachers. Chap. 11, on the Glendale Lutheran Ladies Aid Society, looks at its founding in 1920 to the present, lists members' names, and documents their quilting activities, dances, and World War I relief efforts. Chap. 12, on the Summit Homemaker's Club, narrates the group's establishment in 1930 and its World War II efforts to broaden interest in home care and thoughtful consumerism. Chap. 13 relates the experiences of early pioneer women, particularly those of Scandinavian settlers.

123. Carlson, William H. "Ida Angeline Kidder: Pioneer Western Land-Grant Librarian." *College and Research Libraries* (May 1968): 217-223. Index.

This is a biography of the first professional librarian at Oregon State Agricultural College. Her leadership (1908-1920) was marked by an eight-fold increase in library materials, a new building, and extended hours. In 1918, during World War I, she opened a hospital library for soldiers at Camp Lewis.

124. Carp, Wayne E. "The Sealed Adoption Records Controversy in Historical Perspective: The Case of the Children's Home Society of Washington, 1895-1988." *Journal of Sociology and Social Welfare* xix: 2 (June 1992): 27-57. Notes, bibliography.

Washington state is used as a case study for this general history of adoption rights on a national scale. The paper samples 21,000 adoption case records of the Children's Home Society between 1895-1988, in order to document and analyze three distinct eras in the history of twentieth-century post-adoption contact for adult adopted persons and their birth parents. Women are present in the account both as social workers and mothers.

125. Carson, Joan. *Tall Timber and the Tide.* Poulsbo, Washington: *Kitsap Weeklies*, 1971. 113 pages. Photos of E. Mary DeShaw, great granddaughter of Chief Sealth; Vinland Schoolhouse; Helvor Swenson family; Island Lake School; Lemolo pioneers.

This is a sketchy, anecdotal history of north Kitsap County. The author does not highlight any women, but they are mentioned in passing: Mrs. Pickerell, postmistress of Suquamish in 1906; E. Mary DeShaw, great granddaughter of Chief Sealth; and Mrs. Ekstedt, first white woman in Keyport.

126. Case, Robert Ormand. *The Empire Builders.* Portland: J. K. Gill Company, 1947. x, 333 pages.

This is an example of popular uses of historical material. The author, having read fifty collections of primary sources at the Oregon Historical Society, recounts the migration of Cornelius and Elizabeth Smith and seven children, aged sixteen to infant, from Missouri to The Dalles in 1843. He also discusses Tabitha Brown, who came to the Willamette Valley in 1845 and taught at Tualatin Academy. Both selections quote from diary entries.

127. Caswell, John E. "The Prohibition Movement in Oregon." *Oregon Historical Quarterly* 39 (September 1938): 235-261; 40 (March 1939): 64-82. Notes.

Part 1 of this work covers the years 1836-1904, beginning with missionaries who founded the movement for temperate use of alcohol. There is mention of Elizabeth A.P. White and her mother, Rebecca Clawson, leaders in establishing a branch of the Women's Christian Temperance Union (WCTU) in Oregon in 1880. Part 2 of the Caswell piece discusses the years 1904 through 1915, the year statewide Prohibition was passed in Oregon. Women's efforts are not much discussed, but women used their newly won vote 2:1 in 1912 to support Prohibition.

This article emphasizes the alliance between the Anti-Saloon League, the Prohibition Party, and the WCTU between 1904-1915 to oppose saloons in Oregon. The bulk of the discussion revolves around initiatives, referenda, and legislative struggles. There is considerable focus on the senators and bills passed by prohibitionists. There is little mention of the women working in the movement, but women's vote in the 1912 election is credited as influential in the Prohibitionist fight.

128. Catt, Carrie Chapman, and Nettie Rogers Shuler. *Woman Suffrage and Politics: The Inner Story of the Suffrage Movement.* 1923. Reprint, Seattle: University of Washington Press, 1970. xxiii, 504 pages. Index.

This work, rich with quotations, does not fail to document the contributions of Washington and Oregon women to the suffrage fight. Catt knew the story firsthand, having lived in Seattle during the late 1880s.

129. Chambers, Margaret White. "Reminiscences." In *Recollections,* ed. Andrew Jackson Chambers, 1904. Reprint, Fairfield, Washington: Ye Galleon Press, 1975, pp. 41-59.

Margaret White Chambers's account relates her overland journey from Indiana to the Pacific Northwest, undertaken when she was a child. She describes settlement in Milwaukie and Chamber's Prairie, marriage to Andrew J. Chambers in 1854, the Indian War of 1855-56, and raising ten daughters.

130. Chandler, Milford G. "Sidelights on Sacajawea." *The Masterkey* 43 (1969): 58-66.

This biography of Native American guide Sacajawea and her family was based on information the author collected in 1938 from Dr. Charles A. Eastman. Eastman was commissioned in 1925 by the U.S. Department of Indian Affairs to investigate Sacajawea's biography. This essay asserts her importance to the Lewis and Clark expedition, discusses the debate over her name and its meaning, relates the brutality of her husband Charbonneau, and informs us of her baby-care practices. His position on her later life, in debate by scholars, agrees with that of Dr. Grace Hebard, that Sacajawea married a Comanche warrior, and died in 1884 at the age of one hundred years.

131. Chapman Publishing Company. *Portrait and Biographical Record of Western Oregon.* Chicago: Chapman Publishing Company, 1904. 1,033 pages. Index.

This encyclopedia includes hundreds of biographies of men and fifteen entries on women. Even in these portraits of pioneer women, their male relatives play a prominent part. The women included are Mrs. Mary Minerva Hill Dunn, Mrs. Mary Case, Mrs. M.M. Cooksay, Elizabeth Graham, Mrs. J.H.D. Gray, Pauline A. Hines, Mrs. Myra Highey, Mrs. C.A. Kamm, Mrs. L.C. Kinney, Mrs. N.W. Kinney, Mrs. S.R. Lane, Mrs. Mary E. McCall, Mrs. J.K. Reades, Mrs. Mattie Shaw, and Mrs. W.H. Wilson. Both men's and women's biographies offer the names of the subject's mother, spouse, and daughters.

132. Chase, Cora G. *The Oyster Was Our World; Life on Oyster Bay 1898 to 1914.* Seattle: Shorey Book Store, 1976. 94 pages. Photographs: frontispiece of Gingrich children, Gingrich family album at end.

This is a personal memoir of life as a girl on Oyster Bay, near Shelton, Washington. The Gingrich family lived on houseboats and earned a living by oystering, with everyone helping out. The details of the story relate to family history, and to Cora's experiences as a live-in domestic servant.

133. ————. *Unto The Least: A Biographical Sketch of Mother Ryther.* Seattle: Shorey Book Store, facsimile reproduction, 1972. 75 pages. Photos of Olive H. S. Ryther; first circular publicizing the Ryther Foundling Home; Ryther family; Ryther daughters; Emma Long and Mae Bird Ryther; Theresa and Mary Himmelsbach, 1902; girls at Denny Way Home, 1906; Ryther Home employees.

This book is the history of the Ryther Child Center and its founder, "Mother" Ryther. Based on the reminiscences of the Ryther family and of former residents of the orphanage, it is anecdotal in character and includes reproductions of letters and newspaper articles by and about Mother Ryther.

134. Chittenden, Elizabeth F. "By No Means Excluding Women." *The American West* 12 (March 1975): 24-27. Bibliography. Two photographs of Abigail Scott Duniway.

This four-page essay is a brief summary of the life and work of Abigail Scott Duniway. While well written, it contains no new information, relying instead on the best known facts and anecdotes about the Oregon suffragist's life.

135. Chuinard, E.G. "The Actual Role of the Bird Woman." *Montana: Magazine of Western History* 26 (Summer 1976): 18-29. Bibliography. Four

photographs of Sacajawea statues: in Portland and Salem, Oregon; and Helena and Fort Benton, Montana.

The purpose of this essay is to determine whether Sacajawea was a purposeful member of the Lewis and Clark expedition or merely a "tagalong" who accompanied her husband Charbonneau.

136. Chused, Richard H. "The Oregon Donation Act of 1850 and Nineteenth Century Federal Married Women's Property Law." *Law and History Review* 2 (Spring, 1984): 44-78.

The author, a law professor, recounts the biography of Samuel R. Thurston, Oregon Territory's first delegate to Congress and the probable author of the Oregon Donation Act in 1849. This law gave land grants to married women in their own right, by federal and not state law. His work is situated in the context of federal land law and state laws regarding married women's property rights. His relationship to his wife and daughter is included.

137. Clar, Reva, and William M. Kramer. "The Girl Rabbi of the Golden West: The Adventurous Life of Ray Frank in Nevada, California, and the Northwest, Part I." *Western States Jewish History* 18 (January 1986): 99-111. Notes.

Here is a biography of Ray Frank, sometimes called the first woman rabbi in America. The San Francisco-born woman served the Spokane, Washington, Jewish community in 1890, during High Holy Days, and visited the Pacific Northwest as a newspaper correspondent.

138. ———. "The Girl Rabbi of the Golden West: The Adventurous Life of Ray Frank in Nevada, California, and the Northwest, Part II." *Western States Jewish History* 18 (April 1986): 223-236. Notes, photograph of Ray Frank.

The second part of the Ray Frank account discusses her preaching in California and does not deal with her Northwest experiences.

139. Clark, Ava Melan, and J. Kenneth Munford. *Adventures of A Home Economist.* Corvallis: Oregon State University Press, 1969. xii, 432 pages. Bibliography, index. Photographs of the author and her teachers.

This is an autobiography, introduced by Betty E. Hawthorne, and a history of the School of Home Economics at Oregon State University in Corvallis, Oregon. There is considerable detail about students and curriculum in the school's home economics program during the early twentieth century.

140. Clark, Ella Elizabeth, and Margot Edmonds. *Sacajawea of the Lewis and Clark Expedition.* Berkeley: University of California Press, 1979. vii, 171 pages. Footnotes, bibliography, index, one map. Appendices on memorials, oral tradition, and pronunciation of Native American names. One photograph of the Bismarck, North Dakota statue of Sacajawea.

This is a serious account, avoiding embroidery, of Sacajawea's expedition to the Northwest with explorers Lewis and Clark in the early nineteenth century.

141. Clark, Keith, and Cowell Tiller. *Terrible Trail: The Meek Cutoff, 1845.* Caldwell, Idaho: The Claxton Printers, Ltd., 1966. 244 pages. Notes, bibliography, index, roster of names of travelers with brief biographical data. Photograph of Sarah King Chambers's grave stone.

Stephen Meek was hired to pilot a company of emigrants from Missouri to Oregon in 1845. The author quotes from diaries and reminiscences of men and women to narrate the trials of the expedition. Lucy Hall Bennett and Sarah Hunt Steeves are among those whose accounts are considered.

142. Clark, Malcolm H., Jr. *Eden Seekers: The Settlement of Oregon, 1818-1862.* Boston: Houghton Mifflin Company, 1981. ix, 327 pages. Footnotes, bibliography, index. Portrait of Anna Maria Pittman Lee and of the Deady family.

This book is primarily about men. Women are frequently mentioned, but only in passing as wives and mothers. Two women, Anna M. P. Lee and Margaret Smith Bailey, are described at greater length. They were members of the earliest missionary settlement, and their personalities and roles in the community are discussed. The historic struggle of Polly Holmes and her husband to free their enslaved children is also told.

143. ———. "The Lady and the Law: A Portrait of Mary Leonard." *Oregon Historical Quarterly* 56 (March 1955): 126-39. Notes.

This biography of Mary Gissen Leonard details the life of the first woman lawyer in Oregon, who was disbarred in 1912 at the age of seventy. In 1884, she was admitted to the Washington Territorial

Bar. Two years later, she was the first woman admitted to practice in the state of Oregon. A fiery personality, she was arrested several times for wild behavior.

144. ———. "The War on the Webfoot Saloon." *Oregon Historical Quarterly* 58 (March 1957): 48-62. Notes. Photographs of the crusades of women at the Portland jail in 1874.

Frances Fuller Victor led Portland's fight to rid the city of liquor. She inspired the temperance crusade, which threatened to burn the Webfoot Saloon in 1874.

145. Clark, Malcolm H., Jr., and Kenneth W. Porter. *The War On The Webfoot Saloon and Other Tales of Feminine Adventures.* Portland: Oregon Historical Society, 1969. 52 pages. Notes. Photographs of Francis Fuller Victor and a Chinook maiden.

The pamphlet contains three essays reprinted from the *Oregon Historical Quarterly.* The first, by Malcolm Clark, is a spirited but patronizing account of the temperance crusade of the Women's Temperance Prayer League in Portland in 1874. The second essay, also by Clark, tells of flamboyant Mary Leonard, the first woman admitted to the Oregon Bar in 1886. The final essay, by Kenneth Porter, is a patronizing account of Jane Barnes, the first white woman in Oregon.

146. Clark, Norman H. *The Dry Years; Prohibition and Social Change in Washington.* Seattle: University of Washington Press, 1965. ix, 304 pages. Notes, bibliography, index. Drawings, charts. Photos include members of the Women's Christian Temperance Union and Augusta Trimble.

This history of the Prohibition movement in Washington state includes the role of the Women's Christian Temperance Union and the Woman's Organization for National Prohibition Reform. Chap. 7 analyzes the disassociation of the woman suffrage movement from the anti-saloon movement.

147. ———. *Washington: A Bicentennial History.* New York: W.W. Norton and Company, Inc., 1976. xix, 204 pages. Notes, index.

This concise history of Washington state rarely mentions women, except for chap. 3, which contains the story of Narcissa Whitman and praises her for her commitment and devotion to missionary work.

148. Clark, Robert Carlton. *History of the Willamette Valley, Oregon.* Chicago: S.J. Clarke Publishing Company, 1927. xviii, 888 pages. Notes, bibliography, index. Photos: two portraits, one of Elizabeth Smith, one of Mrs. Joshua S. Walton; photo of pioneers of Lebanon, Oregon, 1914; late 1800s picture of graduating class at University of Oregon (three out of six students are women).

This book covers the history of the Willamette Valley from the 1700s to the early 1900s. It emphasizes geography, Indian tribes, exploration, fur trade, Hudson's Bay Company, settlements, economy, government, education, churches, and politics. Women appear occasionally. For example, the book describes the dress of Indian women along the Columbia River; a Chinook wedding ceremony; the Indian woman's work (cook, carrier, basketweaver, root-digger); the schedule of Mrs. Elkanah Walker's work week, taken from her journals; food used by pioneers and the ways it was prepared; women teachers from the mid-nineteenth century; wages and number of women teachers in the valley during 1874 and 1924; laws regarding rights of women (i.e., property, voting, contracts); and provides remarks on women's rights advocates Abigail Scott Duniway and Bella W. Cooke.

149. Clarke, Ida Clyde. *American Women and the World War.* New York: D. Appleton and Company, 1918. xviii, 545 pages.

Part 1 records relief work undertaken by women's voluntary organizations such as the Young Women's Christian Association, Congress of Mothers, General Federation of Women's Clubs, Daughters of the American Revolution, Colonial Dames, United Daughters of the Confederacy, and the National Council of Jewish Women. They all united under the Woman's Committee of the Council of National Defense during World War I.

Part 2 documents the work of the state branches of the Woman's Committee of the Council of National Defense. The section on Oregon identifies the president, Mrs. Charles H. Castner, president of the Oregon Federation of Women's Clubs, and other officers in the state. The Washington section highlights Mrs. Winfield R. Smith as chair of the National League for Woman's Service. Her workers established classes for women in telegraphy, salesmanship, running elevators, general office work, the French language, motor driving, Civil Service Exam preparation, cooking and canning, rifle corps for home defense or patrol work, and establishing home clubs for soldiers and sailors, including the Fort Lewis Hostess House.

150. Clarke, S.A. *Pioneer Days of Oregon History.* 2 vols. Portland: J.K. Gill Co., 1905. vii, 729 pages. Brief bibliography.

Women appear briefly in this account. There is mention of the cruelty of Blackfoot men to captives they took as wives; of a Flathead bride who married Pierre Michel in 1814; of polygamy among Okanogans; of Anne Maria Pittman, Susan Downing, and Elvira Johnson, missionaries at Jason Lee's Methodist mission, all of whom became his wives. Clarke catalogues the names of male and female settlers in pre-1842 Oregon. He includes an eye-witness account of the 1847 Whitman massacre at Waiilatpu by a thirteen-year-old who experienced it, Catherine Sager (Pringle), along with her account of her captivity.

151. Cleland, Lucile. *Trails and Trials of the Pioneers of the Olympic Peninsula, State of Washington.* Hoquiam, Washington: The Humptulips Pioneer Association, 1959. 312 pages. Photos of Grace Estelle McNutt and Lucile Cleland.

Hundreds of pioneer women are represented in this history/memoir/oral history of the north Olympic Peninsula. Many, such as Kate Hottois Murhard, tell their own stories, and others are discussed by their spouses and children. The stories of the pioneers include their travels to the Olympic Peninsula, their housing, livelihood, schooling, entertainment, marriages, and children.

152. Clifford, Geraldine Jongich. *Lone Voyagers: Academic Women in Co-educational Institutions, 1870-1937.* New York: The Feminist Press at the City University of New York, 1989. xii, 311 pages. Notes. Photograph of Theresa McMahon.

Included here is a brief biography of University of Washington political science professor Theresa Achmid McMahon (1878-1961) by Florence Howe. The book covers the major influences on her life and mind and her political activism outside the classroom.

153. Cline, Walter, and Rachel S. Commons, May Mandelbaum, Richard Post, and L.V.W. Walters. *The Sinkaietk or Southern Okanagan of Washington.* General Series in Anthropology, no. 6, ed. Leslie Spier. Menasha, Wisconsin: George Banta Publishing Company, 1938. 266 pages. Notes, bibliography.

May Mandelbaum contributed "The Individual Life Cycle," pp. 101-128, an essay based on interviews with adult members of the Sinkaietk community. She provides an overview of many topics relating to Native American women, including childhood, puberty and adolescence, marriage, sex life, childbirth, and adult life. She

elaborates on the puberty rites for girls, including seclusion, swimming, prayer, basketmaking, and use of a special sweat lodge.

154. Cloud, Barbara. "Laura Hall Peters: Pursuing the Myth of Equality." *Pacific Northwest Quarterly* 74 (January 1983): 28-32. Notes. Map of the Puget Sound Cooperative colony.

Peters (1840-1902) moved to Seattle in 1864 with her husband, Isaac Hall, and their daughter Eudora. Her career as housewife, mother, and supporter of social movements in the region is detailed. Woman suffrage, temperance, Knights of Labor, Chinese expulsion, populism, communitarianism, and spiritualism occupied her attention. She divorced Hall in 1883 and married Charles J. Peters at the Puget Sound Cooperative in Port Angeles in 1888.

155. Coburn, Catharine Amanda Scott. "Woman's Station in Pioneer Days." In *History of the Oregon Country*, vol. I, pp. 315-322. Cambridge, Massachusetts: The Riverside Press, 1924. Notes.

A eulogistic reminiscence of pioneer women by Catharine A.S. Coburn, herself a pioneer, this article originally appeared in the August 12, 1890 Portland *Oregonian*. The author speaks particularly of women in Lafayette, Yamhill County, where she resided in the 1850s. In connection with their educational contributions she mentions the missionaries Narcissa Whitman, Mary R. Walker, Anna Maria Pittman, Mary Augusta Dix Gray, and Eliza Hart Spalding. She also discusses Tabitha Brown, founder of a boarding school that grew into Pacific University. She mentions Elizabeth Jan, Martha A., and Rebecca Barlow as particularly generous hostesses.

156. Cole, Jean Murray, "Success or Survival? The Progress and Problems of the Tshimakain Mission." *Idaho Yesterdays* 31 (Spring/Summer 1987): 86-94. Notes. Photograph of Mary Richardson Walker.

Cole examines the backgrounds, goals, and tensions in the lives of four founders of the Oregon Territory mission. Mary Walker's diary, in addition to material about Mary Richardson Walker, Elkanah Walker, the Rev. Cushing Eells, and Myra Fairbanks Eells, discusses their journey to the West, the formation of the Columbia Maternal Association at Narcissa Whitman's mission, life among the Spokane Indians between 1839-1848, Jane Klyne McDonald, a part-Indian wife of a white settler, and housekeeping assistance from Native American servant girls.

157. Collins, June McCormick. *Valley of the Spirits: The Upper Skagit Indians of Western Washington*. Seattle: University of Washington Press, 1974. xiii, 274 pages. Bibliography, index. Photographs of Alice Cuthbert and Regina Boome, and two of Agnes Jones Martin.

Chap. 4, on economic life, addresses the division of labor between the sexes and property rights. Chap. 5 explores the household, parent-child relationships, husband-wife relationships, and family law. Chap. 12 addresses the life cycle and describes pregnancy and childbirth, naming the baby, childhood, puberty, marriage, old age, and death.

158. Conant, Roger. *Mercer's Belles, The Journal of a Reporter*. Ed. Lenna A. Deutsch. Pullman: Washington State University Press, 1992. 147 pages. Notes, index. Photos of Occidental Hotel in Seattle, S.S. *Continental*, cartoon from *Harper's Weekly* (February 3, 1866) satirizing the Mercer expedition and one cartoon from *Puck, the Pacific Pictorial* (1866) of "Mercer's Belles."

This is a useful edition of Roger Conant's journal, *The Cruise of the Continental or An Inside View of a Life On the Ocean Wave*, which he wrote during the 1866 voyage of the S.S. *Continental*. The ship carried single women from New York to the Pacific Northwest. Editor Lenna A. Deutsch has added explanatory footnotes to his narration of the passengers' experiences, as well as a list of the passengers, their biographies, newspaper announcements, and circulars pertinent to the recruitment of female settlers. The book includes an introduction by historian Susan Armitage.

159. Confederated Tribes of the Warm Springs Reservation of Oregon. *The People of Warm Springs*. Warm Springs, Oregon: Confederated Tribes of Warm Springs, 1984. 80 pages. Dozens of photographs of women, with cornhusk bags, at boarding school, in families.

The text in this volume does not stress the experiences of Native American women from the Confederated Tribes of the Warm Springs Reservation of Oregon, including Wasco, Paiute, and Warm Springs women, but the photographs portray numerous women in a variety of settings.

160. Connelly, Dolly. "Bloomers and Blouses Plus Waving Alpen-Sticks." *Smithsonian* 7 (October 1976): 126-131. Three photographs of women mountain climbing.

On July 19, 1894, thirty-eight women joined with 155 men in the Portland, Oregon, area to form the Mazamas Club. This was the first climbing club to accept women on equal standing with male mountaineers. The members climbed Mt. Hood, Mt. Jefferson, Three Sisters, Mt. Shasta, Mt. Rainier, and, in 1906, Mt. Baker. In 1906, the Mountaineers formed as an auxiliary to the Portland club. The new group contained fifty-five men and fifty-five women.

161. Cook, Beatrice. *Till Fish Do Us Part; The Confessions of a Fisherman's Wife*. New York: William Morrow, 1949. 249 pages.

162. ———. *More Fish to Fry*. New York: William Morrow, 1951. 280 pages.

Here are chatty autobiographical accounts of life with a fanatical Northwest sport fisherman. The wife of a Seattle physician describes the San Juan Island and Skagit River salmon fishing trips her husband and two sons initiated.

163. Coonc, Elizabeth Ann. "Reminiscences of a Pioneer Woman." Ed. William L. Lewis. *Washington Historical Quarterly* 8 (January 1917): 14-21. Notes.

This is a well written narrative covering the entire life of Elizabeth Coonc from girlhood in the 1840s in Linn County, Oregon, to old age in Spokane County, Washington. She remembers specific events in her family history and describes the farming and ranching activities of her husband. There is detailed discussion of relations between Indians and whites.

164. Coons, Frederica B. *The Trail to Oregon*. Portland, Oregon: Binfords and Mort, 1954. ix, 183 pages. Notes, index.

This is a chatty account of what it was like to purchase supplies and make the overland journey from Missouri to Oregon. Coons quotes many diaries and letters of the mid-nineteenth century, including those by women and girls. She provides a list of markers along the trail, including women's graves.

165. Corning, Howard McKinley, ed. *Dictionary of Oregon History*. Portland, Oregon: Binfords and Mort, 1956. xiv, 281 pages. Bibliography.

This dictionary makes occasional reference to Oregon women and their organizations. Among those included are Abigail Scott Duniway, Narcissa Prentiss Whitman, the Columbia Maternal Association, Eliza H. Spalding, Congresswoman Edith Green, Normal Schools to educate teachers, writer Anne Shannon Monroe, Indian guide Sacajawea, and early school teacher Julia A. Carter Smith.

166. Cornish, Nellie C. *Miss Aunt Nellie; The Autobiography of Nellie C. Cornish*. Ed. Ellen Van Volkenburg

Browne and Edward Nordhoff Beck. Seattle: University of Washington Press, 1964. xvi, 283 pages. Index. Photos of Cornish students, staff and events, among them are photos of Nellie Cornish.

Nellie Cornish (1876-1956) founded the Cornish School in Seattle in 1914. She directed the institution until 1939, developing an innovative program in music, theater, puppetry, diction, dance, painting, and design by tapping the resources of such renowned artists as Mark Tobey, Martha Graham, Florence and Burton James, Maurice Browne and Ellen Van Volkenburg Browne, and a wave of talented white Russian refugees after 1917. Her narrative provides great detail on the story of her life and her associates at the school.

167. Corsilles, D.V., ed. *Rizal Park: Symbol of Filipino Identity; Glimpses of 'Pinoy' Life in the Pacific Northwest.* No city: Magiting Corporation, 1983. xvi, 280 pages. Photographs: Dolores Sibonga, Seattle city councilwoman; Roselie Pagulayan-Montero, president of the Veterans of Foreign Wars Ladies Auxiliary; members of Fil-American Teachers' Association, 1966.

This collection contains essays on the role of women in the Philippines, the Filipino Nurses Association of Seattle (formed in 1963), interview with teacher Nina O'Keefe, Philippine Women's University Alumnae Association, Veterans of Foreign Wars Ladies Auxiliary, Philippine war brides, history of the Fil-American Teachers' Association, and Gabriela Silang Lodge No. 89 honoring a woman martyr, Maria Josefa G. Silang.

168. Crawford, Charles Howard. *Scenes of Earlier Days In Crossing the Plains to Oregon and Experiences of Western Life.* Chicago: Quadrangle Books, Inc., 1962. 186 pages.

In the mid-nineteenth century, Crawford headed west. He mentions the women who cooked and collected buffalo chips on the trail, their impressive handling of hardships, the bigamy of male pioneers, and the return of women to the East when daunted by the difficulties of western life.

169. Crawford, Helen. "Sacajawea." *North Dakota Historical Quarterly* 1 (April 1927): 5-15. Notes. Photograph of the Sacajawea statue in Bismark, North Dakota.

This brief account of Sacajawea's life draws heavily on references to the Indian scout in Lewis' and Clark's journals on their exploration of the West. In discussing her later life, Crawford places Sacajawea's death at Fort Manuel in 1812,

disagreeing with Grace Hebard's account. A well reasoned, scholarly article.

170. Croly, Mrs. Jane Cunningham. *The History of the Woman's Club Movement in America.* New York: Henry G. Allen, 1898. 1,185 pages. Index. Photographs of Oregon club women: Adeliea D. Wade, Jennie E. Wright, Mrs. J.L. Cavana, and seven members of the Thursday Afternoon Club; Washington club women: Abbie H.H. Stuart, Charlotte S. Brintnall, Ella K. Arsons, Laura Shellabarger Hunt, Esther A. Jobes, Rebecca J. Ely, Mrs. C.L. Slauson, Frances Knapp, Mrs. A.J. Ross, Carrie L. Allen, Alice C. Baird, Dr. Sarah Kendall, Amy P. Story.

The chapters on Oregon clubs and Washington clubs provide extraordinary details on the founders and supporters of literary clubs, their activities, and goals. The Oregon section features the history and achievements of the Thursday Afternoon Club of Pendleton; Twentieth Century Club of Portland; Woman's Club of Portland; Neighborhood Club of La Grande; and Musical Club of Portland. The Washington section catalogues the founding and development of the Woman's Club of Olympia, Aloha Club of Tacoma, Sorosis in Spokane, Nesida Club of Tacoma, Classic Culture Club of Seattle, Woman's Century Club of Seattle, Nineteenth Century Literary Club of Seattle, Everett Book Club, Society of Literary Explorers of Port Angeles, Woman's Club of North Yakima, Woman's Reading Club of Walla Walla, St. Helena Club of Chehalis, Fortnightly Club on Queen Anne Hill in Seattle, Woman's Industrial Club in Seattle, Woman's Club of Snohomish, PEO and the Washington State Federation of Women's Clubs.

171. Cross, Mary Bywater. *Treasures in the Trunk: Quilts of the Oregon Trail.* Nashville: Rutledge Hill Press, 1993. xvii, 174 pages. Notes, bibliography, index. Photographs of fifty-one quilts representing forty-six different quilt patterns (including crazy quilt, eight-pointed star, road to California, Oregon rose, and Oregon Trail) from twenty-two Northwest museums and historical societies, the Smithsonian Institution's National Museum of American History, and the Daughters of the American Revolution quilt collection in Washington, D.C.; 30 photographs of women quilters.

This volume celebrates the 150th anniversary of the Oregon Trail journeys of 300,000 pioneers who traversed the West from Independence, Missouri, to Oregon City, Oregon, by wagon. Cross provides biographies of several women who made the trip, discussing for each her origins, her family, her experiences moving west, her daily life in Oregon, and the quilts she created en route and on the frontier. The author quotes from seven diaries and many letters by the pioneer women quilters.

172. Cumming, William. *Sketchbook: A Memoir of the 1930's and the Northwest School.* Seattle: University of Washington Press, 1984. 239 pages. Photographs of Margaret Callahan, Betty Bowen, Agatha Kirsh (WPA Federal Arts Project Secretary in Seattle), Esther Olson, Denise Farwell, Emma Stimson, Betty Willis, Betty MacDonald, Viola Patterson, Cumming's grandmother and mother, his painting of stripper Ginger Dare.

This Seattle painter's autobiography describes the arts environment of the 1930s, where he learned to paint, met artists like Morris Graves, Mark Tobey, and Kenneth Callahan, and worked for the WPA Arts Project. He mentions several women briefly, including project sculptor "Buxom" Irene McHugh; Margaret Callahan; patrons Mrs. Fuller, Joanna Eckstein, Emma Stimson, Betty Bowen; Seattle Repertory Playhouse director Florence James; Xenia Cage (the Russian wife of the Cornish School composer John Cage); the stripper Ginger Dare; author Betty MacDonald, who was also Seattle's director of the Division of Information, National Youth Administration; Cumming's daughters, mother-in-law and wife Lofty; and Mrs. Harold Davis.

173. Cummins, Sarah J. *Autobiography and Reminiscences of Sarah J. Cummins.* La Grande, Oregon: La Grande Printing Company, 1914. 63 pages. One photograph of herself, aged ninety-one years, eleven months.

The autobiography and remembrances concentrate on the making of a home in a new region, the Willamette Valley in 1845. It includes tales of being robbed by American Indians, crossing the Rocky and Cascade mountains and arriving in The Dalles, Oregon, September 14, 1845.

174. Curtis, Edward S. *The North American Indian: Being a Series of Volumes Picturing and Describing the Indians of the United States and Alaska.* [Seattle]: Edward S. Curtis; [Cambridge, Mass.: The University Press], 1907-1930. Reprint, New York: Johnson Reprint Company, 1970. Vol. 7: 210 pages; vol. 8: 227 pages; vol. 9: 227 pages; vol. 13: 316 pages; vol. 15: 225 pages; vol. 19: 270 pages. Notes, index. Many photographs of Indian women and Indian dwellings.

Vols. 7, 8, 9, 13, 15 and 19 include Oregon's American Indians (Cayuse, Chinookan, Klamath, Klickitat, Shasta, Shoshoneans [Plateau], Tolowa, Tututni, Umatilla) and Washington Indians (Cayuse, Chehalis [Lower and Upper], Cowlitz, Chimakum, Chinookan, Clallam, Colvilles, Kalispel, Klickitat, Lakes, Lummi, Methow, Nespilim, Nez Perces, Nooksack, Okanogan, Puget Sound Tribes, Quilliute, Quinault, Salishan [Interior], Samish, Sanetch, Shoalwater Bay, Sinkiuse [Interior Salishan], Sanpoel, Semiahoo, Songish, Spokan, Twana, Walla Walla, Wenatchee [Interior Salish], Willapa, Wishram, and Yakama). There is discussion of women as chiefs in Wishram mythology; women in winter ceremonies; Rock Woman; the clothing of the Chinook, Shasta, and Yakama; songs; women in puberty rites; arts; games; marriage; tattoos; Salish hair-dressing; Klamath bathing customs; singers in healing rites; and mourning.

175. Cutting, Maria Cable. "After Thoughts." *Oregon Historical Quarterly* 63 (June-September 1962): 237-241. Notes.

This short, jumbled reminiscence is by an English emigrant to Cowlitz County, Washington. Maria Cutting, her husband, and daughter homesteaded Cutting Prairie in 1853. Maria describes the hardships of the voyage from England to San Francisco, the building of the homestead, in which she participated, relations with American Indians, which were friendly, and the meager diet of the first pioneering years.

176. Dalgliesh, Elizabeth Rhodes. *History of Alpha Chi Omega.* 6th edition. Menasha, Wisconsin: Banta Publishing Company, 1948. 499 pages. Photographs of Rho's University of Washington chapter house in 1926 and the sorority's twelve charter members and Whitman College's Beta Zeta chapter house and twenty-nine charter members.

This collection contains a portrait of Rho Chapter of the Alpha Chi Omega sorority, founded in 1910. It describes the furnishings of the chapter house, which opened in 1926, and activities of the membership.

177. Daly, Ida F. *Adventure in a Wheelchair; Pioneering for the Handicapped.* Philadelphia: Whitmore Publishing Company, 1973. 79 pages. Bibliography, index.

This is Ida Daly's story of her life dealing with muscular dystrophy. It tells of her desire to lead an independent life and her work to help other disabled people. Through her efforts, the first apartment house and center especially designed for the handicapped was built. Born in Iowa (1901), Ida Daly spent most of her life in Seattle.

178. Daugherty, James. *Marcus and Narcissa Whitman, Pioneers of Oregon.* New York: Viking Press, 1953. 158 pages. Footnotes.

This is a romanticized biography of Marcus and Narcissa Whitman from the time of their marriage in 1836 to their deaths in 1847.

Includes details of the day-to-day life at the mission, troubles with the American Indians, hardships endured by Narcissa, and controversy surrounding the Whitmans. It makes some use of Narcissa Whitman's letters and diary.

179. Daughters of the American Revolution, Multnomah Chapter. *History and By-Laws of the Multnomah Chapter, Daughters of the American Revolution.* Portland: Irwin-Hudson Co., 1903. 32 pages.

This is a history of one Oregon chapter of the patriotic women's organization, from its founding in 1896 through its first seven years of operation. Six pages of by-laws, a list of officers by year, and a list of members is included.

180. Daughters of the American Revolution, Washington State Society. *Bicentennial Commemorative.* Seattle: Commercial Printing Company, 1976. 109 pages.

This resource guide for Daughters of the American Revolution lists members, officers, awards, and ceremonies. While it contains no narrative history of the DAR in Washington state, it chronicles, through its lists, the accomplishments, activities, leadership, and membership of the patriotic society through its formative years.

181. Daughters of the Pioneers of Washington. *Incidents in the Life of Pioneer Women.* No city: Washington State Association of the Daughters of the Pioneers, 1976. 173 pages.

Members of the organization have written brief biographies of pioneers. Vivian Spurrell Jordan's account deals with the 1882 wedding of her grandmother, Alice Newell (Mrs. Henry) Williams. Willa Morgan Leighton contributed an entry on Nettie Connet Dempsey, the aunt of her mother, an independent woman who did a variety of jobs, including ranching. Lois Cain records material about her grandmother's encounters with Native Americans. Poems and excerpts from diaries are used.

182. Davidson, Sue. "Aki Kato Kurose: Portrait of an Activist." *Frontier* 7 (1983): 91-97. Notes.

Here are lengthy excerpts from an interview of Aki Kato Kurose, a Japanese American from Seattle who was a sixteen-year-old citizen when Pearl Harbor was bombed in 1941. She and her family were interned during World War II, first in Puyallup, Washington, and then in Hunt, Idaho. She describes the internment, child-bearing and raising children, teaching school, volunteerism, and activism.

183. Davidson, Sue. "The Liberal Ladies' Beach." *Backbone* 3 (1981): 57-67.

Sue Davidson reminiscences about her own experiences and those of her Seattle friends who combined activism with marriage, running a household, and raising a family in the 1960s. She discusses Carla Annette Chotzen, a mother of eight and a professional photographer of children who worked to oppose nuclear arms testing and promote peace; Carolyn Kizer, founder of *Poetry Northwest*, who worked on an anti-bomb film; Ginny NiCarthy Crow, who was involved in the peace, feminism, and civil rights movements; Ruth Karnofsky Crow, in civil rights organizations, the Progressive Party, Labor Youth League, American Civil Liberties Union, and feminism; and Jeri Ware, who dealt with African American issues through the Negro Labor Council and Central Area School Council.

184. Davis, Elizabeth (Lindsay). *Lifting as They Climb: The National Association of Colored Women.* Washington, D.C.: National Association of Colored Women's Clubs, 1937. 424 pages. Index. Photographs of Nettie J. Asberry, Mrs. N.J. Simms, Mrs. Susan Curd, and Mrs. Katherine Gray, all officers of the Northwest region of the organization.

This general history of the National Association of Colored Women's Clubs contains a brief overview of the history of the Oregon Federation of Colored Women's Clubs and the Washington State Federation of Colored Women's Clubs.

185. Davis, Lenwood G. *The Black Woman in American Society: A Selected Annotated Bibliography.* Boston: G. K. Hall and Company, 1975. xi, 150 pages. Index.

This is a listing of 701 books, articles, general reference works, reports, pamphlets, speeches, and government documents relating to the experiences of black women in the United States past and present. This is a valuable resource, but only four of the entries specifically relate to black women in the Pacific Northwest. Entries are listed by author, and a subject index is included in the back.

186. Dawson, Jan. "Sacagawea: Pilot or Pioneer Mother?" *Pacific Northwest Quarterly* 83 (January 1992): 22-28. Notes. Photographs of Eva

Emery Dye, statue of Sacagawea, and suffragists at the dedication of the statue.

This historian examines the efforts of early twentieth-century suffragists to mythologize the contributions of Sacagawea to the Lewis and Clark expedition of 1805. Their motive was to secure heroines for the woman suffrage movement.

187. Dearborn, Mary V. *Queen of Bohemia: The Life of Louise Bryant.* New York: Houghton Mifflin, 1996. xiii, 365 pages. Notes, bibliography, index. Thirty-two photographs of Bryant, but only one of her Portland years.

This complimentary biography of journalist, artist, and sculptor Louise Bryant (1885-1935) documents her colorful life associated with radical causes. Her most famous husband was Portland-born John Reed, publicizer of the Russian Revolution of 1917. The book gives most attention to the Northwest, however, in its account of her college experiences at the University of Oregon and her first marriage in 1909 to Portland dentist Paul Trulliger. Bryant left Trulliger in 1916 to follow Reed to Greenwich Village. After Reed's death, Bryant married William C. Bullitt, with whom she had a daughter.

188. De Barros, Paul. *Jackson Street After Hours: The Roots of Jazz in Seattle.* Seattle: Sasquatach, 1993. xi, 238 pages. Notes, bibliography, index. Photographs of Jimi Hendrix' grandmother Nora Hendrix, Billie Holiday performing in Seattle, and Seattle's African American blues singers, including Freda Shaw, Evelyn Bundy, Mildred Bailey, Evelyn Wiliamson, Betty Marshall, Janet Thurlow, Wanda Brown, Ernestine Anderson, Patti Brown, Juanita Cruse, Melody Jones, and Cathi Hayes.

While "girl singers" receive more print here than women do in any other role in the Seattle jazz scene, quotations from interviews with women vocalists provide rich details about the entire music world.

189. Debow, Samuel P., and Edward A. Pitter, eds. *Who's Who in Religious, Fraternal, Social, Civic and Commercial Life on the Pacific Coast.* Seattle: Searchlight Publishing Company, 1926/27. Index. 244 pages. Numerous photographs of black women.

This volume consists mainly of brief biographies of prominent black Seattle citizens. Out of 179 biographies, 59 are of women. Also listed are women members of various clubs, organizations, and churches, including several chapters of the Order of Eastern Star, Sojourner Truth Home, Citizen's Council, The First A.M.E. Church, Mt. Zion Baptist Church, Grace Presbyterian Church, and others.

190. Defenbach, Byron. *Red Heroines of the Northwest.* Caldwell, Idaho: The Caxton Printers, Ltd., 1929. 309 pages. Photos of the Sacajawea statue in Portland, of Barbara Myers, grandchild of Sacajawea, an Indian girl child, and of Jane Silcott.

This book contains three biographies of Native American women: Sacajawea of the Lewis and Clark expedition; Madame Dorion, involved in the exploration of the Snake River; and Jan Silcott, associated with gold digging in Idaho in the 1860s. The author is primarily interested in the relationship of these women to Idaho history, but they were all involved in Washington and Oregon history as well. In reference to research about Sacajawea, the work is dated; Defenbach declares that her death occurred in 1884, at Fort Washakie, based on the research of Grace Raymond Hebard, but recent scholars have established her death as decades earlier, before 1820.

191. Delaney, Matilda J. Sager. *A Survivor's Recollections of the Whitman Massacre.* Spokane: Esther Reed Chapter, Daughters of the American Revolution, 1920 edition. Reprint, Seattle: The Shorey Book Store, 1967. 50 pages. Photograph of Matilda J. Sager Delaney and drawing of the Whitman mission.

This is an account of the Whitman massacre by one of the survivors, Matilda J. Sager Delaney. She relates the story of her journey west on the Oregon Trail, including the death of her parents and her adoption by the Whitmans.

192. Del Mar, David Peterson. *What Trouble I Have Seen: A History of Violence Against Wives.* Cambridge: Harvard University Press, 1996. xi, 244 pages. Notes.

Del Mar surveys domestic violence in the mid-nineteenth century period of Oregon settlement, in early towns of the 1890s, in the mid-twentieth century, and in the era since World War II. Chap. 3 (pages 72-96) provides a history of Oregon's whipping post law for wife beaters (1905-1911), which subjected three offenders to twenty lashes for domestic violence. The section serves as a vehicle for the author to examine the general topic of family violence in early twentieth-century Oregon, drawing on court records for moving personal testimonies.

193. Delta Kappa Gamma. *Alpha Sigma State, Washington. Alpha Sigma State's Centennial Salute to Washington's Pioneer Women Teachers.* Ellensburg,

Washington: Delta Kappa Gamma, 1953. 63 pages. One photograph of Elizabeth Prior.

This booklet is comprised of brief biographies of forty pioneer women educators, most of whom arrived in Washington state prior to 1900 and settled in every geographical region of the state. Each biography features early background, interests, and educational achievements. This material was obtained through interviews of the subject herself and/or family and friends, newspaper articles, old records, and other publications.

194. Dembo, Jonathan. *An Historical Bibliography of Washington State Labor and Laboring Classes.* Seattle: Dembo, 1978. ii, 238 pages. Bibliography, index.

This is a comprehensive bibliography of Washington labor history. Entries include one-sentence annotations. Nearly 100 entries are primarily or significantly related to women and women's issues. In addition, Dembo lists three biographies of radical journalist Anna Louise Strong and six of Elizabeth Gurley Flynn, who was arrested in Spokane for her free speech efforts in 1909.

195. Denny, Arthur A. *Pioneer Days on Puget Sound.* Ed. Alice Harriman. Seattle: Alice Harriman Company, 1908. 103 pages. Index. Photographs of Mary A. Boren Denny, Louisa Boren, Louisa and Leonora Denny, L. Gertrude Boren, Ursula Wyckoff, Olive J. Bell Stearns, Laura K. Bell Coffman, Mary Virginia Bell Hall, the J. N. Low Family, Mrs. Mary J. Russell, and her daughter Bess.

Women are incidental to this history of pioneer days in Seattle. They are mentioned only in passing, as relatives of founding fathers.

196. Denny, Emily Inez. *Blazing the Way; Or, True Stories, Songs and Sketches of Puget Sound and Other Pioneers.* Seattle: Rainier Printing Company, Inc., 1909. 504 pages, plus 50-page typescript index bound with book. Photos of Sarah Denny; Louisa B. Denny; daughters of D.T. and L.B. Denny; Mrs. L.C. Low.

This is an extremely valuable account of pioneer life in Seattle. The author recounts stories of the Denny party and the Oregon Trail experiences of Esther Chambers and Mrs. C.J. Crosby. She also provides biographical sketches of Sarah Latimer Denny, Louisa Boren Denny, Madge Decatur Denny, Anna Louisa Denny, and Mary A. Denny. She has a chapter on "Pioneer Child Life," and one on "The First Wedding on Elliott Bay." The book is a wealth of

narrative and anecdotal detail about the major events and everyday activities of pioneer life.

197. Devine, Jean Porter. *From Settlement House to Neighborhood House, 1906-1976: An Historical Survey of a Pioneering Seattle Social Service Agency.* Seattle: Neighborhood House, Inc., 1976. 48 pages. Footnotes, bibliography. Eighteen photographs of people and places connected with Neighborhood House.

This is a detailed summary of the history of Neighborhood House, Seattle's first settlement house. Founded in 1906, it was sponsored by the Council of Jewish Women until 1956 when it became an independent agency. During its association with the council, Neighborhood House was run and supported primarily by clubwomen, who are highlighted in the text.

198. Dilger, Robert Jay, with the assistance of Anne Maren Moser. "Julia Butler Hansen: The Pragmatic Reformer." *Pacific Northwest Forum* 10, 3/4 (Summer/Fall 1985): 13-21. Notes. One photograph of Julia Butler Hansen.

Here is a biography of legislator Julia Butler Hansen, chairperson of the Democratic Committee on Organizational Study and Review in the U.S. House of Representatives in 1970. She proposed and successfully defended a series of reforms in 1971, 1973, and 1974 which weakened the seniority system and decentralized power in the House by weakening the powers of committee chairmen and strengthening the powers of subcommittee chairmen.

199. Dillion, Richard. *Siskiyou Trail: The Hudson's Bay Company Route to California.* New York: McGraw-Hill Book Co., 1975. xv, 381 pages. Bibliography, index. Illustration of Emelie Picard Laframboise.

While this work focuses on the life and work of Northwest trappers, chap. 12 discusses Emelie Picard Laframboise, one of the many wives of Michel Laframboise, a retired trapper who had a wife in every tribe on the Siskiyou Trail.

200. Dobbs, Caroline C. *Men of Champoeg: A Record of the Lives of the Pioneers Who Founded the Oregon Government.* Portland, Oregon: Metropolitan Press, 1932. v, 219 pages. Bibliography. Photograph of the marker established by the Daughters of the American Revolution to honor these pioneer Oregonians.

Here are fifty-two biographies of early male settlers with only brief mention of their Caucasian or

Native American wives. The author was the historian of the Multnomah chapter of the Daughters of the American Revolution, and the work represented the goal of the women's patriotic organization: to laud the men who made history. Students of women's history will be able to use these clues to women's early contributions to settlement, but will have to explore further to flesh out the women's story.

201. Dodds, Gordon B. *The American Northwest: A History of Oregon and Washington.* Arlington Heights, Illinois: The Forum Press, Inc., 1986. x, 359 pages. Notes, bibliography, index. Photographs: including Joseph Drayton's sketch of two Native American women at Jason Lee's mission in Salem; Paul Kane's sketch of Narcissa Whitman; Nellie Cornish; May Arkwright Hutton; Abigail Scott Duniway at the polls with two other women; Anna Louise Strong; Japanese workers posed at Hood River, Oregon work camp in 1920; Oregon representative Nan Wood Honeyman; and Japanese assembly center at Portland's Livestock Exposition Center on August 30, 1942.

This text discusses several areas of importance to Northwest women, including women's role in trappers' work, wives of missionaries, pioneer women's labor on the homestead, woman suffrage, the women's rights activism of Abigail Scott Duniway, organizational efforts of the Oregon Federation of Colored Women's Clubs, Seattle Ladies Colored Social Circle, the Women's Christian Temperance Union, Prohibitionist efforts to close the Webfoot Saloon, the pacifism of Anna Louise Strong, and Multnomah County librarian M. Louise Hunt's refusal to buy war bonds during World War I.

It looks at women's contributions to the arts and credits Nellie C. Cornish with the founding of the Cornish School. There is mention of paintings by Margaret Tomkins, Hilda Deutsch, and the Spokane Federated Art Center, Portland poets Ada H. Hedges and Mary C. Davies, and Northwest writers Eva Emery Dye, Ella Higginson, Abigail Scott Duniway, Minnie Dyer, and journalist and historian Frances Fuller Victor. Eda Bunce, with her husband Louis, opened the first Northwest art gallery in 1940, in Portland; Zoe Dusanne opened the first Seattle art gallery in 1951. Ursula K. LeGuin is named for her science fiction and fantasy writing. Anna Belle Crocker was the director of the Portland Art Association's museum from 1909 to 1936. Amanda Reed left her family fortune to found Reed Institute (now Reed College) in 1911.

In Oregon politics, there is reference to Edith Green, a representative to the Oregon House from 1954 to 1973 and a moving spirit in the War on Poverty and in writing the National Defense Education Act of 1958. Helen Frye was the first woman appointed to the federal bench from Oregon, in 1980. Norma Paulus was elected secretary of state in 1976, the first woman to hold an elective state-wide office.

In Washington, Dixy Lee Ray was elected governor in 1976. Catherine May of Yakima was the first woman elected representative to Washington, D. C., in 1958.

202. ———. *Oregon: A Bicentennial History.* New York: W. W. Norton and Company, Inc., 1977. xiv, 240 pages. Notes, bibliography, index.

This history contains a careful discussion of the fight for woman suffrage, led by Abigail Scott Duniway. The Oregon Donation Land Act of 1850 and its impact on women is examined. The grange of the 1890s is explored for its advanced notions of women's participation.

203. Dodge, Orvil. *Pioneer History of Coos and Curry Counties, Oregon.* Salem: Capital Printing Company, 1898. 468 pages of history and 103 pages of biography. Photographs of women.

The first section of this book consists of a general history of the region. A memoir by Mrs. Esther M. Lockhart is provided, who came to Coos Bay in 1853, taught at Empire City, and fled to the local fort in 1855 in fear of attack by Rogue River Indians. The biographical section contains hundreds of biographies of early men settlers, and includes only a few women pioneers. Among them are Rachel Moore Ayres, Mrs. August Bender, Ruty Collier, Mrs. S.A. Edmunds, Charlotte Guerin, Mrs. Martha Hall, and Mrs. B. Vonder Green.

204. Douthit, Mary Osborn. *The Souvenir of Western Women.* Portland: Anderson and Duniway Company, 1905. 200 pages. Photos of Abigail Scott Duniway; a Umatilla woman; Mary A. D. Gray; Mrs. Charlotte Cartwright; Miss Mary B. Rodney; Miss Helen F. Spalding; Linda Bronson-Salmon; Frances F. Victor; Eva Emery Dye; Narcissa White Kinney; Emma Wilson Gillespie; an Indian woman; Mrs. Catherine A. Coburn; Lueza Osborn Douthit; a Chinese mother and children.

This is a nonacademic book about pioneer women and the life and activities of women in Oregon, Washington, and Idaho up to the 1890s. It is comprised of 105 short essays about individuals, groups, clubs, and topics. Some representative titles: "Councils of Jewish Women," "Home Life of Chinese

Women in the West," "Women in Medicine," "The Oregon Woman's Flax Industry," "Baptist Women in the Pacific Northwest," "Women's Clubs in Oregon," "A Grandmother's Story of Early Days in Washington," "Babies of the Pioneers," "Susan B. Anthony's Visits to Oregon."

205. Dorr, Rheta Childe. *A Woman of Fifty*. New York: Funk and Wagnalls Company, 1924. 451 pages.

In this account of a feminist reporter who covered Russia's Revolution, World War I in Europe, and English suffragettes, she also describes life and her marriage in Seattle from 1893 to 1899.

206. Drazan, Joseph Gerald. *The Pacific Northwest: An Index to People and Places in Books*. Metuchen, New Jersey: The Scarecrow Press, Inc., 1979. xii, 164 pages. Bibliography, index.

This book indexes 6,830 people and 2,100 places in 320 major Northwest source books. The organization of the book is clear and accessible. Many women, from pioneer to contemporary times, are included.

207. Drew, Harry J. *Maud Baldwin —Photographer*. Klamath Falls, Oregon: Klamath County Museum, 1988. Research Paper no. 10. 143 pages. Bibliography. 134 photographs of Baldwin, her family, and her work.

A brief biography is followed by 134 examples of Maud Baldwin's (1878-1929) work as a photographer, including her images of American Indians, buildings and businesses, agriculture, logging, transportation, schools, the landscape, and portraits.

208. Drury, Clifford M. "The Columbia Maternal Association." *Oregon Historical Quarterly* 39 (June 1938): 99-122. Notes.

The first women's club of settlers west of the Rocky Mountains was founded at the Whitman mission at Waiilatpu in 1838. Six wives of missionaries (Mrs. Narcissa Whitman, Mrs. Henry Harmon Spalding, Mrs. Augusta Dix, Mrs. Elkanah Walker, Mrs. Cushing Eells, and Mrs. A.B. Smith) created the Columbia Maternal Association to discuss topics of interest to mothers, including articles in *Mother's Magazine*, to which they subscribed.

209. ———. *The Diaries and Letters of Henry Spalding and Asa Smith*. Glendale: Arthur H. Clark Company, 1958. 379 pages. Notes, bibliography, index. Three photos—Mary Grant and husband.

This book includes the diaries and letters of Mr. H. Spalding and Mr. A. Smith, 1838-1842, as they journeyed to Oregon. The footnotes include bits and pieces from the Mrs. Elkanah Walker and Mrs. Cushing Eells diaries on their experiences pioneering.

210. ———. *Elkanah and Mary Walker, Pioneers Among the Spokanes*. Caldwell, Idaho: The Caxton Printers, Ltd., 1940. 283 pages. Notes, bibliography, index. Photos of Mr. and Mrs. W.H. Gray; Mrs. Cushing Eells; Colville Indians; Mary Walker; Abigail and Cyrus Walker.

A large proportion of this biography is based on the lengthy and highly personal diaries (1838-1847) of missionary Mary Walker.

211. ———. *First White Women Over the Rockies*. 3 vols., Glendale, California: The Arthur H. Clark Company, 1963. Vol. 1, 280 pages; vol. 2, 382 pages; vol. 3, 332 pages. Notes, bibliography, index. Photos and portraits of Mary Richardson Walker, Myra Fairbanks Eells, Sarah White Smith, Mary Augusta Dix Gray, and Narcissa Prentiss Whitman.

This work presents a mass of information about the Oregon Mission of the American Board of Foreign Missions. Drury has written a detailed biographical sketch of each of the missionary women. He has also excerpted, organized, and introduced their diaries and letters. The majority of all of their writings are included in the three volumes. There is a wealth of detail about the overland journey, relations with American Indians, relations among the missionaries, teaching, daily activities, religious beliefs and motivations, health, and hardships as told by Mary Richardson Walker, Myra Fairbanks Eells, Sarah White Smith, Mary Augusta Dix Gray, and Narcissa Prentiss Whitman.

212. ———. *Henry Harmon Spalding, Pioneer of Old Oregon*. Caldwell, Idaho: The Caxton Publishers, Ltd., 1936. 438 pages. Notes, bibliography, index. Photos of Mrs. Joe Nozer, Eliza Spalding Warren, Martha Jane Spalding Wigle, Amelia Spalding Brown.

While this book is primarily about Henry H. Spalding, his wife Eliza figures in it prominently. Her work as a successful teacher of the Nez Perce Indians is chronicled, and the birth of her children and many aspects of her daily life are included.

213. ———. *Marcus and Narcissa Whitman, and the Opening of Old Oregon.* 2 vols. Glendale, California: The Arthur H. Clark Company, 1973. 911 pages. Notes, bibliography, index. Painting and sketch believed to be of Narcissa Whitman. Photographs of Catherine Sager Pringle, Elizabeth Sager Helm, and Mathilda Sager Delaney.

This is one of the most authoritative biographies of Narcissa and Marcus Whitman. Drury gives lengthy character sketches of Narcissa Whitman and Eliza Spalding, and utilizes Narcissa's letters and diaries fully. He is very even handed in his treatment and assessment of the Whitmans.

214. ———. *Marcus Whitman, M.D., Pioneer and Martyr.* Caldwell, Idaho: The Caxton Printers, Ltd., 1937. 473 pages. Notes, bibliography, index. Drawing of Narcissa Whitman, Mrs. Harriet Prentiss Jackson.

This is Drury's early biography of Whitman. Narcissa does not figure as prominently in this book as she does in his later *Marcus and Narcissa Whitman*, but she, Eliza Spalding, and many other women mission residents are important characters in the book. Narcissa's letters and diaries are a major resource for the book, and one whole chapter and several sections of chapters are devoted to her.

215. ———. "The Spokane Indian Mission at Tshimakain, 1838-1848." *Pacific Northwest Quarterly* 67 (January 1976): 1-9. Notes. Photographs of Mary Walker and Myra Eells with their husbands.

This account of two missionary couples in Tshimakain, twenty-five miles northwest of Spokane, uses diaries to build an important portrait of life in the Inland Empire, including agricultural, domestic, religious, and educational patterns of the Native Americans.

216. ———. "Wilderness Diaries: A Missionary Couple in the Pacific Northwest." *American West* 13 (1976): 4-9, 62-63. Bibliography. Photograph of Mary Walker.

Mary Walker was a faithful diarist for most of her life while her husband Elkanah Walker wrote sporadically. Drury compares their accounts, written while they were missionaries to the Spokane Indians from 1839-1849. He explores their views of the overland journey, household labors, food, housing, furniture, medical practices, relations with the Indians, and raising and educating five children.

217. Drury, Clifford M., comment by. *More About the Whitmans: Four Hitherto Unpublished Letters of Marcus and Narcissa Whitman.* Tacoma: Washington State Historical Society, 1979. 22 pages. Notes. Image of design for a Narcissa Whitman window in the Stewart Memorial Chapel, San Francisco Theological Seminary.

Drury used 302 letters by Marcus and Narcissa Whitman for his 1973 book, *Marcus and Narcissa Whitman and the Opening of Old Oregon.* Then he found these four additional letters. Narcissa wrote to her sister on January 16, 1840, and to her brother-in-law on September 30, 1842. Marcus wrote two in 1847. Drury points out that they contain little new information, but they contribute to a better understanding of Narcissa's assistance to pregnant wives of missionaries and describe her help during the delivery of their babies.

218. Dryden, Cecil P. *Dryden's History of Washington.* Portland, Oregon: Binfords and Mort Publishers, 1968. ix, 412 pages. Bibliography, index. Two photographs of women: Cecilia, an Okanogan Indian, and coastal Indian women weaving baskets.

This study includes references to three missionary women, Narcissa Whitman, Eliza Spalding, and Mary Walker. It also details the spring 1864 Mercer girls expedition, on which East Coast women traveled by ship to Seattle, and mentions the less successful subsequent effort. Dryden explores the fight for women's rights led by Abigail Scott Duniway, Emma Smith DeVoe, and May A. Hutton.

219. ———. *Give All to Oregon!: Missionary Pioneers of the Far West.* New York: Hastings House, 1968. 256 pages. Notes, bibliography, index. Illustrations of Narcissa Whitman, and a Chinook mother with her infant.

In fictional dialogue this book tells the stories of six Belgian nuns, Sisters of Notre Dame de Namur, who accompanied Father De Smet to run a school; Methodist missionary Jason Lee's wife Anna Maria Pittman; Narcissa Whitman; six nuns at St. Paul's, whose mission attracted Chief Harkley, a Yakama Indian; Chief Lateh, an Okanogan Indian; and the conversion of Dr. John McLoughlin to Catholicism.

220. Duke, David C. "Anna Louise Strong and the Search for a Good Cause." *Pacific Northwest Quarterly* 66 (July 1975): 123-137. Notes. Photographs of Strong in 1913 and in 1947.

This article stresses the travels of Anna Louise Strong (1885-1970) through the Soviet Union between World

War I and World War II, and later through Communist China. There is considerable biographical background about her social and political development in Seattle, her election and removal from the Seattle school board in 1916, her reportage of the I.W.W. strike in Everett, Washington, for the *New York Evening Post*, her anti-war activity and support for the Seattle general strike.

221. Duniway, Abigail Scott. *Path Breaking; An Autobiographical History of the Equal Suffrage Movement in Pacific Coast States.* Portland: James, Kerns and Abbott Company, 1914. xvi, 291 pages. Photos of Abigail Scott Duniway writing Oregon's Equal Suffrage Proclamation, signing the proclamation, and registering as Oregon's first woman voter.

This famous, rambling autobiography of Abigail Scott Duniway tells of her entire life, but concentrates on her suffrage work. Duniway draws heavily on her files on the suffrage movement and reproduces in this book a large number of letters, resolutions, and articles relating to the suffrage movement. She names and describes some of her co-workers, friends and foes, thus providing valuable information about other women. There is a lot of discussion about Duniway's conflict with the prohibitionists.

222. Dunn, J. P., Jr. *Massacres of the Mountains: A History of the Indian Wars of the Far West, 1815-1875.* New York: Archer House, 1958. Notes, bibliography, index. Illustrations include "Piute Squaw and Papoose" and a Chinook woman and child.

Chap. 4, "The Murder of the Missionaries," is devoted to the death of Narcissa Whitman, the Sager children, and company. Miss Lorinda Bewley's deposition of December 1848 is quoted, in which she implicates Roman Catholic priests for inciting the Cayuse to violence.

223. Dunn, Mary M. *Undaunted Pioneers: Ever Moving Onward and Westward and Homeward.* Eugene, Oregon: Valley Printing, 1929. 54 pages.

This account draws on stories by Mary M. Dunn, aged ninety-three, and the diary of her mother Elizabeth Fine Hill, who journeyed from Tennessee to Oregon in 1852. There is description of life in Tennessee, the overland journey, a girl's farm life south of Ashland, Oregon, antagonism with the American Indians in 1855, marriage, the building of the first school, and family life. Letters are quoted to friends back home in Tennessee.

224. Durham, N.W. *History of the City of Spokane and Spokane County Washington: From its Earliest Settlements to the Present Time.* Spokane: The S.J.

Clarke Publishing Company, 1912. Vol. 1: xxviii, 661 pages; vol. 2: 831 pages, index. Vol. 3: 755 pages, index.

Women are poorly represented in this study. In vol. 1, a Scottish trapper, McDonald, takes a Spokane wife and the exchange of goods and ceremony are detailed. There is consideration of the work of Protestant missionary wives and the Sisters of the Holy Names, Spokane. The book explores the work of the Spokane Equal Suffrage Association on behalf of women's enfranchisement. In the examination of the National Apple Show, an annual event beginning in 1908, the hostesses and princesses are listed. Lucy A.R. Switzer of Cheney is credited with being the first woman to serve in the Washington territorial government.

Vols. 2 and 3, biographical encyclopedias, mention women only incidentally, as wives and daughters, to the male figures recorded. The single exception is a full biographical sketch of Miss Theo Hall, in vol. 2 (pp. 177-178), who served as the postmistress of Medical Lake, Washington, from 1893-1912 and bought and edited the Medical Lake *Ledger*.

225. Dwelley, Charles M., ed. *Skagit Memories: Stories of the Settlement Years as Written by the Pioneers Themselves.* Mount Vernon, Washington: Skagit Historical Society, 1979. vi, 170 pages. Index. Photograph of Carrie M. White and of a drinking fountain dedicated to Carrie M. White by the Anacortes chapter of the Women's Christian Temperance Union; of authors of many of the essays included in the volume.

This collection includes several brief essays, including one on Louisa Ann Conner using Conner correspondence. Among the other entries are "Kirstena's Memories" by Mrs. Peter Larsen; an account of the Civic Improvement Club of Mount Vernon by May Smith Willes; the Alpha Club by Florence B. Strong; "Those Indomitable Edison Women" on the Edison Ladies Improvement Club of 1909 by Bess Conn Rogers; "Experiences of a Pioneer Woman on the Grand Jury" by Mrs. J. M. Bradley; and "Kate Malory, Born in a Skagit Cabin" by Lucile Mc Donald.

226. Dye, Eva Emery. "Woman's Part in the Drama of the Northwest." *Transactions of the Oregon Pioneer Association, 1894,* 22nd annual reunion, pp. 36-43. Portland: Oregon Pioneer Association, 1894.

The author describes the marriages between white male pioneers in Oregon and Indian women, attributing improved cultural relations to the alliances. She discusses rugged American Indian women who were adaptable to the demands of the environment. Narcissa Whitman and Eliza Spalding, early white women who crossed the Rockies, became missionaries. When the California gold rush lured Oregon men to the mines, the women stayed behind to run the farms.

227. Eagle, Mary Kavanaugh-Oldham. *The Congress of Women, Chicago, 1893.* Philadelphia: J.W. Keeler and Company, 1894. 824 pages. Index. Reprinted New York: Arno Press, 1974. Photographs of Mary Payton, Oregon's representative to the Exposition's Board of Lady Managers, Alice Houghton of Washington, and Abigail Scott Duniway.

Elizabeth M. Wilson contributed "Pioneer Women of Oregon," her personal account of settling in Oregon, presented at the 1893 Chicago exposition. Abigail Scott Duniway's speech, "The Pacific Northwest," was a prose and poetic account of the region's history and beauty, with little mention of women. Jennie F. White delivered "Development in Eastern Washington," enumerating arts and educational facilities for the women of eastern Washington, including Walla Walla, Yakima, Pullman, and Ellensburgh. Her account of Spokane is fullest, with reference to the high school, Ladies brass band, Conservatory of Music, Mozart Club, school of oratory, Young Ladies Seminary, art studios for drawing and painting, Spokane Art League, kindergarten, Cultus Club, Spokane Sorosis, Daughters of Rebekah, Eastern Star, and Daughters of Veterans.

228. Ebey, Isaac Neff, Colonel, and Rebecca W.D. Ebey. "Diary of Colonel and Mrs. I. N. Ebey." Ed. Victor J. Farrar. *Washington Historical Quarterly* 7 (July 1916): 239-246; (October 1916): 307-321; (January 1917): 40-62. Notes.

A six-page introductory essay by Victor Farrar describes early settlements on Whidbey Island and the genealogy of the Ebey family. Brief entries follow by Colonel Ebey about the weather, ships sighted, and his building and farming concerns. In the October publication, paragraph-length entries by Mrs. Ebey, made from June to August 1852, describe pioneer life on Whidbey Island, visiting with neighbors, and hiring American Indians. She discusses loneliness and ill-health as particular problems. The third piece, Mrs. Ebey's diary of September 1852 to January 1853, addresses her lonely life raising children while her husband attends the legislature in Olympia.

229. Edson, Christopher H. *The Chinese in Eastern Oregon, 1860-1890.* San Francisco: R. D. Reed

(R & E Research Association), 1974. xi, 84 pages. Notes, bibliography, maps, and charts.

Statistics are provided on Chinese men and women in Baker, Grant, Umatilla, Union, and Wasco Counties in Oregon.

230. Edson, Lelah. *The Fourth Corner: Highlights from the Early Northwest.* Bellingham: Cox Brothers, 1951. x, 298 pages. Notes, bibliography, index. Numerous photographs including Teresa Eldridge, Mary F. Lysle, Elizabeth Roeder, Nellie Moore Coupe, Isabelle Eldridge Edens, Ella Higginson.

This is the history of Bellingham and Whatcom County from the early nineteenth century until 1904. The backgrounds and experiences of early women settlers such as Teresa Eldridge, Maria Roberts, Mary F. Lysle, Elizabeth Roeder, and Mary Tawes are recounted. The lives and accomplishments of Ella Higginson, "poet laureate of Washington," and Nellie Coupe, first teacher on Whidbey Island and first Whatcom County school superintendent, are also related.

231. Edwards, G. Thomas. "Dr. Ada M. Weed: Northwest Reformer." *Oregon Historical Quarterly* 78 (March 1977): 5-40. Notes. Portraits of physicians Gideon and Ada Weed.

Here is a biography of Ada M. Weed, who lived in Oregon from 1858-1860 and in Seattle from 1870-1890. Weed was a hydropathic physician and with her husband championed hydropathy and improvements in the status of women.

232. ————. *Sowing Good Seeds: The Northwest Suffrage Campaigns of Susan B. Anthony.* Portland: Oregon Historical Society Press, 1990. xxvi, 340 pages. Notes, bibliography, index. Photographs of Susan B. Anthony during her 1871 tour of the West; Abigail Scott Duniway; national leadership in the woman suffrage struggle, including Rev. Anna Howard Shaw and Carrie Chapman Catt; statue of Sacajawea; Oregon newspaper headlines and political cartoons addressing the issue of woman suffrage; Dr. Annice Jeffreys Myers, president of the Oregon State Equal Suffrage Association; local activists with national suffrage experience, including Emma Smith DeVoe and Clara Colby; group gathered for the National American Woman Suffrage Association convention in July 1905 at the Lewis and Clark Exposition in Portland.

Susan B. Anthony made three trips to the Pacific Northwest to stump for woman suffrage. In 1871, she toured for three months, in 1896 for nine days, and in 1905 for two weeks. Professor Edwards argues for the importance of her efforts in winning Northwest women the right to vote, four decades after her initial campaign. Laboring under a scarcity of Washington state and Oregon organizational records from suffrage and temperance associations, the author has drawn largely on newspaper coverage for this account. With astonishing meticulousness, Edwards has compiled Anthony's "reviews" from fifty-seven periodicals. He has pieced together a formidable study of her reception by Northwest editors and audiences. There is also attention to Abigail Scott Duniway, the Portland-based suffragist who accompanied Anthony in the early years.

233. ———. *The Triumph of Tradition: the Emergence of Whitman College, 1859-1924.* Walla Walla, Washington: Whitman College, 1992. xxiii, 577 pages. Notes, bibliography, index. Photographs of faculty member Louisa P. Anderson; 1886 seniors Lizzie Justice and Emma Stine; administrator Elvira F. Cobleigh; groups of students; groups of teachers; 1896 girls' glee club; 1902 women's basketball team; 1908 Philolithian (literary) Society; 1905 residents of Reynolds Hall; family of President Penrose; Dean Helen Louise Burr; 1924 women's tennis team; Delta Gamma Sorority in 1920; Kappa Kappa Gamma Sorority in 1919.

This history traces the evolution of Whitman Seminary into Whitman College between the years 1859 and 1924. Sections devoted to faculty and student life deal with women more extensively than those addressing administration and physical plant.

234. Edwards, Rev. Jonathan. *An Illustrated History of Spokane County: State of Washington.* No city: W. H. Lever, 1900. xviii, 726 pages.

This study touches on women's role in the Whitman massacre, missionary work among the Spokanes, Spokane County public school educators, and these organizations: Ladies Matinee Musicale, Daughters of the American Revolution, Wednesday Afternoon Literary Club, Ross Park Twentieth Century Club, Sorosis, Cu Hus Club, Floral Association, Amethyst Club, Spokane Kindergarten Association, Red Cross, Art League, and Crocker Kindergarten. Under philanthropies is identified the Ladies Benevolent Society, Woman's Exchange, Rescue Home, Ladies Catholic Benevolent Society, and Ledgerwood Ladies Aid. Under institutions is discussed the fight for woman suffrage in Spokane County, the city librarian—Mrs. Emma Driscoll Wheatly, and a botanist of national reputation, Mrs. Mary P. Olney.

235. Eells, Myron. *Father Eells: Or the Results of Fifty-Five Years of Missionary Labors in Washington and*

Oregon: A Biography of Rev. Cushing Eells, D.D. Boston: Congregational Sunday School and Publishing Society, 1894. 342 pages. Notes, index. Photograph of Myra F. Eells.

Myra F. Eells's biography is woven throughout this account. Her impressions of 1838 Oregon are recorded in a letter she wrote from the Whitman station and are quoted here. She died in 1878, at the age of seventy-three, in Skokomish.

236. ———. *Marcus Whitman, Pathfinder and Patriot.* Seattle: The Alice Harriman Company, 1909. Index, 349 pages.

This early biography of Marcus Whitman contains extensive information about Narcissa Whitman and Eliza Spalding. Their experiences on the trip across country are discussed. Narcissa Whitman's letters and diaries are quoted frequently. Her daily life at the mission, the birth and loss of her daughter Alice, and many of her thoughts and feelings are recorded.

237. Elliott, T.C. "The Coming of the White Women, 1836." *Oregon Historical Quarterly* 36 (June 1936): 87-101; (September 1936): 171-191; (December 1936): 275-290. Notes. Illustration of Flathead family crossing river.

This series, published on the centennial of the early missions, addresses the Northwest careers of Narcissa Whitman and Eliza Spalding, missionary wives. Part 1 uses quotations extensively from Narcissa Whitman's diaries to describe their arrival in August of 1836. Part 2 recounts the women's observations of life at Fort Vancouver, Hudson's Bay Company headquarters on the Columbia River. Part 3 dwells on the Idaho experiences of the Spaldings.

238. ———. "The Grave of Madame Dorion." *Oregon Historical Quarterly* 36 (1935): 102-104. Notes.

Marie Dorion, a full-blooded Iowa Indian, came to Oregon on an overland expedition with trappers headed for Astoria in 1811-12. She wintered at the fur-trading post in 1813-14. This biography details her marriage, Catholicism, and burial at the age of 100 in a St. Louis, Oregon, church in 1850.

239. Ellison, Joseph W. "Diary of Maria Parsons Belshaw, 1853." *Oregon Historical Society Quarterly* 33 (December 1932): 318-333. Notes.

A three and one-half page introduction by Ellison discusses the Oregon Trail and early portions of Belshaw's diary. The diary begins with Maria Parsons Belshaw's experiences on the Snake River and ends at Marysville where Belshaw's family makes a claim. Entries describe the terrain, traveling conditions, commerce along the Columbia, and hardships. Belshaw, a religious person, decried the loose language of the frontier and longed for a church.

240. Elmendorf, William W. *The Structure of Twana Culture with Comparative Notes on the Structure of Yurok Culture by A. L. Kroeber.* Pullman: Washington State University Press, 1960. Reprint, WSU Press, 1992. xviii, 580 pages. Notes and bibliography. Twelve illustrations, including dishes used for serving food.

Anthropologists who conducted research at the Skokomish Reservation in the Hood Canal area of western Washington, between 1939-1956, describe women's clothing, education, puberty rituals of seclusion and fasting, menstruation, pregnancy, delivery, postnatal care, bride-price, adultery, food preparation, gathering of clams and mussels and edible roots and berries, weaving of mats for bedding, and making blankets.

241. Ely, Arline. *Our Foundering [sic] Fathers: The Story of Kirkland.* Kirkland, Washington: The Kirkland Public Library, 1975. 128 pages. Bibliography, index. Photographs of Caroline French, Mary Matilda Curtis, Anna Andrean, Mabel Andrean, Eliza Forbes, Abigail Fish, Bessie Fish, the Houghton School, Mary Ann Kirk, the Kirk daughters, Marie Kirk Bell and her children, Mrs. Newell, Mrs. Churchill, the girls' basketball team (1913-1914), Amelia Newberry, Carrie Shumway, Kirkland High School class in 1912, Emilie Anderson, the Follies Review of 1929.

It is difficult to understand why this book is named for Kirkland "fathers." Women are featured throughout, including Mrs. Nancy McGregor, first resident; Mrs. Caroline French, an important pioneer; Eliza Forbes, first woman justice of the peace in King County; Miss Carrie Shumway, first city councilwoman in Washington, and many more. The book is a well written narrative with many anecdotes of Kirkland from its founding in the 1870s to the 1970s.

242. Engle, Flora A.P. "The Story of the Mercer Expeditions." *Washington Historical Quarterly* 6 (October 1915): 225-237. Notes.

This is a personal reminiscence of the two Mercer expeditions: mid-1860s trips organized by Asa S. Mercer of Seattle to bring women to Puget Sound. Lists of passengers on both trips, and mention of their subsequent lives, are included.

243. Ernst, Alice Henson. "Eugene's Theatres and 'Shows' in Horse and Buggy Days, Part I: 1852-1884." *Oregon Historical Quarterly* 44 (June 1943): 127-139. Notes.

Among the women sprinkled throughout this survey are Sallie Goodrich Thayer, who did dramatic readings in 1865; Lisle Lester of California; General Tom Thumb and his wife Minnie Warren with a celebrated troupe of midgets; elocutionist Mrs. Lusk; and Madame Ursuli, a violinist.

244. ———. "Eugene's Theatres and 'Shows' in Horse and Buggy Days, Part II: 1884-1903." *Oregon Historical Quarterly* 44 (September 1943): 232-248. Notes.

This survey enumerates women in Eugene theatre, including campus women at the University of Oregon who did recitations, Delsartian tableaux mouvantes, and drills with fans and dumb bells, visiting actress Clara Morris, the Caroline Gage Theatrical Company, the Eutaxion Society (a woman's literary club which in 1891 studied the Age of Elizabeth), and New York actress Catherine Coggswell Thorne visiting her Oregon cousin Lischen Miller and enacting Greek statues at the Rhinehart Theater.

245. ———. *Trouping in the Oregon Country: A History of Frontier Theater.* Portland: Oregon Historical Society, 1961. 197 pages. Bibliography, index. Photographs of the cast of "Pirates of Penzance," Blanche Bates (Portland), Lotta Crabtree (Oregon), Jeanie Winston (Oregon), Minnie Tittel (Oregon), Minnie Pixley (Seattle).

This book draws on newspaper and magazine accounts to focus on the history and development of the theater and acting in the Northwest from 1846-1950. Women are mentioned throughout, mainly as actresses and theater owners. Included were Miss Lotta, juvenile actress, 1862; Julia Hayne, actress, 1864; Madame Holt, a hostess in 1880 of Holts Hall, an auditorium; and Emma Abbott. Bess Whitcomb and Doris Smith directed the Portland Labor College players of the 1920s. Nellie C. Cornish founded the Cornish School in Seattle, where Ellen Van Volkenberg directed theater productions. Volkenberg also directed productions at the Tacoma Little Theater and presented puppet theater for children. Margery Bailey taught summer courses for Angus Bowmer at Southern Oregon College of Education in Ashland. Florence James operated Seattle's Playhouse with her husband Burton James. The index is useful for looking up actresses in Washington, Oregon, and British Columbia.

246. Essex, Alice. *The Stanwood Story*. Stanwood: *The Stanwood News*, 1971. 125 pages. Photos: the L. A. Carson family; Mrs. Harvey and Miss Ida Rygg of Cedarhome; Stanwood Grade School; picnickers along the Stillaquamish in the early 1920s; eighth grade graduating class, 1901; workmen and their families at the Church and Manley Shingle Mill; American Indian family; Mrs. Mary Jordan and children; Ketchum's store, 1911; women workers of the Friday Fish Company, 1909; the Pearson home, 1891; Stanwood High School class of 1911; millworkers in Florence including Mrs. Terry Hendrickson, cook, and Jesse Anderson, waitress; Stanwood Lumber Company employees of the Nicklasom Mill in 1909; the N.M. Lien family, 1909; the Stanwood Lutheran choir; the Norwegian picnic, 1893; congregation of the Lutheran church; picnickers at Juniper Beach; Fourth of July in Norman; Stanwood Grade School in 1891; Cedarhome School in 1890; Pleasant Hill School, 1910; village school, 1907; Cedarhome School, 1908; Island School pupils, 1911; Alice Tomkinson Essex and Alice Essex.

This work recounts the history of Stanwood in pictures and anecdotes. The first white woman to settle in Stanwood was Mrs. Marie Marvin, who arrived and lived in a boat with her husband in 1864. There is a short biographical sketch of Clara Stanwood Pearson who gave the town her name. The earliest teacher and principal of the Stanwood Grade School was Katherine Anderson. Other women are mentioned as teachers, librarians, and hotel operators.

247. Etulain, Richard W. "Novelists of the Northwest: Opportunities for Research." *Idaho Yesterdays* 17 (Summer 1973): 24-32. Notes, bibliography.

This study examines the literary work of Abigail Scott Duniway, Eva Emery Dye, Margaret Jewett Bailey, and Ella Higginson.

248. Evans, John W. *Powerful Rockey: The Blue Mountains and the Oregon Trail*. Enterprise, Oregon: Pika Press, 1990. xv, 375 pages. Notes, bibliography, index.

This professor quotes letters and diaries of men and women who migrated west, organizing them chronologically, by 1811-40, 1841-48, 1849-60, and 1861-83.

249. Evans, Rondeau L. "Fifty Years of A.A.U.W.: The Record of the Seattle Branch." *Pacific Northwest Quarterly* 45 (April 1954): 47-51. Photograph of Dr. Marion Spector and Miss Gertrude Woodcock.

This surveys the history of the Seattle Chapter of the American Association of University Women. It lists most of the thirteen local founders and describes the group's educational efforts. Brief biographies of the University of Washington's women faculty and deans of women, active in the A.A.U.W., are included.

250. Faragher, John Mack. *Women and Men on the Overland Trail*. New Haven: Yale University Press, 1979. xiii, 284 pages. Notes, bibliography, index.

Faragher's history draws heavily on 169 diaries, letters, and other accounts, many of which were created by pioneers headed to Oregon. He examines the sex roles of men and women from the Midwest who moved to the coast in the years 1840s-1870s. He exposes the ways that the difficulties of the overland journey challenged participants' assumptions about those sex roles.

251. Faragher, Johnny, and Christine Stansell. "Women and Their Families on the Overland Trail to California and Oregon, 1842-1867." *Feminist Studies* 2 (1975): 150-166. Notes.

This cites many Oregon women's sources, including the unpublished Helen Marnie Stewart diary, Esther and Joseph Lyman letter, and Mrs. Bryon J. Pengra diary, all in the Lane County Historical Society in Eugene. It discusses the way reluctant women travelers asserted the female subculture in a male-defined journey westward. Preserving the home in transit and performing domestic tasks remained women's work, even though women took on many male jobs as well.

252. Fargo, Lucile F. *Spokane Story*. New York: Columbia University Press, 1950. viii, 256 pages. Notes, bibliography, index.

This is a lively history of Spokane from 1812 until the turn of the century. Several influential women are discussed at some length. Chap. 2 includes many excerpts from the diary of missionary Mary Richardson Walker and discusses the Columbia Maternal Association. Clara Smiley Gray, who with her husband ran one of the first hotels in Spokane, is discussed in Chap. 7. Chap. 8 features Miss Mattie Hyde, an early school teacher, and chap. 12 mentions various women's clubs and organizations including the Women's Exchange, an AA League, a children's home, and the Ladies Benevolent Society. Chap. 14 features Elizabeth Gurley Flynn, labor activist. The remarkable reformer May Arkwright Hutton is discussed in chaps. 15 and 16.

253. Faust, Langdon. *American Women Writers: A Critical Reference Guide from Colonial Times to the Present in Two Volumes* (Abridged). New York: Frederick Ungar Publishing Company, 1979. Vol. 1: xxi, 449 pages; vol. 2: vii, 456 pages. Bibliography, index.

This is a collection of brief factual and descriptive biographies, including such Northwest authors as Ella Rhoads Higginson (vol. 1, pages 310-311) by Jean M. Ward. This is an abridgement of Lina Mainiero, *American Women Writers*, four vols. See Mainiero.

254. Ficken, Robert E., and Charles P. LeWarne. *Washington: A Centennial History*. Seattle: University of Washington Press, 1988. xxi, 216 pages. Bibliography, index. Photographs of Colville Reservation couple, family on Puyallup Reservation, image of girl in apple orchards to promote tourism, suffragists hanging political posters.

This ten-chapter survey of Washington state history, written for the centennial of 1989, contains several references to women. Among those mentioned are suffragists Emma Smith DeVoe and Abigail Scott Duniway, missionary Myra Eells, author Betty MacDonald, professor Teresa McMahan, Governor Dixy Lee Ray, Representative Julia Butler Hansen, and candidate Ruthie McInness.

255. Fields, Ronald. *Abby Williams Hill and the Lure of the West*. Tacoma: Washington State Historical Society, 1989. 120 pages. Notes, bibliography, index. List of 111 of Hill's paintings. Twelve photographs of Hill and 57 of her landscapes, in black and white and in color.

Fields is an art historian at the University of Puget Sound in Tacoma and curator of the Abby Williams Hill art collection. He uses Hill's diary for biographical detail, notably her 1903 to 1906 commissions from the Great Northern and Northern Pacific Railroads to paint landscapes of the Northwest in order to attract tourists to the region. Fields documents the exhibitions and prizes in her career and offers insight into her private life, including marriage, child-raising, and retirement years.

256. ———. "Abby Williams Hill: Northwest Frontier Painter." *Landmarks* 3 (Winter, 1984): 2-7. Notes. Photograph of Hill, five color representations of her paintings, seven in black and white.

Hill (1861-1943), a Tacoma painter of nature and American Indian studies, was commissioned by the State of Washington and Great Northern and Northern Pacific Railroad companies to produce works for national fairs and exhibitions at the turn of the century. The article reviews her biography, including education in Chicago and New York, teaching in French Canada, marrying a Tacoma physician in 1888, and raising a family.

257. Fitch-Brewer, Annette. *The Story of a Mother-Love*. Akron, Ohio: New Werner Company, 1913. 289 pages. Photos throughout of Mrs. Fitch-Brewer.

This book is the tale of a woman who kidnapped her son and fled with him to Washington in 1906. Her ex-husband sent detectives to find the boy, but Mrs. Fitch-Brewer and her son successfully eluded them until 1910. In two chapters, "Local Characters" and "More Local Characters," the author provides character sketches of her cleaning woman and of the proprietor of the confectionery shop.

258. Flynn, Elizabeth Gurley. *The Rebel Girl, an Autobiography: My First Life (1906-1926)*. New York: International Publishers, 1955. 352 pages. Index. Sixteen photographs of Flynn, including one of her in Seattle in 1926.

Introduced with remarks by editor James S. Allen, this autobiography includes remarks about Flynn's activism in the Spokane Free Speech movement of 1909, the Everett massacre of 1916, the Centralia massacre of 1919, and the activism of Northwest physician and suffragist, Dr. Marie Equi.

259. Foreman, Carolyn Thomas. *Indian Women Chiefs*. Washington, D.C.: Zenger Publishing Company, Inc., 1954. 90 pages. Notes, index. Photograph of Nancy Ward, Cherokee Chief.

This book is a survey of women Indian chiefs. There is a short essay of Queen Mary of the Modocs in southeastern Oregon. There are two essays about Osage Chiefs, Rosana Chouteau and another unnamed woman chief. The period covered is the 1840s to 1870s for the Northwest women.

260. Fowler, Catherine S. "Sarah Winnemucca." In *American Indian Intellectuals*, ed. Margot Liberty, pp. 32-42. New York: West Publishing Company,

1978. ix, 250 pages. Notes, bibliography. Photograph of Sarah Winnemucca.

This biography of Sarah Winnemucca emphasizes the feistiness of this activist for Native American rights. After her career as interpreter for General O.O. Howard, Winnemucca lectured widely on Yakama and Malheur reservation conditions in Washington and Oregon, educating the public in 1883 and 1884 about federal Indian policy and government agent corruption. The following year, she managed a school for Paiute children.

261. Fowler, William Worthington. *Woman on the American Frontier: A Valuable and Authentic History of the Heroism, Adventures, Privations, Captivities, Trials, and Noble Lives and Deaths of the "Pioneer Mothers of the Republic."* Hartford, Connecticut: S.S. Scranton, 1878. 527 pages. Notes.

This overview provides little material that is specific to the Pacific Northwest woman. One section, entitled "A Missionary Wife's Experience in Oregon," examines Mrs. White, of the Methodist mission in the Willamette Valley. It is probably based on the diary she wrote with her husband. There is also a brief recounting of the Whitman massacre. The study provides general anecdotes about pioneers from the seventeenth to the nineteenth centuries. Chapter headings include "Woman's Work in Floods and Storms," "Patriot Women of the Revolution," "Home Life in the Backwoods," and "Women in the Army."

262. Frank, Dana. "'Food Wins All Struggles': Seattle Labor and the Politicization of Consumption." *Radical History Review* 51 (1991): 65-89. Notes. Photograph of Bon Marche department store.

Consumer organizing among Seattle's American Federation of Labor members in the post World War I era included women's boycotts of stores, formation of cooperatives, and support for the union label. The Seattle Women's Card and Label League was instrumental in agitating for union issues.

263. ———. "Gender, Consumer Organizing, and the Seattle Labor Movement, 1919-1929." In *Work Engendered: Toward a New History of American Labor*, ed. Ava Baron, pp. 273-295. Ithaca: Cornell University Press, 1991. Notes.

Frank argues that labor tactics have been deeply gendered in history. American Federation of Labor unionist women in Seattle took up three consumer tactics in the 1920s. These were support of cooperatives, especially for food; boycotts, including one

against the Bon Marche; and promotion of the union label by the Women's Card and Label League. Married women, aged thirty to sixty, who performed unpaid work at home or were employed in traditional wage-earning jobs for women, participated.

264. ———. *Purchasing Power: Consumer Organizing, Gender, and the Seattle Labor Movement, 1919-1929.* New York: Cambridge University Press, 1994. xii, 348 pages. Notes, index. Photographs of women serving meals in a labor-managed dining hall during the February 1919 Seattle general strike; a Japanese American couple in front of their cleaning and dye shop; the Bon Marche department store; lady barbers in a barber shop; garment workers eating in the Black Manufacturing Company cafeteria.

Asking what became of Seattle's labor movement after its famous general strike of 1919, Frank looks at the American Federation of Labor as a case study for the demise of the U.S. labor movement. She examines consumer tactics used by women, such as boycotts, cooperatives, promotion of the union label, and labor-owned businesses. Using a sophisticated analysis, she addresses the gender dynamics of the labor movement and the racism which divided it. She explores the new unions for women in World War I (laundry workers, telephone operators, lady barbers) and growing unions (waitresses, bookbinders, musicians). She identifies the work of women's voluntary organizations, including the Women's Cooperative Clubs, Women's Cooperative Guilds, Women's Card and Label League, and Women's Trade Union League. There is brief mention of individual women in the labor movement, including journalist Anna Louise Strong, president of the Seattle Waitress Union Alice Lord, and AFL organizing staff Blanche Johnson, Myrtle Howarth, Jean Stovel, and Sophie Pugsley.

265. ———. "Which 'Women' and the Labor Movement? Women's Roles in the Seattle, Washington AFL, 1917-1929." In *Geschlect-Klasse-Ethnizitat*, ed. Gabriella Hauch, pp. 189-197. Vienna: Eurpaverlag, 1993. Bibliography.

This general essay summarizes Seattle's American Federation of Labor from 1917 to 1929. It treats the women union members, telephone operators, and waitresses, who became "wives" of the movement, "serving the men in ways that replicated the sexual division of labor in the family." For example, women decorated and cooked for union events. However, Frank asserts that they used their "sex-segregated activities to challenge inequities and fight for equality in the workplace" even if they excluded Japanese, Chinese, and African American women from their circle.

266. Freeman, Olga, ed. "Almira Raymond Letters, 1840-1880." *Oregon Historical Quarterly* 85 (Fall, 1984): 291-303. There are two photographs of scenes Almira Raymond describes, cattle grazing at Tansy Point and a ship.

Two pages by the editor explain that the New York-born author came to Oregon in 1840 with her husband, as part of a contingent of fifty-two missionaries. Here are Raymond's letters to her parents, sister, and brother about her sea travels, her arrival in Oregon, and her missionary work.

267. Fridlund, Paul. *Prosser 1910-20: Going Back.* Fairfield, Washington: Ye Galleon Press, 1985. 172 pages. Notes, index. Photographs of Kathryn Severyns, who was elected Benton County auditor in 1918; two operators at Benton Independent Telephone Company; four champions in the 1915 Kona-Benton City Canning Club, with 1,457 jars of fruit; cooks who fed threshers at harvest; members of the PEO; and Mrs. Verda Moffat, queen of the First Community Carnival in 1911.

This study deals with women entering politics, describing the 1910 celebration for woman suffrage in Benton County in 1910, the women selected for jury duty in 1911, and Maude Chapman's unsuccessful race for Prosser City Council. It mentions the Women's Christian Temperance Union, organized in 1910 in Prosser, for its war against "booze," and leisure time activities including voluntary activity in women's groups like the Prosser Women's Club, Women of Woodcraft, and Camp Fire Girls. A memoir by Elizabeth Lushbaugh Capps is included.

268. Friedlander, Alice G. "A Portland Girl on Women's Rights—1893." *Western States Jewish Historical Quarterly* 10 (January 1978): 146-150. One photograph of Alice Friedlander.

The introduction of this piece contains a biography of Kentucky-born Alice Friedlander (1875-1947). Here is a reprint of a speech she delivered on women's rights at the Portland Press Club for the Washington and Oregon Editorial Associations' meeting when she was eighteen years old. She urged women to enter the field of jour-

nalism, arguing that they were capable of achieving distinction in intellectual work. The essay was also published in the Portland *Oregonian* on October 8, 1893.

269. Friedman, Ralph. *This Side of Oregon.* Caldwell, Idaho: Claxton Printers, Ltd., 1983. xiii, 316 pages. Index. Photographs of Mary Day Brown; Abbie C. Brown; grave of Cynthia Ann Parker; two women of Grant County with two Chinese men, Hung On and Doc Hey; and two women office workers and men laborers at Central Oregon Sawmill.

In a chatty style which relies on diaries and reminiscences, this account divides women into pioneer women, heroic women, and battered brides. It discusses Marie Dorion's historical marker, near North Powder, commemorating the birth of a son by an Iowa Indian woman on the Wilson Price Hunt expedition to Astoria. Friedman narrates two heroic stories about pioneer women published by William W. Fowler in 1879 and believed at the time to be true. The book discusses Clara Larrson, one-quarter Indian, and the first woman elected mayor of Troutdale, Oregon, in 1913. There is also mention of Mayor Laura Harlow; Mary Leonard, who was the first woman admitted to practice law before the Oregon Supreme Court in 1886; and Lola G. Baldwin, the first woman law enforcement officer in Oregon (1908).

270. Friesen, Jennifer, and Ronald K. L. Collins. "Looking Back on '*Muller v. Oregon.*'" *American Bar Association Journal* 69 (March 1983): 294-298. Photographs of Josephine C. Goldmark and Florence Kelley.

This article deals with the 1908 Supreme Court case of *Muller v. Oregon.* Emma Gotcher worked for the Grand Laundry owned by Curt Muller of Portland. He violated Oregon's 1903 statute limiting the work day of laundry women to ten hours. Gotcher was backed by the National Consumer's League and National Women's Trade Union League, under the leadership of Josephine Goldmark and Florence Kelley, who assisted Gotcher's attorney, Louis D. Brandeis, to see Muller's conviction upheld. The case upheld the right of Oregon to limit the workday of women, thus enabling a wave of protective legislation to be passed during the early twentieth century.

271. ———. "Looking Back on '*Muller v. Oregon.*'" *American Bar Association Journal* 69 (April 1983): 472-477. Part 2. Photographs of Frances Perkins, secretary of labor under Franklin Delano Roosevelt, and a modern

demonstration in favor of the Equal Rights Amendment.

This article studies the history and effect of the 1908 Supreme Court decision in *Muller vs. Oregon,* which upheld the right of Oregon to limit the workday of women in commercial laundries to ten hours a day. It commends the efforts of the Oregon branch of the National Consumer's League and Caroline Gleason (later Sister Miriam Theresa) for arguing for the minimum wage law, passed by the Oregon legislature in 1913.

272. Frost, Mary Perry. "Experiences of a Pioneer." *Washington Historical Quarterly* 7 (April 1916): 123-125.

Frost traveled in spring 1854 with her family, from Iowa to Nebraska, then on to the Territory of Oregon. In the last stretch her father lost his life in an attack by American Indians in Idaho. After his burial, they traveled with several other families to Puget Sound via Naches Pass, by wagon. She and her brother then herded sheep for the Hudson's Bay Company to earn money for provisions.

273. Frost, O. W. "Margaret J. Bailey: Oregon Pioneer Author." *Marion County History* 5 (June 1959): 64-70.

This biography of Margaret Jewett Bailey details her 1837 arrival in Oregon at the age of twenty-five to become a missionary. It includes discussion of her autobiographical novel, *The Grains,* which detailed the scandal of her divorce, and includes three of her poems, "Love," "Affliction," and "It Charms Me that I Hope to Live."

274. Fuller, George W. *The Inland Empire of the Pacific Northwest: A History.* 4 vols. Spokane: H.G. Linderman, 1928. Vol. 1: xiii, 240 pages; vol. 2: viii, 262 pages; vol. 3: viii, 262 pages; vol. 4: 288 pages. Index in vol. 3.

Vol. 1 discusses the Native American family, medicine women, and the controversy over Sacajawea's name and biography. Vol. 2 mentions Narcissa Whitman and the Mercer girls. In vol. 3 is material on the social life of the pioneers, the missionary efforts of the McBeth sisters, the women who organized the Spokane Library in 1883, and Mrs. Burgess Lee Gordon's effort to create an art gallery in 1926 as a memorial to her daughter, Mrs. William Powell. Vol. 4 consists of biographies, mostly of men, whose mothers, wives, and daughters are mentioned in passing. However, there are full biographies of Clara Hughes (Mrs. Joel) Ferris, for her club activity, and Rebecca Jane Hurn, lawyer.

275. Gallagher, Dorothy. *Hannah's Daughters: Six Generations of an American Family, 1876-1976.* New York: Crowell, 1976. 343 pages. One hundred family photographs.

This study is based on a series of 1974 interviews with six generations of women from the Lamberston family of Washington state. They discuss, candidly and movingly, their experiences in marriage, family, work, and survival through hard times. There is an introduction by Dorothy Gallagher, interviewer, and an afterward by Robert Coles.

276. Gardner, Virginia. *"Friend and Lover": The Life of Louise Bryant.* New York: Horizon Press, 1982. 390 pages. Notes, bibliography, index. Photographs of Bryant and her friends.

Brief attention is given to the Portland years (1905-1916) of Louise Bryant, playwright (*The Game*) and journalist/supporter of the Russian Revolution (*Six Red Months in Russia*). There she participated in Oregon's 1912 woman suffrage campaign and met Greenwich Village radicals Emma Goldman and John Reed, through Rev. Albert Ehrgott's wife, Sara Bard Field.

277. Gaston, Joseph. *The Centennial History of Oregon.* 4 vols. Chicago: The S.J. Clarke Publishing Company, 1912. Vol. 1: xxiii, 684 pages, bibliography, photographs of five women founders of the Home for the Aged, twelve foundresses of St. Mary's School for Girls in Portland, and Tabitha Brown at Pacific University. Vol. 2: 1,060 pages, index; vol. 3: 1,096 pages, index; vol. 4: 1,100 pages, index.

Vol. 1 lists the orders of Catholic Sisters who ran early schools, discusses Narcissa Whitman and the Whitman massacre, and discusses women in the development of "Moral and Educational Agencies." Vol. 2 provides biographical sketches of Theckla Bright, Sarah A. Cantrall, Mrs. C.G. Copeland, Lena R. Hodges, Rhoda Johnson, Josephine V. Jones, Emma Lammert Kennedy, Mary Miller, Elisha Morcom, Mrs. C.W. Mumford, Mrs. A.C. Patterson, Elizabeth A. Simerville, Mrs. S.A. Underwood, Emma C. Warren, Caroline E. Watts, and Susan Whitney. Vol. 3 provides biographies for May B. Anderson, Maggie Buckley, Katie N. Byrne, Clara Collins, May De Lamter, Mrs. W.H. Gray, Annie Honan, Eliza E. Kelly, Maud Kubli, Margaret Matney, Martha Messinger, Aura Raley, Marjorie Trowbridge, and Elizabeth Watts. Vol. 4 discusses the lives of Sarah M. Applegate, Elsie Boyd, Margaret Edmunson, Eliza Keppinger, Bethenia Owens-Adair, Mary Perkins, Marguerite E. Pomeroy, Lyda Powell, Mary J. Tyler, and Permelia Wilkins.

278. Gates, Charles Marvin. *The First Century at the University of Washington, 1861-1961*. Seattle: University of Washington Press, 1961. xviii, 252 pages. Notes, index. Photographs of Professor Effie Raitt, Professor Elizabeth Soule, 1862 student body, biology class, cheerleaders, university singers, and the 1903 women's basketball team.

Women do not enjoy great attention in this work, with the exception of Dean Martha Hansee and Professor Theresa McMahan. There are also one-paragraph descriptions of the Women's League, a campus club, and even briefer mention of women's dormitories. Women's names appear at about a one to twenty ratio to men in the index. The passing references are to women as benefactors, authors of books, or student leaders.

279. Gay, Theressa [sic]. *Life and Letters of Mrs. Jason Lee, First Wife of Rev. Jason Lee of the Oregon Mission*. Portland: Metropolitan Press, 1936. 224 pages. Notes, bibliography, index. Portrait of Anna Maria Pittman Lee, frontispiece.

The first half of this book is a biography of missionary Anna Maria Pittman Lee. Her early life, travels to Oregon, and daily activities are detailed. The second half of the book is Anna Lee's letters and poems, upon which the biography is based.

280. Gedney, Elizabeth. "Cross Section of Pioneer Life at Fourth Plain." *Oregon Historical Quarterly* 43 (March 1942): 14-36.

The author self-consciously stresses the "woman's angle" on pioneer clothing, houses, parties, gardens, superstitions, housewifery, food, and doctoring with home-grown medicines.

281. Geer, Elizabeth Dixon Smith. "Diary of Mrs. Elizabeth Dixon Smith Geer." *Transactions of the Oregon Pioneer Association*, 35th annual session, pp. 153-179. Portland: Oregon Pioneer Association, 1907.

The diary and letters cover the journey to Oregon in 1848 and the first two years of Mrs. Geer's pioneer experience. Entries include brief descriptions of the weather, landscape, and hardships encountered. There are references to the Whitman massacre and early Portland.

282. Gellatly, John A. *A History of Wenatchee: The Apple Capital of the World*. No city: no publisher, 1957. vi, 400 pages. Photographs of Apple Queens from 1921-1962. Index of individuals and index of subject matter.

This volume enumerates the programs of the Wenatchee branch of the American Association of University Women from 1939-1957 and lists the nineteen charter members who founded the organization in 1938. It deals with the history, officers, and projects of the Wenatchee branch of the Rotary Anns (Women of Rotary), Soroptimist, Altrusa, Venture Club, Girl Scouts, Young Women's Christian Association, Women's Christian Temperance Union, Ladies of Elks, Business and Professional Women's Club, Royal Neighbors of America, Apple Capital National Secretaries Association, Native Daughters of Washington, Daughters of the American Revolution, and Daughters of Union Veterans of the Civil War. The book provides biographies of Belle Culp Reeves of the Women's Democratic Club, and Rose Reeves Mann, who organized the Wenatchee Music Club.

283. Gibson, Lillian. *My God Teacher: I Can Read*. Olympia: Washington State Retired Teacher's Association, 1976. 212 pages. Index of almost 700 submissions, not all used in this volume.

Here are anecdotal accounts of former days in Washington's schools, unsigned by the contributors. Topics covered include classroom experiences in small towns and on the Yakama Reservation; regulations for teachers; Teachers' Institutes; foreign students; teachers' cottages for residences; interaction with parents; and structural changes in administration over the years.

284. Gilbert, Adelaide Sutton. "Letters of Adelaide Sutton Gilbert." Ed. Michael A. Page. *Pacific Northwest Forum* 5 (Winter-Spring 1992): 3-96. Photographs of Adelaide Sutton Gilbert.

Editor Michael A. Page offers selections from 300 of the letters of Adelaide Sutton Gilbert, on deposit at the Eastern Washington State Historical Society in Spokane. She wrote these to her parents while she lived in Spokane, from 1891 to 1893. Her accounts relate the life of an upper middle class wife and mother who raised her children and brought culture to her community. These selections are only part of the special issue of the journal devoted to her life. See also entries under Michelle Hanson and Gina Hames.

285. Gilbert, Frank T. *Historic Sketches of Walla Walla, Whitman, Colombia and Garfield Counties, Washington Territory*. Portland, Oregon: A.G. Walling, 1882. 460 pages. Index.

There is mention of Joe Lewis's attack on Narcissa Whitman at the Whitman massacre. The book lists the lodges for four counties in Washington, including those to which women belong, such as these Walla Walla County organizations: the Pioneer Lodge #16, founded in 1867, the International Order of Good Templars, and the grange. Women's names appear in the lists of officers.

286. Gill, Frances. *Chloe Dusts Her Mantel: A Pioneer Woman's Idyl.* New York: Press of the Pioneers, Inc., 1935. 88 pages.

In 1874, Chloe Willson remembers her voyage to Portland in 1839, at the age of twenty-one, on the *Lausanne.* She left New York to become a Methodist missionary in the West. She recalls her work with Indians, her marriage, daily life raising a family, and farming.

287. Gleason, Caroline Joanna. *Oregon Legislation for Women in Industry, by Sister Miriam Theresa, Ph.D.* Washington, D.C.: U.S. Government Printing Office, 1931. v, 40 pages.

The U.S. Women's Bureau sponsored this expansion of a Catholic University dissertation of 1924 by Minneapolis-born Caroline Gleason. Her doctoral research expanded investigations she had conducted on Power Laundries in Portland (1915) and dealt with the political rights of women (including suffrage and office holding) and civil rights of women. She treated the latter subject by examining the early status of women in Oregon, property rights, administration of estates, the power to make wills, the age of majority, support, personal rights of women, education, marriage and divorce, and women in industry, including child labor laws, the ten-hour law for women, and the minimum-wage law.

288. Glenn, Evelyn Nakano. "The Dialectics of Wage Work: Japanese-American Women and Domestic Service, 1905-1940." *Feminist Studies* 6 (Fall 1980): 432-471. Notes.

While most of the evidence explores California women, the piece makes reference also to Seattle domestic workers who were Issei women. The study covers the entry and socialization process, conditions of work, employer-employee relations, and work and family life.

289. Gogol, J. M. "Columbia River Indian Basketry." *American Indian Basketry* 1 (1979): 4-9. Bibliography. Photographs of Umatilla family on the Columbia River with two beaded and one corn husk bag; a Klickitat basket of 1920; Cowlitz basket of 1890; Wasco woman and girl at The Dalles with bags; Clatsop basket of 1945; and Wasco-Wishram bags.

Gogol asserts that Columbia River basketry reached its greatest heights among Native American women near The Dalles, Oregon. Two traditions met there, the coiled basketry of the Klickitats and the twined basketry of the Upper Chinook/Wasco/Wishram women. The author traces the designs and materials employed in the baskets of the region.

290. ———. "Cornhusk Bags and Hats of the Columbia Plateau Indians." *American Indian Basketry* 1 (1980): 4-11. Bibliography. Photographs of Cayuse woman weaving a cornhusk bag in 1900; examples of woven bags, hats, and beaded belt pouch; Se-cho-wa, aged 110, on the Umatilla Reservation in 1900 with cornhusk bag; two Plateau Indian girls with bags in 1902; Umatilla woman weaving a bag in 1900.

Hunting and gathering societies need strong and flexible containers to collect, store, and transport roots, berries, and fish. Native barks, roots, and grasses offer suitable materials for weaving bags for this purpose. Women wove round and flat bags in winter and decorated them with distinctive designs.

291. Goodfriend, Joyce D. *Published Diaries and Letters of American Women: An Annotated Bibliography.* Boston: G.K. Hall and Company, 1987. xiv, 230 pages. Index.

Listing entries by year, from 1669-1982, this reference work provides twelve citations to Northwest women. These include, for 1836, Mrs. Marcus Whitman and diaries, letters, and biographical sketches of six women of the Oregon mission who made the overland journey.

292. Grant, Frederic James. *History of Seattle, Washington.* New York: American Publishing and Engraving Company, 1891. 526 pages. Notes, index.

Women receive scant attention. There is mention of white women's impressions of the American Indians, Abbie J. Hanford, Miss Nellie Powell, the origins of the Seattle fire in Mrs. M. J. Ponties's building, businesswomen who advertised in the 1861 city directory, teachers, and organizers of churches.

293. Grant, Howard F. *The Story of Seattle's Early Theatres.* Seattle: University of Washington Bookstore, 1934. 47 pages. Bibliography, index. Six woodcuts of early theatres.

This work divides Seattle theatre history into three episodes: 1852-1876, 1876-1890, 1890-1900. Entries under each year enumerate details on theatre history, excerpted from Seattle newspapers. This is rich in details regarding the names of women who performed, the titles of their plays, reviews, sizes of theatres, and audiences.

294. Gray, Dorothy. *Women of the West*. Millbrae, California: Les Femmes Publishers, 1976. 179 pages. Notes, bibliography, index. Photos of pioneer family enroute; statue of Sacajawea; portrait of Narcissa Whitman.

Three women associated with the Northwest—Sacajawea, Narcissa Whitman, and Dr. Bethenia Owens-Adair—are covered in this general anthology of women west of the Mississippi. The essays about Sacajawea and Narcissa Whitman are adequate for the general reader. However, the author tends to lionize their roles, offers questionable conclusions, and occasionally makes factual errors. The essay about Dr. Owens-Adair is more down-to-earth, telling the often heartbreaking but ultimately triumphant story of a woman's struggle to make her own way in nineteenth-century Oregon.

295. Gray, William Henry. *A History of Oregon, 1792-1849, Drawn from Personal Observation and Authentic Information*. Portland, Oregon: Harris and Holman, 1870. 624 pages.

Women receive little attention in this volume, although they are mentioned as staff members at the Hudson's Bay Company, participants at the Ladies Table at Fort Vancouver in 1836, and wives of missionaries. Lorinda Bewley's account of the Whitman massacre is included.

296. Green, Giles S. *A Heritage of Loyalty; the History of the Ashland, Oregon Public Schools*. Ashland, Oregon: Ashland Public Schools, 1966. 220 pages. Index. Photographs of women teachers and the female-dominated graduating class in 1892, 1893, 1894, and 1895.

While this survey of Ashland, Oregon, public schools spans 1857-1966, it dwells more on buildings, the school board, and the superintendent than on staff. In lists of teachers, women figure prominently. They also appear in connection with references to the school nurse, Parent-Teacher Association sponsorship of tuberculosis tests, and the 1961 policy on pregnant students.

297. Greenwald, Maurine Weiner. "Working-Class Feminism and the Family Wage Ideal: The Seattle Debate on Married Women's Right to Work, 1914-1920." *Journal of American History* 76 (June 1989): 118-149. Notes. Photographs of lady barbers; the officers of a women's union, the Card and Label League; women telephone operators on strike; Mrs. Minnie Ault at a fund-raising affair.

This article examines attitudes toward working women in early twentieth-century Seattle. The author finds liberal attitudes toward feminism among working-class activists. She draws on letters to the workers' newspaper, *The Seattle Union Record*, and the "Woman's Page" with Ruth Ridgeway's column to examine the debate over married women's employment during the years 1914 to 1920. She explores the history of the Women's Card and Label League and quotes Lorene Wiswell Wilson, president of the Seattle Women's Trade Union League and member of the Waitresses' Union to illuminate economic and ideological reasons for labor's commitment to women. Greenwald documents collaboration with middle-class clubwomen on questions of suffrage and protective legislation.

298. Gridley, Marion E. *American Indian Women*. New York: Hawthorn Books, Inc., 1974. 178 pages. Bibliography, index. Pictures of Sarah Winnemucca, Sacajawea statue at the North Dakota state capitol building, and Winema.

A collection of eighteen biographies, geared to a young adult audience, includes material on Sacajawea, Marie Dorion, Sarah Winnemucca, and Winema or Peacemaker, an interpreter during the Modoc War. In order to engage readers, Gridley sometimes employs undocumentable details in her accounts, but she never invents dialogue for her historical subjects.

299. Grumbach, Doris. *The Company She Kept*. New York: Coward-McCann, Inc., 1967. 218 pages. Photographs of Mary McCarthy between 1949 and 1961.

This biography covers writer Mary McCarthy's girlhood in Seattle and Minnesota. Upon graduation from high school, she left Seattle for good, going initially to Vassar College in Poughkeepsie, New York.

300. Gunther, Erna. *Art in the Life of the Northwest Coast Indians*. Seattle: Superior Publishing Company, 1966. xi, 275 pages. Bibliography, index. Color and black and white photographs of Northwest Coast Indian peoples and art.

This book contains a 174-page essay about Northwest Coast Indian art, and is followed by a catalog of the Rasmussen Collection of Northwest Indian Art in the Portland Art Museum. It discusses women's baskets, their value, variety, design, and use.

301. ———. *Design Units on Tlingit Baskets*. Sitka, Alaska: Sheldon Jackson Museum, 1984. 20 pages. Notes.

This museum exhibition catalog, prepared at the end of Gunther's life, offers the material she collected at the beginning of her career in anthropology for her 1920 M.A. thesis at Columbia University. An overview of the Tlingit baskets in the collection of the American Museum of Natural History in New York City, the pamphlet points out that women made the baskets and controlled the industry. Gunther describes spruce-root basketry in detail, providing illustrations of designs.

302. ———. *Ethnobotany of Western Washington*. University of Washington Publications in Anthropology, vol. 10, no. 1. Seattle: University of Washington Press, 1945. 62 pages. Notes, bibliography, index.

This monograph discusses the uses of plants by western Washington Indians. Comparing sex roles, the author states, "women knew the food and medicinal plants and were more likely to give information on charms and potions; men knew the materials in mats, fishing gear, and wood working" (p. 9). Gunther frequently refers to women informants and also discusses medicinal uses of plants that specifically relate to menstruation, pregnancy, and other women's health concerns.

303. ———. *Indian Life on the Northwest Coast of North America*. Chicago: University of Chicago Press, 1972. xiv, 277 pages. Bibliography, index. Drawing of a Nootka couple; drawings of a Native American family; drawing of a Nootka woman; many photographs of Native American domestic utensils and baskets.

This book is a rich ethnohistorical account of the Northwest Coast Indians that utilizes the diaries of early Europeans in the region. Throughout there are references to customs, stories, and aspects of physical culture that relate to Native American women. Women's roles in relation to textile arts, personal decoration, ceremonies, and household equipment are discussed. The only individual women referred to are the wives of Tatosh, a Nootka chief from Neah Bay. Their portraits were painted by an artist from a Spanish expedition.

304. ———. *Klallam Ethnography*. University of Washington Publications in Anthropology, vol. 1, no. 5. Seattle: University of Washington Press, 1927. Notes, bibliography, index.

Gunther's chapter entitled "The Cycle of Life" deals with birth customs, including pregnancy taboos, delivery, treatment of infant and mother, nursing, cradle boards, flattening the head of the child, birth control and abortion, aids to fertility, and twins, as well as the care and training of children, names, puberty and menstrual customs, marriage, burial and mourning customs, and children taken captive in war.

305. ———. *Viewer's Guide to Indian Cultures of the Pacific Northwest*. Seattle: University of Washington, 1955. viii, 57 pages. Bibliography. Photographs of textile art, including Tlingit basketry and weaving.

This is the outline of thirteen lectures Gunther prepared for a television course delivered between September and December, 1955.

306. Haarsager, Sandra. *Bertha Knight Landes of Seattle: Big-City Mayor*. Norman: University of Oklahoma Press, 1994. xv, 334 pages. Notes, bibliography, index. Twenty photographs of Bertha Knight Landes from childhood through retirement, her husband Henry, daughter Katherine, house in Seattle, and official portrait as mayor.

Here is a biography of the first woman elected mayor of a large American city. Bertha Knight Landes (1868-1943) led the city of Seattle from 1926 to 1928, after serving on the city council. The bulk of the story deals with her public life. Most scrutiny is given to her volunteerism in women's clubs, where she developed the leadership skills, Progressive principles, and a devoted following who elected her to the city council and the position of mayor. There is rich discussion of the political and social context in which Landes supported control of dance halls and gambling, clean government, public power, and a municipal railway. Haarsager explores the backgrounds and platforms of Landes's political rivals and explains her defeat in 1928.

307. Haeberlin, Hermann, and Erna Gunther. *The Indians of Puget Sound*. University of Washington Publications in Anthropology, vol. 4, no. 1. Seattle: University of Washington Press, 1930. 84 pages. Notes, bibliography, index. Photograph of an Indian woman, Mrs.

Joshu, spinning, and of Annie Sam, a principal informant.

In brief sections this paper covers a wide range of material about Puget Sound Indians, primarily the Snohomish, Snoqualmie, and Nisqually. There are sections on food varieties and preparation, weaving and basketry, puberty rites, menstrual customs, and marriage. The section on government asserts that women participated only rarely in tribal councils.

308. Hagen, Cecil. "Liberated Women?—Not Those Lewis and Clark Met on their Way." *Pacific Northwesterner* 25 (Spring 1981): 17-25. Notes.

Drawing on the diaries of Northwest explorers Lewis and Clark, this piece categorizes the hardships faced by Native American women, including poor diet, primitive tools for work, drudgery, and long hours of labor. It also rails against arranged marriages, polygamy, and other sexual customs of Native American societies.

309. Haley, Delphine. *Dorothy Stimson Bullitt: An Uncommon Life*. Seattle: Sasquatch Books, 1995. viii, 344 pages. Index. Twenty-five photographs of Bullitt plus others of her family, friends, and estates.

Dorothy Stimson (1892-1989) was born with the proverbial silver spoon in her mouth. Her father had moved to Seattle three years before her birth to expand his Michigan timber empire by spending half a million dollars on old-growth forests. This careful biography traces her privileged upbringing in luxurious houses, with servants, governesses, tutors, show horses, winters in Southern California, and two years of finishing school in New York. During World War I, she headed Seattle's Red Cross Motor Corps and shortly afterward married Kentucky attorney Scott Bullitt. When they started a family, she insisted on relocating to Seattle. She raised three children, joined Seattle women's voluntary associations, and served on the boards of many arts and educational institutions and businesses. She supported Franklin Roosevelt's New Deal and in the 1940s and '50s distinguished herself as a woman in the broadcasting industry. She founded KING radio and television in Seattle and KGW-TV in Portland. This biography also details the experiences of her female relatives, friends, and business associates.

310. Halvorsen, Helen Olson, as told to Lorraine Fletcher, "Nineteenth Century Midwife: Some Recollections." *Oregon Historical Quarterly* 70 (March 1969): 39-49.

This short essay is a well-organized and lively reminiscence by a farm woman, mother and midwife who was interviewed by Lorraine Fletcher in 1952. Helen Halvorsen moved to Silverton, Oregon, in the 1890s. She describes in detail the births of her own seven children, the work she and her older children did taking care of babies, and the assistance she gave as a midwife to neighboring women.

311. Hames, Gina. "'Dear Folks at Home...' The Making of a Western Woman." *Pacific Northwest Forum* 5 (Winter-Spring 1992): 113-117. Notes.

This essay discusses Adelaide Sutton Gilbert as representative of patterns in western women which have been identified by scholars of western women's history. Among the categories analyzed are rebel, lonely figure, wife, mother, homemaker, entrepreneur, friend, daughter, and sister.

312. Hanford, Cornelius Holgate, ed. *Seattle and Environs, 1852-1924*. 3 vols. Chicago, Seattle: Pioneer Historical Publishing Company, 1924. Vol. 1: 626 pages; vol. 2: 635 pages; vol. 3: 621 pages. Index in each volume. Numerous photographs of people and places.

Vol. 1 of this three-volume history of Seattle tells the history of the city itself. Women played important roles in the cultural and civic life of Seattle as discussed in chap. 11, "Civic Associations," chap. 18, "Learned Professions, the Press, Literature, Music and Art," and chap. 19, "Fine Arts." Vols. 2 and 3 are comprised of short biographies of important Seattle citizens. Included in vol. 2 are the biographies of Henrietta S. Crofton, Lady Willie Forbus, Evelyn H. Hall, Gertrude Kelsay, Etta C. Martin, Marjorie V.C. Nottingham, and Ann B. Rudy. Vol. 3 includes the biographies of Helen Ardelle, Estelle E. Bright, Carolyn K. Chambers, Helen Igre, Bertha K. Landes, Mrs. J.M. Lightfoot, Jean Seymour, and Violet Tatum.

313. Hanify, Mary Lou. *The Light in the Mansion*. Seattle: privately printed, 1971. 60 pages. Bibliography. Photographs of every Washington state first lady from 1889 to 1970.

In chronological order, a two-to-five-page biography is provided for each first lady of Washington state. There is so much information about children, pets, traditional virtues, and the governors themselves, that material on the wives is quite skimpy.

314. Hansen, Julia Butler. *Cathlamet Pioneer: The Paintings of Maude Kimball Butler*. Tacoma: Washington State Historical Society, 1973.

39 pages. Notes. Thirty photographs, including five paintings Butler completed after she was seventy years old: *Chinese Workers Gathering Wapatoes, Home of J. B. Hansen, First Schoolhouse in Cathlamet, Fourth of July,* and *Sunday School Picnic.*

Here are descriptive notes by Julia Butler Hansen, who owned the paintings her mother, teacher and clubwoman Maude Kimball Butler, exhibited in August 1973 at the Washington State Historical Society Museum.

315. Hanson, Michelle Alward. "Adelaide Sutton Gilbert, 1873-1893." *Pacific Northwest Forum* 5 (Winter-Spring 1992): 97-112. Notes. Photograph is Gilbert's 1873 wedding picture.

This biography of painting instructor Adelaide Sutton Gilbert is assembled from details in letters she wrote from Spokane to her parents in De Ruyter, New York, between the years 1873 and 1893.

316. Hanson, Signe, and Judith Yarrow. "Some Details." *Backbone* 3 (1981): 9-11. Two photographs: Signe with her two daughters, Frederikke and Sylvia Friis; and with her husband, Oley Friis, in front of the house he built.

Signe Hanson remembers her upbringing in the rural area of Green Valley, eastern Washington, where she was born in 1892 and raised.

317. Hargreaves, Sheba. *The Cabin At the Trail's End; A Story of Oregon.* New York: Harper and Brothers Publishers, 1928. 341 pages. One photograph of a statue of a woman and boy.

This is the story of Martha Bainbridge and her family, who lived in the Willamette Valley, Oregon. It reveals details on weaving, spinning, cooking, relations with Native Americans, neighbors, and politics in the community.

318. ———. *Heroine of the Prairies; a Romance of the Oregon Trail.* New York: Harper and Brothers, 1930. vi, 288 pages.

This narrative details a family's 1848 journey from the Blue Mountains of Oregon to Oregon City, through the eyes of their woman guide, Salita. She discusses interactions with Native Americans, lack of receptivity to her masculine attire, and marriage to John Barfield.

319. Harmon, Florence. "Reminiscence: Florence Harmon on Depression-Era Homesteading in Lincoln County." *Oregon Historical Quarterly* 89, No. 1 (1988): 46-69. Three photographs of Florence Harmon.

This is Florence Thuirer Harmon's account of her life in Oregon, beginning in 1933, when she established a homestead of 160 acres with her husband Wendall, south of Elk City, Oregon. Rick Harmon, editor of the *Oregon Historical Quarterly*, provides background based on a 1983 oral history with the Harmons, on file at the Oregon Historical Society Research Library.

320. Harris, Minnie. "The Women Build a Museum: The Story of the Seattle Historical Society." *Pacific Northwest Quarterly* 43 (April 1952): 158-169. Notes, index.

English-born Emily Carkeek moved to Seattle with her husband and coaxed her friends to join her in creating the Seattle Historical Society in 1914. In 1952, it evolved into the Museum of History and Industry. The role of Carkeek's daughter, Guendolen (Mrs. Theodore) Plestcheeff, is highlighted.

321. Harrison, Cynthia E., ed. *Women in American History: A Bibliography.* Santa Barbara, California: Clio Press, Inc., 1979. xi, 374 pages. Bibliography, index.

This bibliography treats American women from colonial to contemporary times. There is geographical access in the subject index and many entries relating to Washington and Oregon are included.

322. Hawthorne, Julian, ed. *History of Washington: The Evergreen State, from Early Dawn to Daylight.* 2 vols. New York: American Historical Publishing Company, 1893. xv, 676 pages. Index to biographies.

In vol. 2, chap. 34 discusses the Mercer girls, who were recruited by Asa Mercer to embark on a six-month steamship voyage from the East Coast to Seattle. Included is Mercer's account of the adventure for the *San Francisco Chronicle* and biographies of some of the participants, including Mary A. Woodruff of Waitsburg.

323. Hayden, Mary Jane. *Pioneer Days.* San Jose, California: Murgotten's Press, 1915. Reprint, Fairfield, Washington: Ye Galleon Press, 1979. 49 pages. One photo of the author.

Mary Jane Hayden's (1830-1919) account of the years 1850 to 1866 discusses overland trail adventures, relations with Yakama and Klickitat Indians during the 1855 Indian War, the beauty of the

West, and the details of raising twin girls and running a household in Oregon. The volume also contains a biography of Hayden written by Edmund S. Meany and published in the *Seattle Post-Intelligencer* when she was eighty-six, in 1916.

324. Haywood, Mike. "Behind Senate Bill 2431." *Good Work: Sisters of Providence* 4 (July 1977): 1-6.

Here is an account of the effort to put Mother Joseph's statue in Washington, D.C. This Roman Catholic nun founded over two dozen Northwest hospitals and schools, and hers is one of two statues representing the state of Washington in Statuary Hall at the capitol building in Washington, D.C.

325. Hazard, Joseph Taylor. *Pioneer Teachers of Washington.* Seattle: Retired Teachers Association, 1955. 144 pages. Notes.

This book discusses the early history of teaching in Washington state. It names numerous women who were teachers or wives of teachers. It treats educational opportunities for girls and conditions for educators, including wages, job opportunities, and marriage patterns of women teachers.

326. Hebard, Grace Raymond. *Sacajawea, A Guide and Interpreter of the Lewis and Clark Expedition, with an Account of the Travels of Toussaint Charbonneau, and of Jean Baptiste, the Expedition Papoose.* Glendale, California: The Arthur H. Clark Company, 1933. 340 pages. Notes, fourteen pages of annotated bibliography, index. Several paintings reproduced including *Race of the Cheyenne Maidens,* by Mollhausen, October 26, 1851; photo of Sacajawea's "grave," Wind River, Wyoming; photo of author and Indian woman on Shoshone Reservation, Wyoming, September 1926.

Wyoming historian Grace Hebard spent decades researching Sacajawea. Hebard's goal was to resurrect the Indian guide of Lewis and Clark from obscurity. This scholarly biography gives a great amount of detail about Sacajawea's role in the expedition and then recounts the supposed subsequent years of Sacajawea's life until her death in 1884.

Later historians dispute many of Hebard's theories, and majority opinion today is that Sacajawea died of a fever a few years after the expedition. The book still has important early biographical material and historiographic value.

327. Heckman, Hazel. *Island in the Sound.* Seattle: University of Washington Press, 1967. xii, 284 pages. Bibliography.

This is a chatty memoir about the residents of Anderson Island in Puget Sound. Women are important figures throughout. Settled in the 1870s by Scandinavians, Anderson Island's population in the 1960s consisted mainly of their descendants. There is a chapter devoted to Ellen Ehriche, the storekeeper, and another to Bessie Cammon, a lifetime resident. There is also a chapter entitled "The Distaff Side" about the Island's social organizations, all of which were founded and run by women. These include the Cemetery Association, The Anderson Island Social Club (which owned the island's telephone system), and the Anderson Island Community Club.

328. Helms, Irene H. *Remembering—School Days of Old Crook County.* Prineville, Oregon: by the author, 1980. vi, 380 pages. Photographs of teachers with pupils, school buildings, documents, reports, and school registers.

The history of each of Crook County, Oregon's, ninety-two school districts is covered in detail, listing teachers and administrators, expansion of school properties, and anecdotes by alumni and alumnae of the schools.

329. Henderson, Alice Palmer. *The Ninety-First: The First at Camp Lewis.* Tacoma: John C. Barr, 1918. xii, 518 pages. Seven photographs of women, including Miss Jenny Booth, Chief of Nurses at the base hospital; Miss Ethel Allen, First Red Cross Nurse's Aid; Camp Lewis Hospital Nurses; Mrs. William Mac Master; Mrs. Constance H. Clark; Mrs. McCrackin; nine women hostesses socializing at Hostess House.

This book emphasizes the male experience at Camp Lewis. Chap. 5, however, is dedicated to Army nurses, 200 of whom served at the base hospital. There is discussion of their duties, schedules, good nature, and substantial contribution to World War I. In addition, chap. 23 explores "Hostess House," or guest houses for families visiting soldiers at camp. These were staffed by Young Women's Christian Association members. Mrs. William Mac Master of Portland organized the project, a homelike structure with a porch, easy chairs, and nursery facilities for children, so reunions could take place.

330. "Her Honor, the Mayor." *Woman Citizen* 6 (March 25, 1922): 10 and 19.

Fourteen mayors of small towns are briefly discussed, including Miss Helen B. Coe of Langley, Washington.

331. Herbst, Joyce. *Discovering Old Oregon Series: Oregon Coast.* Vol. 2. Portland, Oregon: Frank Amato Publications, 1985. 95 pages. Bibliography. Entire text is photographs, many of women.

This illustrated history of the Oregon coast offers numerous images of women, many of them taken before 1930. It includes photographs of women bathers at the seaside in 1910, camping, and working in a cannery. Annie Miner Peterson of Coos Bay is a Native American teller of oral history. A Chinook family fishing is also portrayed.

332. Hiatt, Richard G. "Lady Troupers Along the Oregon Trail." *Dutch Quarterly Review of Anglo-American Letters* 19, no. 2 (1989): 113-123. Notes.

Quoting from rave reviews in local Northwest newspapers, Hiatt documents the actresses who toured in Oregon theaters from the 1880s through 1909. Among the women treated are Fannie Janauschek, Nellie Boyd, Katie Putnam, and Jolly Della Pringle and Her Merry Company. The author lists the names of the plays they performed in each town.

333. Hicks, Arthur. "A Tribute to Mabel Zoe Wilson." *PNLA Quarterly* (Pacific Northwest Library Association) 29 (January 1965): 127-128.

The author, a professor at the Bellingham state normal school in Washington state, worked with Mabel Zoe Wilson from 1933 to 1945. He describes her achievements as the school librarian: securing a grant from the Carnegie Foundation in 1938, helping to organize the original Washington Library Association, serving as its first vice-president, helping to survey her state for its library needs, and recodifying library laws to create a rural library service in 1935.

334. Hill, Pauline Anderson Simmons. *Too Young to be Old.* Peanut Butter Publishing, 1981. xiv, 58 pages. Photographs of Bertha Pitts Campbell and clippings about her activities.

This is a biography of Bertha Pitts Campbell, African American founder of Delta Sigma Theta Sorority in 1913. It draws on interviews for much of its material.

335. Hinding, Andrea, ed. *Women's History Sources: A Guide to Archives and Manuscript Collections in the United States.* New York: Bowker, 1979. Vol. 1: xix, 1,114; vol. 2: x, 391. Index.

This important but now-outdated reference work lists primary materials available to researchers in public archives. The chapter on Oregon identifies 447 collections of papers dealing with women in Aurora, Beaverton, Coos Bay, Corvallis, Eugene, Forest Grove, Jacksonville, Maryhurst, Mount Angel, Portland, Roseburg, and Salem. Records are available which deal with such women's organizations as the Ladies Coffee Club, Portland Woman's Club, Lutheran Women's Missionary League, Sisters of the Holy Name, and local branches of the American Association of University Women, Women's International League for Peace and Freedom, Women's Christian Temperance Union, and Young Woman's Christian Association. Individuals treated include teacher Ellen Pauline Walton, song writer Nell Seely, journalist and suffragist Abigail Scott Duniway, missionary Mary Richardson Walker, and journalist Dorothy Sterling.

For Washington state, the work cites 298 holdings in Bellingham, Chehalis, Cheney, Edmonds, La Conner, North Bend, Olympia, Port Townsend, Pullman, Seattle, Spokane, Tacoma, Vancouver, Walla Walla, and Yakima. The clubs covered include the Walla Walla Women's Reading Club, National Organization of Women of Seattle, Daughters of the Pioneers of Skagit County, Bellingham Women's Music Club, Burlington Garden Club, Seattle Business and Professional Women's Club, and the Women's Christian Temperance Union. Individuals' papers are from anthropologist Erna Gunther, legislator Julia Butler Hansen, art gallery owner Linda Farris, and painter Myra Albert Wiggins. Vol. 2 is an index to the first volume, listing material by name of person or organization, subject matter, or geographical location.

336. Hines, Celinda E. "Diary of Celinda E. Hines." *Transactions of the Oregon Pioneer Association* (1918), 46th annual reunion, pp. 69-125. Portland: Oregon Pioneer Association, 1921.

Here is a detailed account of Hines's overland journey to Oregon in 1853. She observes weather, scenery, road conditions, and domestic responsibilities along the way. She also comments on the Native Americans and Caucasian settlers she meets.

337. Hines, Rev. H. K. *An Illustrated History of the State of Oregon*. Chicago: Lewis Publishing Company, 1893. xii, 1,300 pages.

The beginning of this work contains a conventional history of the state, covering climate, American Indians, claims, missions, statehood, and the Indian Wars. The remaining pages contain hundreds of biographies, only seventeen of which feature women. Even those accounts dwell on the lives of their pioneer husbands. The women include: Alphia L. Dimick, Mrs. A.M. Elkins, Mrs. E. Elliott, Martha L. Hansee, Gertrude Holmes, Mrs. N.C.B. Kelly, Mrs. L.E. Marrs, Mrs. F.B. Martin, Emma W. McKenzie, Mrs. S.J. Mull, Lucretia Overturf, Mrs. S.A. Sloan, Miss H.F. Spalding, Phoebe A. Stephens, Sarah A. Talbot, Mrs. E. Whitman, and Elsia Wright. All biographies contain the names of the women who are mothers, spouses, and daughters of the subjects.

338. *History of the Pacific Northwest: Oregon and Washington*. 2 vols. Portland, Oregon: North Pacific History Company, 1889. Vol. 1: xiv, 656 pages; vol. 2: vii, 709 pages. Index. Photographs of a few pioneer wives.

Vol. 1 discusses the Whitman massacre in detail and includes a listing of all the children who were held captive afterward. Vol. 2 consists of biographical sketches, mainly of men, and women are mentioned as wives, mothers, and daughters. Dr. Berthenia [sic] Angelina Owens-Adair, physician, receives her own biography.

339. Hitt, Helen. "History in Pacific Northwest Novels Written Since 1920." *Oregon Historical Quarterly* 51 (September 1950): 180-206.

Here are plot summaries of novels by women that draw on Northwest history for their subject matter. Among the works featured are *Shadow on the Plain* by Alice Wheeler Greve about the Whitman massacre; *From Out this House* by Greve on early Portland; *Chloe Dusts Her Mantel* by Laura Francis Gill about a twenty-one-year-old Methodist missionary of 1839; *The Cabin at the Trail's End* by Sheba Hargreaves about the Bainbridge family's first year in Oregon, in 1844; *Each Bright River* by Mildred Masterson McNeilly from 1845 to 1855; *Light Down, Stranger* and *The Bitter Country* by Anita Pettibone about Johnny Painter in Washington Territory of the 1870s; *Eliza* by Patricia Campbell; *Rock and the Wind* by Vivien Bretherton; *The New House* by Nancy Noon Kendall; *Trail of the Plow* by Marie Goffin; *The Color of Ripening* by Matthea Thorseth about the Industrial Workers of the World; *The Day Will Come* by Elizabeth Marion; and *Marching! Marching!* by Clara Weatherwax.

340. Hoar, Jay S. "Susan Haines Clayton, American Lady, 1851-1948." *Oregon Historical Quarterly* 84 (Summer 1983): 206-210. Notes. Two photographs of Susan Haines Clayton.

Here is a biography of Susan Haines, who was born in Bethlehem, Indiana, to Quakers and nursed Union soldiers in the Civil War. In 1875, she organized the first Women's Relief Corps in Kansas. In 1905, she moved to Portland, Oregon, and in 1921 to Talent, Oregon, where she belonged to the Daughters of Union Veterans.

341. Hoffert, Sylvia D. "Childbearing on the Trans-Mississippi Frontier, 1830-1900." *Western Historical Quarterly* 22 (August 1991): 273-288. Notes.

This is a survey of pioneer birth control, pregnancy, mid-wifery, and absence of eastern medical resources for Anglo American, Native American, and Mormon women. Among the materials tapped include the experiences of Anna Maria Pittman Lee, Mary Richardson Walker, Eliza Spalding, and Narcissa Whitman.

342. Hogue, Jadee, Anna Margaret Kalhar, and Mae Turner. *Green Bluff's Heritage*. Fairfield, Washington: Ye Galleon Press, 1984. 318 pages. Bibliography, index. Photographs of Ethel Keck in Keck's Market, majorettes in Spokane's Lilac Festival Parade, members of Green Bluff Home Economics Club, family portraits.

This work provides biographies of many local families and women are mentioned throughout. The Green Bluff Home Economics Club history before 1915 is featured and officers and members are listed for 1936, 1958, and 1983. The Green Bluff Grange is mentioned, as are school teachers and women who served in World War I and World War II.

343. Holmes, Kenneth L., ed. *Covered Wagon Women: Diaries and Letters from the Western Trails, 1840-1890*. Vol. 1 (1840-1849): Glendale, California: Arthur H. Clark Company, 1983. Notes and bibliography. 278 pages. Photographs of Rachel Fisher Mills and Tabitha Brown. Vol. 3 (1851): Glendale, California: Arthur H. Clark Company, 1984. 283 pages. Photographs of Harriet Talcott Buckingham, Lucia Loraine Williams, and Eugenia Shunk Zieber. Vol. 5 (1852): David C. Duniway, co-editor. Glendale: Arthur H. Clark Company, 1986. Notes. 312 pages. Photographs of Abigail Scott Duniway; Harriet, Margaret, and Catherine Scott; Amos and Frances Scott

Cook; Polly Coon and pages of her 1852 diary; Martha Reed. Vol. 7 (1854-1860): Glendale: Arthur H. Clark Company, 1988. Notes, 295 pages. Photograph of Elizabeth Austin. Vol. 8 (1862-1865): Spokane: Arthur H. Clark Company, 1989. Notes. Photograph of Nancy C. Glenn. Vol. 9 (1864-1868): Spokane: Arthur H. Clark Company, 1990. Notes. 249 pages. Photograph of Elizabeth Lee Porter. Vol. 10 (1875-1883): Spokane: Arthur H. Clark Company, 1991. Notes, 273 pages. Photograph of Mary Riddle, Laura Wright, and M.M. Surfus. Vol. 11 (1879-1903). Spokane: Arthur H. Clark Company, 1993. 276 pages.

Several of the volumes in the series entitled *Covered Wagon Women* include diaries and letters by women who crossed the overland trail by covered wagon to make a new life in Oregon. For every traveler, Kenneth Holmes has provided considerable biographical detail about the author and her family, their lives before they embarked on their journey west and their accomplishments after they settled in the Pacific Northwest. The context he offers, in order for readers to interpret the primary documents collected here, is impressive.

Vol. 1 contains commentary with diaries or letters of seven women who journeyed to Oregon in the 1840s. While full biographical material is unavailable for all his subjects, Holmes includes background and documents on Betsey Bayley, who came to Chehalem Valley, Oregon, in 1845; Anna Maria King, whose destination was the Luckiamute River area; Tabitha Brown, a sixty-six-year-old widow from Brimfield, Massachusetts; Phoebe Stanton, who traveled to the Willamette Valley in 1847 while she was pregnant; Rachel Fisher Mills, a Quaker, who arrived in 1847 at the Tualatin Valley in Washington County, Oregon; Elizabeth Dixon Smith, who traveled in 1848; and Keturah Belknap, who also made the move in 1847 while she was pregnant.

Vol. 2 includes no Pacific Northwest women, but vol. 3 draws from diaries, journals, and letters of eight figures who made the westward journey in 1851. Among them were Harriet Talcott Buckingham, Amelia Hammond Hadley, Susan Amelia Marsh Cranston, Lucia Loraine Williams, Elizabeth Wood, and Eugenia Shunk Zieber.

Vol. 4 addresses women who moved to California. Vol. 5, however, deals with women's 1852 experiences on the Oregon Trail. The bulk of this volume consists of the diary of Abigail Jane Scott Duniway, which she kept as an adolescent, moving with her family from Illinois to the Willamette Valley. The volume also contains documents by Polly Coon (1825-1896), describing her journey from Wisconsin to Oregon; Martha S. Read (1811-

1891); twin sisters—Cecilia Adams (1829-1867) and Parthenia Blank (1829-1915)—who kept a diary together.

Vol. 7 considers 1854-1860. It includes Sarah Sutton's travel diary of 1854, documenting her Illinois to Oregon trip. Sarah died en route, in Tygh Valley, east of Mount Hood in eastern Oregon, but the family reached the Willamette Valley a month later. Vol. 7 also includes the Vermillion wagon train diaries of 1854 by Anna Maria Goddell, aged twenty-three, and Elizabeth Austin, aged twenty-seven. Both left Vermillion, Ohio, for Grand Mound, Washington Territory.

Vol. 8 contains a long letter written by Nancy Cordelia Glenn to her parents, in 1862. Vol. 8 also contains letters home to Ohio by Louisa Cook, who, with her daughter, interrupted her westward journey to teach children of officers of the First Oregon Cavalry, at Fort Walla Walla; "Travel and Incidents, 1864" by Harriet A. Loughary, who kept a diary in 1864 while she traveled west with her six children; and Harriet Hitchcock's "Thoughts by the Way, 1864-65," written when she traveled from St. Joseph, Missouri, to Colorado with her family. She was only thirteen years old at the time.

Vol. 9 offers two Oregon diaries. Elizabeth Lee Porter left Lacelle, Iowa, for Linn County, Oregon, in 1864, with her husband and five children. Her travel journal is reprinted. Mary Louisa Black spent seven months on the Oregon Trail in 1865. Holmes's biography adds a family genealogy and a list of medicines used by overland travelers.

Vol. 10 contains five Oregon contributions. Mary Riddle left Coon Grove, Iowa, in 1878 and arrived in Baker City, Oregon. Her overland diary inspired her to keep a diary for forty-five years, until 1923. She died in 1929 at the age of eighty-nine. Lucy Ide took a Prairie Schooner from Omaha, Nebraska, to Dayton in eastern Washington in 1878, even though a railroad was available. Laura Wright, her husband, and three children, left Carthage, Missouri, for Weston, Oregon, in 1879. Sarah J. Collins (1845-1913) kept a diary in 1883, when she and her husband left McCune, Kansas, for North Powder, Oregon. Mary Matilda Surfus made the trip from Vallonia, Kansas, to Oregon City, Oregon, in 1883. Her diary and Holmes's commentary provide an extensive narration of her experiences.

Vol. 11, the most recent in Holmes's series, contains three Oregon entries. Viola Springer's 1885 diary describes her journey from Missouri to Harvey Valley, Oregon; Mrs. Hampton's 1888 diary covers her trip from Kansas to Oregon; and Anna Hansberry's 1903 letter details her Oregon journey.

344. Hood, Brenda. "'This Worry I Have': Mary Herren Journal." *Oregon Historical Quarterly* 80 (Fall 1979): 229-257. Notes. Photograph of Mary Herren.

This is an autobiographical account of Mary Herren's (1858-1887) journey from Oregon to Pasadena, California, by wagon, in 1885, to find a cure for tuberculosis. The account draws on Herren's journal for details about Chinese miners, Native Americans, weather, food, and local sites. Her health seemed to improve and she returned to Oregon in 1887, but she died there at the age of 28.

345. Hopkins, Danielle L. *Fruit and Flower: The History of Oregon's First Day Care Center.* Portland, Oregon: Fruit and Flower Child Care Center, 1979. vi, 103 pages. Bibliography, index. Photographs of founders, buildings where day care was offered, children with staff.

This narrates the history of the founding of the Children's Flower Mission of Portland from 1885-88, and details the changing services offered over a century and the expansion of its facilities. Appendices offer a chronology of events, a map of structures in Portland, budget totals, and a list of past presidents from 1893 to 1979.

346. Hopkins, Sarah Winnemucca. *Life Among the Piutes: Their Wrongs and Claims.* Ed. Mrs. Horace Mann. Boston: G.P. Putnam's Sons, 1883. 268 pages.

Here is a memoir of a Native American woman, born in 1844 and granddaughter of the chief of the entire Piute nation, who served as an interpreter and guide for the U.S. Army near the Vancouver barracks in Washington Territory, at Malheur Reservation fifty miles east of Camp Harney in Oregon in 1875, and during the Piute and Bannock War near Juniper Lake, Oregon, in 1878. She describes the interactions of Native Americans with whites and details many promises broken.

347. Horner, John B. *Oregon: Her History, Her Great Men, Her Literature.* Corvallis: Press of Gazette-Times, 1919. Index. 408 pages. Photograph of Abigail Scott Duniway.

This overview sprinkles in references to women, including the movement for woman suffrage, the Oregon State Industrial School for Girls, and Tabitha Brown's Orphan School as a seed for Pacific University. The literature section contains a brief biography, bibliography, and writing sample for Ella Higginson and Eva Emery Dye.

348. Horner, Pat. "Mary Richardson Walker: The Shattered Dreams of a Missionary Woman." *Montana: The Magazine of Western History* 32 (Summer 1982): 2-31. Notes. Five photographs of Walker.

This biography of missionary Mary Richardson Walker (1811-1897) makes extensive use of the diary Walker kept for forty-five years, notably during her nine years as a missionary at Tshimakain in Spokane Indian country. Her accounts record her relationships with the Native American community and the responsibilities of raising eight children and running a household.

349. ———. "May Arkwright Hutton: Her Life and Thought." *Pacific Northwest Forum* 3 (Spring-Summer 1978): 23-40.

This essay contains much of the same biographical material from the author's essay in Karen Blair's collection, *Women in Pacific Northwest History: An Anthology.* This is a biography of Hutton, a suffragist and Democratic politician in Idaho and Washington from the 1890s to 1915. The article discusses in detail her role in the Washington Equal Suffrage Association and her falling out with Mrs. Emma Smith DeVoe in 1908-1909.

350. ———. "May Arkwright Hutton: Suffragist and Politician." In *Women in Pacific Northwest History: An Anthology,* ed. Karen J. Blair, pp. 25-42. Seattle: University of Washington Press, 1988. Notes. Four photographs of Hutton.

This biography of Spokane women's rights activist May Arkwright Hutton emphasizes her conflict with the more sedate suffragists of Washington state, notably Tacoma's Emma Smith DeVoe. Hutton's strategies to win public support for women's enfranchisement before 1910 were notably more flamboyant than those deemed appropriate by most other activists of her day.

351. Howard, Harold P. *Sacajawea.* Norman: University of Oklahoma Press, 1971. xiii, 218 pages. Informational footnotes, bibliography, index.

In the spring of 1805, the Lewis and Clark expedition left for the Pacific Coast with Sacajawea, her French-Canadian spouse, and her infant son. This succinct report, however, is mistitled, for it describes the entire company's experience rather than focusing on that of Sacajawea. The last chapters address the debate about the facts of her later life.

352. Howard, Helen Addison. "The Mystery of Sacajawea's Death." *Pacific Northwest Quarterly* 58 (January 1967): 1-6. Notes. One photograph of Grace Raymond Hebard.

Howard evaluates the contribution of Shoshone interpreter Sacajawea to the Lewis and Clark expedition from 1804-1806. The author quotes the journals of the two explorers to collect and evaluate the advice that Native American guide Sacajawea offered to the band of travelers. Howard explains that the spelling and meaning of Sacajawea's name are in dispute, as is her death date and place. Historian Grace Hebard's scholarship is employed to document the roots of the argument.

353. Howell, Erle. "Chloe Aurelia Clarke Willison." *Pacific Historian* 14:3 (1970): 50-62. Notes. Photograph of Chloe Aurelia Clarke Willison.

Here is a biography of Puget Sound's first teacher. Willison taught in 1840 at the Indian mission established by Jason Lee at Nisqually, near Olympia, Washington. In 1844, she was the first instructor at the Oregon Institute (later Willamette University in Salem, Oregon). She also sailed from New York around Cape Horn to Vancouver, Washington. She kept a ten-year diary describing her eight-month journey by ship, her teaching schedule and curriculum, and her travel in the Pacific Northwest.

354. Howell, Erle. *Methodism in the Northwest.* Nashville: Parthenon Press, 1966. 468 pages. Index to names. Photographs of women.

Chap. 12 of this study explores "Women of Dedication," or those who raised money for ministers' salaries and promoted home and foreign missions. The Northwest Ladies Aid Societies are featured. In chap. 9, on "Men of Learning," the examination of educational efforts in elementary schools, Sunday schools, and Bible-study groups, makes no mention of women's contributions, but two women are pictured among the ten executive directors. These are Mrs. Gerie Brown and Mrs. Bertha Pease Hartsell. At the back, the names of 409 women missionaries are listed, plus twenty sent to foreign countries. A list of Seattle-area deaconesses contains 186 names.

355. Hughes, Babette. *Last Night When We Were Young.* New York: Rinehart and Company, 1947. 251 pages.

This is a chatty autobiography of a University of Washington co-ed who fell in love with her drama professor and married him. Of interest are her efforts to secure the Showboat for a campus theatre.

356. Hulbert, Archer Butler. *Marcus Whitman, Crusader.* Denver: Denver Public Library, 1941. Vol. 1: xii, 341 pages, notes, index. Vol. 2: xii, 342 pages, notes, index.

This biography of missionary Marcus Whitman generously uses the letters and diary of his wife, Narcissa, for material. Vol. 1 excerpts her remarks about his early life and education and their overland trail experiences. Vol. 2 draws on her accounts of the routine at the mission, the Cayuse Indians, Marcus's activities, news of other missionaries, Rev. Eells and Rev. Walker's opposition to women praying in the presence of men, and the birth in 1837 of Alice Clarrisa, their daughter, who drowned in 1839.

357. Hunt, Herbert. *Tacoma: Its History and Its Builders, A Half Century of Activity.* 3 vols. Chicago: S.J. Clarke Publishing Company, 1916. Vol. 1: xxiii, 563 pages, index. Photographs of Janet Elder Steele and Lena Tacoma Baker, first white child born in Tacoma. Vol. 2: xiv, 608 pages, index. Photograph of Tacoma Chorus of Women in 1915. Vol. 3: 705 pages, index. Photograph of Bernice A. Newell, society editor, writer, impresario; Emma Smith DeVoe, suffragist; and Mrs. A.P.S. Stacy, clubwoman.

Vol. 1 describes Janet Elder Steele, who established a hotel in 1869; Native American wives; temperance activism and passage of woman suffrage in the territorial constitution; women called for jury duty; Supreme Court's consideration of woman suffrage in the 1870s; equal suffrage overthrown; suffrage activity revived; and the organization of a Woman's Exchange, with a list of officers.

Vol. 2 considers the founding of the Tacoma Ladies Musical Club in 1890 and the work of such women's clubs as Aloha, Nesika, Women's Inn, Young Women's Christian Association, the Anderson Home created by the Club House Association, Parent-Teachers Association, suffrage, and Mrs. Amy P. S. Stacy's leadership in organizing women for the Pure Food Campaign.

358. Hunt, Herbert, and Floyd C. Taylor. *Washington: West of the Cascades.* 3 vols. Chicago: S. J. Clarke Publishing Company, 1917. Vol. 1: xix, 536 pages. Photographs of Mrs. Michael T. Simmons, early settler on Puget Sound; Mrs. Mary Ann Plomodon St. Germain, Washington state's oldest white daughter; Mrs. Charles Prosch; Emma Smith DeVoe, suffragist. Vol. 2: 675 pages, index. Vol. 3: 654 pages.

Vol. 1 is a general history of western Washington which contains the standard story of the Whitman massacre and the settling of the Pacific Northwest. In addition, the story of the Mercer girls is related and the failure of woman suffrage and Prohibition to pass with statehood in 1889. Chap. 38 is devoted to the battle for woman suffrage and mentions the contributions of Abigail Scott Duniway, Susan B. Anthony, and Emma Smith DeVoe.

Vol. 2 contains biographies, mostly of men. The women included are Mrs. Bennett W. Johns, suffragist and assistant postmistress who ran a book bindery and was twice the Republican Convention delegate in the 1880s; Miss L.C. Nicholson, proprietor of Snohomish General Hospital; and Alma Smith, towboat captain of Raymond. Vol. 3 deals with women only as wives of men featured in biographies.

359. Hussey, John A. "The Women of Fort Vancouver." *Oregon Historical Quarterly* 92 (Fall 1991): 265-308 and *A Columbia Reader*, ed. William L. Lang, Tacoma: Washington State Historical Society (1992): 25-32. Notes, photographs of Marguerite Wadin McKay McLoughlin, Eloisa McLoughlin, and Marguerite's tombstone in Oregon City.

In 1825, the Hudson's Bay Company established a fort on the north side of the Columbia River at present-day Vancouver. European fur traders married Indian women "in the custom of the country." John McLoughlin married Marguerite McKay, who was half Cree. James Douglas married Amelia Connoly, a full-blooded Cree. Sarah Ogden, daughter of Peter Skene Ogden, married Archibald McKinley. In 1845, the fort's residents peaked at 210 men, 160 women, 210 children, and slaves of both sexes. Most of the female residents were American Indians. The article explores the living patterns at the fort, dress, food preparation, furnishings, and women's roles on trapping expeditions and in child-raising. Tension arose between these women and pure-blooded Euro-American women who later arrived. Men demonstrated a preference for "European" brides as they gradually arrived in significant numbers.

360. Ichioka, Yuji. "Amerika Nadeshiko: Japanese Immigrant of the U.S., 1900-1924." *Pacific Historical Review* 49 (1980): 339-357. Notes.

Using interviews conducted in 1978 with retired Issei women at a Los Angeles retirement home, this article catalogues the ways Japanese American women came to the United States to marry Japanese American men. The women discuss their problems of acculturation and their work and living conditions. Cases of spousal desertion in the Seattle/Tacoma area of Washington, and Medford, Oregon, were reported in the Japanese American press.

361. *An Illustrated History of Baker, Grant, Malheur and Harney Counties.* Spokane: Western Historical Publishing Company, 1902. 788 pages.

The section on education in Baker County names the women teachers who were hired when the school system was initiated. The Roman Catholic sisters who ran St. Francis Academy are also listed. The section on Grant County schools includes the names of early teachers as well. The material on fraternal organizations makes reference to such women's groups as the Julia chapter of the Order of the Eastern Star, Daughters of Rebeccah, Women of Woodcraft, and Native Daughters of Oregon. Thumbnail biographies of upstanding male citizens in the four counties provide the names of wives and children.

362. *Illustrated History of the Big Bend Country, Embracing Lincoln, Douglas, Adams and Franklin Counties: State of Washington.* Spokane: Western Historical Publishing Company, 1904. 1,028 pages. Many photographs of women with husbands.

This massive work begins with a general history of the region, followed by specific histories of Lincoln, Douglas, Adams, and Franklin counties. The bulk of this work is constituted from biographical sketches, which mention women only in conjunction with their husbands. In the education section for each county, women are mentioned as educators.

363. *An Illustrated History of Klickitat, Yakima and Kittitas Counties: With an Outline of the Early History of the State of Washington.* Chicago: Interstate Publishing Company, 1904. xxiii, 941 pages. Index. Photographs of Mrs. Lysander Coleman and Mrs. Martin Fuhrman of Klickitat County; Dr. Bethenia Owens-Adair, Martha Cheney, Mrs. Charles Beach, and Mrs. James B. Clements of Yakima County; Mrs. John Oldings, Mrs. H. Doty, Mrs. John Shoudy, and Mrs. Tillman Houser of Kittitas County; public school buildings with classes and specific teachers in Goldendale, Prosser, Roslyn, the State normal school at Ellensburg; Sas-we-As,

wife of Chief Spencer; and pupils at Fort Simcoe Indian School.

Here are brief biographies of these Kittitas County women: Rebecca N. Bull, Margaret E. Clymer, Susan E. Cooke, Hannah Doty, Mrs. John Ellison, Catherine Morrison, Anna M. Pease, and Mary S. Rugg. Yakima County is represented with biographies of Mrs. Lysander Coleman, Dr. Bethenia Owens-Adair, Elizabeth Cochrane Carmichael, Martha A. Cheney, and Catherine F. Lynch. This contains no biographies of women from Klickitat County.

364. *An Illustrated History of Southeastern Washington: Including Walla Walla, Columbia, Garfield and Asotin Counties.* Spokane: Western Historical Publishing Company, 1906. xxii, 878 pages. Biographical index only. Twenty-six photographic portraits of women, alone or with their husbands.

This survey makes brief reference to missionary Narcissa Whitman, teacher Mrs. A. J. Minor in Walla Walla County (1861-1862), early women teachers and pupils in Columbia County, and includes the early roster of teacher Miss Blanche Marsilliott's 1881 class of boy and girl pupils.

365. *Illustrated History of Stevens, Ferry, Okanogan and Chelan Counties: State of Washington.* Spokane: Western Historical Publishing Company, 1904. xxii, 870 pages. Index of biographies by county. Photographs: an Okanogan medicine woman, Mrs. Enoch P. Morris, Mrs. J. McFarland, Mrs. George H. Gray, Mrs. William S. Cagle, Mrs. John Olsen, Mrs. Joseph Roberts, and Mrs. Joseph Lapray.

Like other histories of the period, this work is concerned mainly with the contributions of men. An account of the Whitman massacre mentions the presence of women. Mrs. Jennie Bottomly, pioneer homesteader, is noted. The history of Stevens County documents the wage differential for twenty-eight teachers in 1891, men averaging $46.76 to women's $46.00. The Ferry County educational history names early women teachers of 1888.

366. *An Illustrated History of Whitman County: State of Washington.* No city: W. H. Lever Publishers, 1901. xx, 474 pages. Index of portraits and index of biographies. Photographs of Mrs. Benjamin T. Boone, Mrs. Daniel W. Boone, Mrs. Alexander Canutt, Mrs. John L. Canutt, Mrs. Charles D. Cram, Mrs. Jay B.

Cram, Mrs. C. F. Crampton, Mrs. William V. Ewing, Mrs. Joan W. Imbler, and Mrs. William Mood.

Women receive scant attention in this historical study. Catherine Sager Pringle is mentioned for her capture by Indians during the Whitman massacre. In the chapter on education, the wage differential between men ($58/year) and women ($47.37) teachers is observed. Among the fraternal organizations recognized are two women's groups cited in 1887, Order of the Eastern Star and Daughters of Rebekah.

367. Imman, Margaret Windsor. "My Arrival in Washington in 1852." *Washington Historical Quarterly* 18 (October 1927): 254-260.

This is a rather sketchy account of Mrs. Imman's life along the Columbia River in the 1850s. She discusses at length the strained relations between Native Americans and white settlers—notably, a battle between them at Powder Island in 1856. She makes no mention of other women.

368. Ito, Kazuo. *Issei: A History of Japanese Immigrants in North America.* Trans. Shinichiro Nakamura and Jean S. Gerard. Seattle: Japanese Community Service, 1973. xxviii, 1,016 pages. Bibliography, index, chronological table. Maps of old Japanese districts in Seattle, Tacoma, Spokane, Portland, and Vancouver, British Columbia, Canada. Photographs of women.

This records the struggles of the Japanese in the Northwest. Women appear throughout, in chapters on entertainment, business, poetry clubs, prostitution, church organizations, midwives, and workers on farms and in business. Non-Japanese women who were respected by the Issei communities are cited in the "Pro-Japanese" chapter and elsewhere.

369. Jackson, Gary L. *Remembering Yakima: By Those Who Were There.* 5 vols. Yakima, Washington: Golden West Publishing Company, Inc., 1975. Vols. 1-5: 128 pages each. Photographs of 1935 board of directors at groundbreaking for Young Women's Christian Association Building, and of Bertha Johnson, Martha Tidland, Ann Smith, Cowiche telephone operators in 1947, and Mabel Steele Morgan.

This collection of brief accounts conveys women's contributions to Yakima, Washington. Patty Rose offers "They Told the Girls They Couldn't Play Basketball at the Men's Y So they Formed the YWCA." Gary Jackson details Bertha Johnson's management of the Yakima Hotel in

1899, Sis Anthon's experiences as city editor of the *Yakima Herald Republic*, Ann Smith's founding of the Yakima Valley Museum and Martha Tidland's pioneer story. Other women featured are Irene Eschbach, who founded Eschbach Park in 1920 and operated it until 1942; teachers Grace Bigford, Mildred McLean, and Anna Hahn; Grange member Mabel Steele Morgan; the Lower Naches Garden Club members who preserved the cemetery; Jessamine Van Amburg, charter member of the PEO; and Hilda Engdahl Meystre, superintendent of schools.

370. Jacobs, Melville. "The Romantic Role of Older Women in the Culture of the Pacific Northwest Coast." *Kroeber Anthropological Society Papers* 18 (Spring 1958): 79-85.

This male Caucasian anthropologist developed rapport with older native women in Washington and Oregon coast Indian tribes. Tillamook widows or divorced women of post-menopausal age described the affairs with unmarried younger men they sought and enjoyed, with acceptance by their culture in the pre-contact era. He observes a similar pattern from oral literature in Clackamas, Chinook, and Coos Indians.

371. James, Edward T., Janet Wilson James, and Paul S. Boyer. *Notable American Women 1607-1950.* 3 vols. Cambridge: Harvard University Press, 1971. Notes, bibliography, index in vol. 3. Vol. 1, 687 pages; vol. 2, 659 pages; vol. 3, 729 pages.

This reference tool contains 1,337 short biographies of American women who died before 1951. It includes coverage on Northwest women such as Abigail Scott Duniway (by L. C. Johnson), Bertha Knight Landes (by Robert Burke), Sacajawea (by Merle W. Wells), Eliza Hart Spalding (by Clifford M. Drury), and Sarah Winnemucca and Narcissa Whitman (by Thurman Wilkins).

372. James, Sister Mary. *Providence: A Sketch of the Sisters of Charity of Providence in the Northwest, 1856-1931.* Seattle: Sisters of Charity of Providence, 1931. ix, 88 pages. Two photographs of women.

This history of the Sisters of Charity of Providence begins in Montreal in the eighteenth century with the foundress, Emily Tavernier Gamelin. Using inheritance money, as a widow, she cared for the poor. She founded a Catholic order, Sisters of Charity of Providence. The book features the Northwest, providing a description of Mother Coron's Fort Vancouver settlement. The account devotes a chapter to Mother Joseph of the Sa-

cred Heart, their most famous member, who founded many Northwest hospitals, orphanages, and schools.

373. Jefferson County Historical Society. *With Pride in Heritage: History of Jefferson County.* Portland, Oregon: Professional Publishing, Inc., 1966. xii, 440 pages. Bibliography, index. Photographs of Native American couple, Kate Hill Plummer, author Mary Ann Lambert Vincent.

This collection contains Irene J. Grady's essay "Garden Club Achievements"; Helen D. Burns's account of "May B. Smith," a biography of the librarian who wrote *Picturesque Port Townsend* in 1929; and Sallie Hill's "Pioneer Women in the Puget Sound Country." Lists of officers of the Nordland Garden Club, Quilcene Garden Club, Chimacum Garden Club, Gardener Garden Club, and Port Townsend Club are provided, with details on community projects. Hill has also written a general essay on pioneer housing and domestic responsibilities, with few details specific to the region.

374. Jeffrey, Julie Roy. *Converting the West: A Biography of Narcissa Whitman.* Norman: University of Oklahoma Press, 1991. xvii, 238 pages. Bibliography, index. Fourteen sketches and photographs of Cayuse Indians, the Whitman Mission, Prentiss House in Prattsburg, New York.

This is the most ambitious biography undertaken of pioneer missionary Narcissa Prentiss Whitman. Jeffrey explores the ways Narcissa's mother shaped her values during her youth, and is sophisticated in viewing Whitman's difficulties with her mission, examining her assumptions about Cayuse and examining their views of her.

375. ———. "Empty Harvest at Waiilatpu." *Columbia* 22 (Fall 1992): 22-32. Photograph of Mary Richardson Walker.

Jeffrey asserts that male and female missionaries adopted differing strategies to cope with the stresses of their work and looks especially at Narcissa Whitman, who read biographies of other Christian missionary women for support. Jeffrey articulates the subjects on which Whitman clashed with Native Americans and suggests that she diffused her frustration by corresponding, creating a cozy household, and adopting orphans.

376. ———. *Frontier Women: The Trans-Mississippi West, 1840-1880.* New York: Hill and Wang, 1979. xvi, 240 pages. Bibliography, index.

This is a valuable social history of women on the western frontier. Jeffrey believes that the frontier experience reinforced rather than liberated women from their traditional nineteenth-century domestic role, and that women, as well as men, wanted it that way. She draws generously on the writings of many Northwest women to illustrate her point. The book is analytical in nature, rather than a narrative of experience or anecdotal.

377. ———. "The Making of a Missionary: Narcissa Whitman and Her Vocation." *Idaho Yesterdays* 31 (Spring/Summer 1987): 75-85. Notes. Illustrations of pages from Narcissa Whitman's journal.

This article examines the religious background of Narcissa Whitman, an early Protestant missionary in Waiilatpu (now Walla Walla, Washington). Her mother, Clarissa, was an evangelical Christian and served as Narcissa's role model.

378. ———. "Narcissa Whitman: The Significance of A Missionary's Life." *Montana* 41 (Spring 1991): 2-15. Notes, illustrations of sites pertinent to Whitman, including her parents' farm in Prattsburg, New York, and the mural in the Oregon state capitol rotunda depicting Dr. John McLoughlin welcoming Narcissa Whitman and Eliza Spalding in 1836.

This biographical essay on missionary Narcissa Whitman enumerates the difficulties she faced on the frontier, including a failure to convert any Cayuse Indians to Christianity, an antagonism with the Cayuse, and the drowning of her only daughter.

379. Jensen, Hazel Addie. *Across the Years: Pioneer Story of Southern Washington.* No city: No publisher, 1951. 124 pages. Two photographs of women.

Here is an account of early settlers who moved east from Rock Creek to establish communities on the eastern Klickitat frontier and in Bickleton, Washington. Women are listed in the section on frontiers (pp. 51-53 and 94-98). The list of supplies from the mercantile business of Bickle and Flower includes foodstuffs and household supplies.

380. Jensen, Joan M. *Promise to the Land: Essays on Rural Women.* Albuquerque: University of New Mexico, 1991. xix, 326 pages. Notes, index. Photographs of women included a Yakama Indian group in fields, 1904.

One essay in this collection, co-authored by Jensen and Susan Armitage, addresses "Women in the Hop Harvest from New York to Washington." An interview with Margaret Keys offers a first-hand perspective on the job, including details about the wagons which came through to sell food and the cooperation of the public school system, which delayed the opening of the academic year to accommodate the youthful employees.

381. Jensen, Joan M., ed. *With These Hands: Women Working on the Land.* New York: McGraw-Hill Book Company, 1981. xxiii, 298 pages. Notes, bibliography, index. Photographs: women working in peat in Oxflat, Oregon; Yakama Indians picking crops; celery workers in Oregon.

An essay entitled "Pioneering in the Northwest" provides excerpts from the autobiography of Abigail Scott Duniway, offering remarks about homesteading in Oregon in the 1850s. Jensen provides editorial comment.

382. Johnson, Claudius O. "George Turner of the Supreme Court of Washington Territory." *Oregon Historical Quarterly* 44 (December 1943): 370-385. Notes.

This portrait of Judge George Turner gives considerable attention to his opposition to woman suffrage in Washington Territory in the 1880s.

383. Johnson, Harry. *Washington Schools in the Good Old Days.* Olympia: State Superintendent of Public Instruction, 1969. 56 pages. Photographs of school buildings, teachers with pupils, Catherine Henry, Josephine Corliss Preston, and Pearl Wanamaker.

Although there is considerable attention to institutional, impersonal educational history, this includes a chatty portrait of Catherine Henry, called "Sagebrush Schoolmarm," in Kahlotus, Washington, in 1917. Among the state superintendents of schools discussed are Josephine Corliss Preston and Pearl Wanamaker.

384. Johnson, Ruth, and Elna Peterson. "The Swedish Women's Chorus of Seattle." *Swedish-American Historical Quarterly* 34 (1983): 294-305. Notes. Three photographs of the Swedish Women's Chorus in 1952, 1980, and 1982.

The Swedish Women's Chorus of Seattle was organized in 1951, the first American chorus for women only that was devoted primarily to singing in Swedish. Their performances are documented here.

385. Jones, Nard. *Evergreen Land: A Portrait of the State of Washington.* New York: Dodd, Mead and Company, 1947. x, 276 pages. Index.

This general account offers mention of women in the sections on missionary wives, the Mercer girls, and Jane Barnes—a barmaid from England who sailed to Astoria in 1814.

386. ———. *The Great Command; the Story of Marcus and Narcissa Whitman and the Oregon Country Pioneers.* Boston: Little, Brown and Company, 1959. 398 pages. Notes, index. One drawing of Narcissa Whitman.

The purpose of this book is to provide a biography of the Whitmans for the general reader, based on the research of Clifford M. Drury, and Archer B. and Dorothy P. Hulbert. These scholars have in recent years tried to revise the history of the Whitmans to debunk the myths surrounding their missionary experience.

387. ———. *Puget Sound Profiles.* Seattle: Puget Sound Power and Light Company, 1961-62. Vol. 1: iii, 100 pages; vol. 2: iii, 90 pages.

Vol. 1 mentions the Mercer girls who did not marry, and Anna Curtis, for whom Anacortes, Washington, is named. Elizabeth M. Ordway (1828-1897) is named, educator on Bainbridge Island, Port Gamble, Port Madison, and Port Blakely.
Vol. 2 discusses pioneer childhood, drawing on Emily Inez Denny's account *Blazing the Way.* It uses letters from Mary Walker, missionary, and considers the life of a Native American girl, her dress, village, dwellings, and transportation by canoe.

388. ———. *Seattle.* Garden City, New York: Doubleday and Company, Inc., 1972. Bibliography, index. 371 pages. Photographs of Bertha K. Landes and Anna Louise Strong.

This overview of Seattle's past deals with sports, culture, racial climate, Boeing, the expositions of 1909 and 1962, politics, and the general strike of 1919. Throughout the book there is very brief mention of women except for Mayor Bertha K. Landes, journalist and radical Anna Louise Strong, and the Mercer girls of the 1860s and their descendants.

389. Jones, Sylvia Case. *Early Laws Pertaining to Women in the State of Washington.* Seattle: National Society of the Colonial Dames of America, 1972. 62 pages. Bibliography.

This book contains lists of laws on civil action, civil rights, marriage, and land claim laws pertaining to women in Washington.

390. Jordan, Teresa. *Cowgirls: Women of the American West.* Garden City: Doubleday and Company,

Inc., 1982. viii, 301 pages. Notes, bibliography, index. Photographs of twenty-eight interviewed cowgirls.

In a text sprinkled with song lyrics, poems, and newspaper clippings, the daughters and wives of ranchers and independent cowgirls discuss their work, private lives, and Girls Rodeo Association. One woman interviewed is from the Northwest: Mildred Kanipe, of Oakland, Oregon (pp. 117-123).

391. Judson, Katharine Berry. *Early Days in Old Oregon.* Portland: Metropolitan Press, 1936. 275 pages. (Reprint of Chicago: A. C. McClurg and Company, 1916. 263 pages). Bibliography, index.

This is a well-written and researched history of the Oregon Territory. The author was one of the early frontier historians to have access to the records of the Hudson's Bay Company. Narcissa Whitman and Sacajawea are listed in the index and their roles in Oregon history described. Chap. 21, "Life of the Children," contains details and anecdotes about girls and their mothers.

392. ———. *Myths and Legends of the Pacific Northwest, especially of Washington and Oregon.* Chicago: A. C. McClurg and Company, 1916. xvi, 159 pages. Classic photographic portraits of a basket maker; Umatilla "squaw" and child; Yakama maiden; an Indian Madonna (Yakama); and Indian mother and child.

This is a collection of legends of Northwest Native Americans, illustrated with marvelous photographs of women.

393. Judson, Phoebe Goodell. *A Pioneer's Search for an Ideal Home.* Bellingham: Union Printing, Binding and Stationery Company, 1925. 314 pages. Photo of Mr. and Mrs. Judson at their Lynden home, 1899.

This is a well-organized and well-written reminiscence by Phoebe Judson, one of Whatcom County's earliest and most respected pioneers. She and her husband and children crossed the plains in 1853 and lived in several areas of Washington before settling in Lynden in 1871 as its first white residents.

394. Kaiser, Leo M., and Priscilla Knuth, eds. "From Ithaca to Clatsop Plains: Miss Ketcham's Journal of Travel." *Oregon Historical Quarterly* 62 (December 1961): 237-287. Notes.

A twelve-page introductory essay by the editors provides the historical context of the diary of New York-born Rebecca Ketcham, who left Missouri for the Pacific Northwest in 1853. The diary recounts women's jobs making tents and wagon-covers, "overseeing the men," and cooking. She also describes members of the troupe, encounters along the way, and scenery she observed en route.

395. Kaminkow, Marion J., ed. *The West.* Vol. 4 of *United States Local Histories in the Library of Congress: A Bibliography.* Baltimore: Magna Carta Book Company, 1975. 1,130 pages. Bibliography, index. (Vols. 1-3 deal with eastern states.)

This is an unannotated bibliography of local histories in the Library of Congress through 1972. Entries are arranged geographically. Entries dealing with the Pacific Northwest in general are on pages 725-738. Oregon is covered on pages 1027-1085 and Washington on pages 1087-1128. Entries within the states are further subdivided into regions, cities, and towns.

396. ———. *United States Local Histories in the Library of Congress: A Bibliography.* Volume 5. Supplement and Index. Baltimore: Magna Carta Book Company, 1975. Bibliography, index, 569 pages.

The supplementary volumes to the above-mentioned work list local histories catalogued in the Library of Congress between 1972 and January 1976. Pacific Northwest coverage begins on page 337, Oregon on page 365, and Washington on page 369. Within the states, entries are further subdivided by region, city, and town. This volume also contains a personal name index to vols. 1-5 of the local history bibliography.

397. Kaplan, Louis, comp. *A Bibliography of American Autobiographies.* Madison: University of Wisconsin Press, 1961. xii, 372 pages. Bibliography, index.

This bibliography lists published autobiographies only and excludes those which are "episodic" in nature, such as overland trail stories. The subject index provides access by geographic region (Pacific states), and by occupation (nursing, suffragette). Many women are included.

398. Kaplan, Shirlie, ed. *Pots and Politics: An Historical Cookbook from the Suffragists to the Equal Rights Amendment.* Tacoma: Washington State Women's Political Caucus, 1976. 115 pages. Notes, one index to 1909 recipes and another for the present edition. No photographs, but graphics and fashions from turn-of-the-century ads.

This is a reprint of the 1908-1909 *Washington Women's Cook-book,* edited by Linda Deziah Jennings for the Washington Equal Suffrage Association. The book was originally published to raise money for the Washington state campaign for woman suffrage. Both before and after the original recipes and household hints are biographies of May Arkwright Hutton and Ellen Swinburne Leckenby, a history of the woman suffrage fight in Washington, the Declaration of Sentiments from the women's rights convention in Seneca Falls, New York of 1848, and an assortment of early women's rights materials. For example, there is a reprint of a 1907 Charlotte Perkins Gilman article from *Women's Home Companion,* but it has no special relevance for Northwest women. The book contains twenty-one new recipes for the "Busy Political Worker, Elected Official, or Candidates" (pp. 49-56) of 1976.

399. Karolevitz, Robert F. *Doctors of the Old West; A Pictorial History of Medicine on the Frontier.* Seattle: Superior Publishing Company, 1967. 192 pages. Bibliography, index. Photograph of Catherine Maynard; Providence Hospital; Mother Joseph; nurses in Portland.

This book is primarily about men, but it provides one chapter about women doctors, nurses, pharmacists, and midwives. Northwest women mentioned are: Mrs. E. Perry, "Doctress" of St. Helens, Oregon; the Sisters of Providence, who arrived at Fort Vancouver in 1856; and Angela L. and Ella A. J. Ford, two sisters who were the first women graduates of Willamette University Medical Department in Salem in 1877.

400. ———. *Newspapering in the Old West; A Pictorial History of Journalism and Printing on the Frontier.* Seattle: Superior Publishing Company, 1965. 191 pages. Index. Eighteen women's photos: Nellie Watson, Washington; Abigail Scott Duniway, Oregon; and Fay Fullerton, Washington.

One brief chapter is devoted to women printers of the entire western United States. The Northwest women it mentions are Florence Apponyi Loughead, first woman reporter; Abigail Scott Duniway, editor and reporter; and Duniway's sister, Catherine A. S. Coburn, editor. It includes Lily and Dolly Wright and Gertrude and Laura Huntington.

401. Kaufman, Polly Welts. *Women Teachers on the Frontier.* New Haven: Yale University Press, 1984. xxiii, 270 pages. Notes, bibliography,

index. Four appendices about the lives of pioneer women teachers. Photographs include Mary Almira Gray McLench and Elizabeth Millar [sic] Wilson.

This account includes information about five Northwest teachers: Mary A. Gray McLench of Tualatin, Oregon; Elizabeth H. Lincoln Skinner of Oregon City and Astoria, Oregon; Elizabeth Millar [sic] Wilson of Forest Grove, Oregon; Sarah Smith Kline of Oregon City, Oregon; and Margaret B. Wands Gaines of Oswego, Oregon, all of whom taught in 1851 and 1852.

402. Kellogg, Jane D. "Memories of Jane D. Kellogg." *Transactions of the Oregon Pioneer Association* (1913), 41st annual reunion, pp. 86-94. Portland: Oregon Pioneer Assoc., 1916.

The Jane D. Kellogg reminiscence discusses living conditions, landmarks, geography, and hardships while crossing the plains in the nineteenth century to settle in the West.

403. Kesselman, Amy. *Fleeting Opportunities: Women Shipyard Workers in Portland and Vancouver During World War II and Reconversion.* New York: State University of New York Press, 1990. xii, 192 pages. Notes, bibliography, index. Photographs: women workers in wartime, day care center, and eight cartoons.

Kesselman's study is based on thirty-five interviews she did in 1981 with women who were defense workers during World War II. They were all employed in three Kaiser shipyards built in the Portland, Oregon, and Vancouver, Washington, area. These "Rosie the Riveters" are used as representative of the 40,000 women employed in war-work at the time in this region. Quoting generously from the oral histories, the author describes the recruitment of women workers and the position of labor unions in women's entrance into this labor force and provides a portrait of the white and African American women who were hired. She describes life in the yards, including the sexism faced by female employees and the tasks undertaken, particularly welding. She bares the tensions of handling domestic responsibilities alongside wage work and praises the two twenty-four-hour Kaiser Child Service Centers funded by the U.S. Maritime Commission. She documents both the women's interest in staying on in the work force after World War II and the magnitude of post-war layoffs that quickly removed women from the defense industry.

404. ———. "Hidden Resistance: Women Shipyard Workers after World War II." In *Hidden Aspects of Women's Work*, ed. Christine Bose et al., pp. 283-298. New York: Praeger, 1987. x, 384 pages. Notes, bibliography, index.

After World War II, women employed in industrial trades were dismissed. Through interviews with women workers, Kesselman determines that women in Portland, Oregon, and Vancouver, Washington, resisted this exclusion from shipyard employment, but only as individuals, in an unorganized and therefore hidden fashion. They avoided pink collar work as long as possible. Specific work histories are included.

405. ———. "Women on the Oregon Trail." In *America's Working Women*, ed. Rosalyn Baxandall, Linda Gordon, and Susan Reverby.

See Baxandall, Roslyn, *America's Working Women.*

406. Kesselman, Amy, Tina Tsu, and Karen Wickre. "'Good Work Sister!' The Making of an Oral History Production." *Frontiers: A Journal of Women Studies* 7 (1983): 64-70. Notes. Pictures of women in the defense industry and one World War II poster.

This describes the 1978-1982 creation of the oral history project with women defense workers from Portland, Oregon, and Vancouver, Washington, who were employed during World War II. The study culminated in a twenty-minute slide-tape production now available to educators. Both the film and this article use extensive quotations from the women, reporting on such themes as wages, skills, job satisfaction, family, dismissal after the war, and unions. The authors self-consciously bare the problems of interpreting the interviews with integrity.

407. Kessler, Lauren. "A Siege of the Citadels: The Search for a Public Forum for the Ideas of Oregon Woman Suffrage." *Oregon Historical Quarterly* 84 (Summer 1983): 117-149. Notes. Photographs of Abigail Scott Duniway, two suffrage handbills, front page of *New Northwest.*

This outlines the forty-two-year fight for woman suffrage in Oregon. Kessler offers considerable background on the history of the eastern suffrage movement and provides a portrait of the Oregon suffrage leader, Abigail Scott Duniway. Her efforts through two newspapers, *The New Northwest* and *Pacific Empire*, plus those of editor Clara Bewick Colby at the *Woman's Tribune* in Portland (1906-1909), are documented.

408. ———. "The Ideas of Women Suffrage and the Mainstream Press." *Oregon Historical Quarterly* 84 (Fall 1983): 257-275. Notes. Photographs of Abigail Scott Duniway, suffragist, voting in the 1914 election; Mrs. Edna Shooks, Susan B. Anthony, and Rev. Anna Shaw at the unveiling of the Sacajawea statue at 1905 Lewis and Clark Exposition.

The Oregon press shut its doors on woman suffrage issues during the six campaigns which came before the voters, in 1884, 1900, 1906, 1908, 1910, and 1912. Enhanced by tables, this work surveys the inattention to suffrage ideas in thirteen Oregon newspapers, two months prior to each vote. Harvey Whitefield Scott, powerful editor of *The Oregonian* and anti-suffragist, is cited as particularly influential. That his sister (Abigail Scott Duniway) led the woman suffrage movement in Oregon did not sway him in his opposition to women's enfranchisement.

409. ———. "The Ideas of Woman Suffragists and the Portland *Oregonian*." *Journalism Quarterly* 57 (Autumn 1980): 597-605. Notes.

Kessler argues that suffrage ideas were reported by the premier Portland newspaper, *The Oregonian*, only after woman suffrage was perceived as a legitimate movement. Advocates of the franchise for women campaigned from 1870-1912, bringing the matter to the voters six times. The newspaper was consistent in its lack of commentary about the issue, however, until the 1904-05 campaign.

410. ———. *Stubborn Twig: Three Generations in the Life of a Japanese American Family.* New York: Random House, 1993. xvi, 352 pages. Bibliography, index. Sixteen photographs of women from the Yasui family.

Through the technique of oral histories, Kessler has assembled a detailed portrait of a Japanese American family in Oregon. She has divided her story into three parts, addressing the first generation immigrants or Issei, then the children or Nisei, and finally the grandchildren or Sansei. The account begins with Masuo Yasui, who came to Portland from Japan in 1903, at the age of sixteen.

411. Kingsbury, Mary E. "Mary Frances Isom." In *Dictionary of American Library Biography*, ed. B. S. Wynar, pp. 261-263. Littleton, Colorado: Libraries Unlimited, 1978. Bibliography.

This biography of Mary Frances Isom, a librarian in Portland, Oregon, explores her career from 1901 to 1918 and accusations of her disloyalty during World War I.

412. Kingsbury, M.E. "'To Shine in Use': The Library and War Service of Oregon's Pioneer Librarian, Mary Frances Isom." *Journal of Library History* 10 (1975): 22-34. Notes.

Here is a detailed biography of a controversial Portland librarian. Mary Frances Isom was born in Tennessee in 1865 and attended Wellesley College for one year. At the age of thirty-four, she attended Pratt Library School and worked briefly at the Cleveland Public Library. In 1901, she moved to Portland and assumed full responsibility for the transition of its library from private subscription to public facility. She organized the Oregon Library Association in 1904, hosted the American Library Association (ALA) meeting in 1905, founded the Pacific Northwest Library Association in 1909, served as its second president from 1910 to 1911, sat on the ALA Council in 1912 and 1913, and supervised the construction of the Central Library Building in 1912. During World War I, she established camp libraries for soldiers and hospital libraries. During the Liberty Bond drives, she protected an employee, M. Louise Hunt, a pacifist, who refused to buy war bonds. Her own loyalty in question, she resigned from her position and went to Europe to volunteer for war-related activities. She died of cancer at home, shortly after the war, and left a bequest for a pension fund for the library staff.

413. Kingston, C.S. "Sacajawea as Guide: The Evaluation of a Legend." *Pacific Northwest Quarterly* 35 (January 1944): 3-18. Notes.

This author asserts that Sacajawea was not a significant contributor to the Lewis and Clark expedition. Challenging the work of other scholars, Kingston minimizes her assets to the Northwest exploration and reminds readers that her knowledge of the terrain was limited.

414. Kitsap County Historical Society Book Committee. 6 books. *Kitsap County History: A Story of Kitsap County and Its Pioneers.* Silverdale, Washington: Kitsap County Historical Society, 1977. Book 1, 64 pages; book 2, 177 pages; book 3, 119 pages; book 4, 134 pages; book 5, 144 pages, book 6, 162 pages. Bibliography, index. Photographs of groups of men and women celebrating July 4, 1890, in Kingston, Washington; school teachers with their classes of boys and girls; Daughters of the American Revolution

markers; individual portraits of women; family groups; and the Princess Angeline monument.

This collection is divided into five parts, narrating the histories of Kitsap County, North Kitsap, Bremerton, Puget Sound Naval Shipyards, Central Kitsap, South Kitsap, and Bainbridge Island. Many of the sections are written by women. The text includes reference to Chief Sealth's daughter Angeline, teacher and suffragist Lizzie M. Ordway, woman schoolteachers and female pupils, the Elizabeth Ellington chapter of the Daughters of the American Revolution, and women who participated in Burley's Cooperative Colony of 1898. Here is reprinted the biography of "Martha John, Grand Lady of S'Klallam, Speaks Three Tongues" from the *Bremerton Sun*, April 23, 1977. An account of midwifery is based on an oral history.

415. Kittitas County Centennial Committee. *A History of Kittitas County, Washington, 1989.* Dallas: Taylor Publishing Company, 1989. Vol. 1: ii, 696 pages. Bibliography, indices, hundreds of images of women. Vol. 2: 80 pages. Solely photographs, many of women, including John and Mary Ellen Shoudy on the porch of their Ellensburg store in 1870; Barge Hall of the Ellensburg normal school; the normal school campus in 1895; normal school library with students; Laura So-Happy in the 1890s; street scenes and dwellings with women in the landscape; children at a Sunday school picnic.

The collection compiles autobiographies and biographies of individuals or families in Kittitas County history with surveys of organizations. Among the women's groups mentioned are the Kittitas County Dairy Wives, Kittitas County Cattle Women, Genealogical Society, the Ladies Lounge, Ellensburg Federation of Business and Professional Women's Clubs, Arvida Club, Gallina Club, Mother's Club of Ellensburg, Rodeo City Grandmother's Club, Ladies Musical Club, Study Club, Garden Club, Princess Patrol and Escorts (a horse-riding club in the junior and high school), Women of the Moose Lodge #1920, Grace chapter #105 of the Order of the Eastern Star, Ellensburg Emblem Club #349, Thorp Home Makers Club, Progressive Club, Women's Thursday Club, Miriam Rebekah Lodge #25, Altrua Rebekah Lodge #298, Badger Pocket Home Economics Club, Jolly Neighbors Club, and Kittitas County Federation of Rural Women's Clubs.

416. Kizer, Benjamin H. "May Arkwright Hutton." *Pacific Northwest Quarterly* 57 (April 1966): 49-

56. Photograph of May and Al Hutton at home in Wallace, Idaho.

This brief essay chronicles the life of May Hutton, a prominent public figure in the Coeur d'Alenes and Spokane from the 1880s until her death in 1915 at age 55. Hutton was a vocal supporter of the Western Federation of Miners, and in 1899 published the propaganda novel *The Coeur D'Alenes*.

417. Knight, Mrs. Amelia Stewart. "Diary of Mrs. Amelia Stewart Knight. An Oregon Pioneer of 1853." *Transactions of the Oregon Pioneer Association* (1928), 56th annual reunion, pp. 38-53. Portland: Oregon Pioneer Association, 1933. Photographs of author.

One woman's brief diary entries describe road conditions on the Oregon Trail, feed for cattle, weather, interactions with Indians, health of travelers, and the cost of provisions.

418. Knight, Margot H., comp. *Directory of Oral History in Washington State.* Pullman: Oral History Office, Washington State University, 1981. viii, 76 pages. Index.

This is a detailed listing by county of 135 oral history projects in Washington. Several projects are specifically about women and women are listed as narrators in many additional entries.

419. Koslosky, Nancy. "A Filipino Nurse in the 'Thirties: An Interview with Maria Abastilla Beltran." *Backbone* 3 (1981): 28-32. Three photographs of Beltran, one as president of the Filipino Woman's Club.

At the age of seventy-two, Maria Abastilla Beltran was interviewed by her niece about her youth in the Philippines, her coming to the United States at the age of twenty-four, her education and career as a nurse, the discrimination she faced, her husband and family, and the Filipino Woman's Club, a social organization which she founded in November 1930.

420. Kovinick, Phil. *The Woman Artist in the American West, 1860-1960.* Fullerton, California: Northland Press, 1976. x, 59 pages. Index of artists. Photographs of examples of art works.

This is a catalog of an art exhibition from 1976 and includes a brief introduction on the significance of women artists in the West. Following are brief biographical sketches of several artists, with one photograph illustrating the work of each. Two Washington area artists represented are Harriet Foster Beecher and Abby Rhoda Williams Hill.

421. Krichmar, Albert. *The Women's Rights Movement in the United States, 1848-1970*. Metuchen, New Jersey: The Scarecrow Press, 1972. ix, 436 pages. Bibliography, index.

An early reference work for researchers in women's political history, this identifies four collections of women's manuscript materials in Washington state and two in Oregon. These collections are also included in Andrea Hinding's more recent study, *Women's History Sources*, which supersedes Krichmar in scope and size.

422. Kuneki, Nettie, Elsie Thomas, and Marie Slockish. *The Heritage of Klickitat Basketry: A History and Art Preserved*. Portland: Oregon Historical Society, 1982. 56 pages. Bibliography. Eighty-three photographs of Native American women and their baskets.

Three Native American women, Nettie Kuneki (born 1942), Elsie Thomas (born 1910), and Marie Slockish (born 1912), are Klickitat basket makers of the Columbia River area near Mount Rainier and Mount Adams in Washington and Oregon. This essay includes a Klickitat legend, "Where the Baskets Got their Designs," and provides details on women's gathering of materials, preparing, designing, and executing their baskets. A 1981 interview with Kuneki and Thomas is available at the Oregon Historical Society in Portland.

423. Lamb, W. Kaye. "The Mystery of Mrs. Barkley's Diary." *British Columbia Historical Quarterly* 6 (January 1942): 31-47. Notes.

Frances Hornby Trevor (1769-1845) married Captain Charles William Barkley in 1786, and accompanied him on his explorations of the Northwest Coast, at Nootka Sound and the Strait of Juan de Fuca. She kept journals in 1787 and 1792, permitting us to contemplate observations of the region by the first white woman to visit there. While many of the records are now lost or destroyed by fire, her account of the Vancouver Islands remains and we have quotations which refer to her long-lost accounts.

424. Lang, Sister Mary Margaret. "The Legacy of Mother Joseph." *The Good Work: Sisters of Providence* 4 (July 1977), entire issue. Fifteen photographs of Mother Joseph, the Sisters of Providence building, the Mother Joseph statue

in the capitol building in Washington, D.C., and the people involved in winning recognition for the nun's work.

This is a brief summary of the life and accomplishments of Mother Joseph in the Northwest, during the years 1854-1902. It outlines her work as an architect, builder, educator, healer, and administrator at the twenty-five schools and hospitals she established in Washington, Oregon, Montana, and Idaho.

425. Larsell, Olof. *The Doctor In Oregon: A Medical History*. Portland: Binfords and Mort, 1947, for the Oregon Historical Society. x, 671 pages. Bibliography, index. Photos: Portland Baby Clinic and Free Dispensary.

Chap. 10, on "Women Physicians to 1900," asserts that women were first admitted to the Willamette Medical Department in 1876. The account provides a list of the names of women physicians who practiced medicine in Washington and Oregon, and the school from which they graduated. There is no mention of women in health positions other than as medical doctors. Among those mentioned are Drs. Mary Cooke Thompson, Mrs. M. Bayler, Sarah D. Cunningham Dodson, Elizabeth Perry, Bethenia Owens-Adair, Callie Brown Charleton, Mae Harrington Whitney-Cardwell, Lydia M. Hunt-King, Emma J. Welty, Bellie J. MacDonald, Margaret Comstock Snell, Clara I. Darr, Margaret N. Quigley, Helena J. Price, Myra Brown-Tynam, Emma M. Linden, Sarah S. Marquam-Hill, Ella Keyes Dearborn, Viola M. Coe, Esther Pohl-Lovejoy, Corilla Gertrude French, Jessie M. Gavin, Belle Cooper Rinehart Gerguson, and Edna Davis Timms.

426. Larson, T. A. "The Woman Suffrage Movement in Washington." *Pacific Northwest Quarterly* 67 (April 1976): 49-62. Notes. Three portraits: Abigail Scott Duniway, Emma Smith DeVoe, and May Arkwright Hutton. One picture of suffragists pasting up posters.

This essay, while brief, provides a thoughtful and concise history of the suffrage movement in Washington. It focuses primarily on the work of activists Abigail Scott Duniway, Emma Smith DeVoe, and May Arkwright Hutton.

427. Laughlin, Mildred. "Teacher on the River." *Cowlitz Historical Quarterly* 24:1 (1987): 3-48. Photographs of Mildred Laughlin and her students in Altoona, Washington, in 1921.

A forward by Virgil Hopkins sets the stage for Mildred Laughlin's memoir of her teaching career between the two world wars. She grew up near Cathlamet, Washington, and reports on the Chinese compound, transportation, shopping, canneries, and her father's role in local government and as pastor of a church.

428. Lavender, David. *Land of Giants: The Drive to the Pacific Northwest, 1750-1950.* Garden City: Doubleday and Co., Inc., 1958. x, 468 pages. Bibliography, index.

The chapter entitled "The First Women" addresses the strength of Eliza Spalding and Narcissa Whitman, wives of Northwest missionaries.

429. Leasher, Evelyn. *Oregon Women: A Bio-Bibliography.* Bibliographic Series No. 18. Corvallis: Oregon State University Press, 1980. 54 pages.

Using the 102 books and journals in *Oregon Biography Index* plus seventy other books and journals, this work makes it possible to locate information and likenesses of Oregon women. Almost 1,700 names are listed in an alphabetical index. The women are also classified by forty-four occupations, the most popular of which are early settlers and educators. Only a few are classified under such categories as architect, aviator, barber, cowboy, criminal, dressmaker, forest lookout, funeral business, genealogist, ghost, Indian trader, interior decorator, miner, photographer, police, school bus driver, scientist, swimmer, telegraph and telephone operator.

430. LeCompte, Mary Lou. *Cowgirls of the Rodeo: Pioneer Professional Athletes.* Urbana, Illinois: University of Illinois Press, 1993. 252 pages. Notes, bibliography. Photograph of Mabel Strickland roping a steer at the Pendleton Rodeo in 1932.

This history of women and the rodeo includes discussion of the Pendleton Rodeo in Oregon. Tillie Baldwin, Fannie Sperry Steele, and Mabel Strickland are among the cowgirls who participated.

431. Lee, W. Storrs, ed. *Washington State: A Literary Chronicle.* New York: Funk and Wagnalls, 1969. xxii, 514 pages.

This digest provides brief biographies and excerpts of writing by a handful of Washington women writers. These are missionary Narcissa Whitman, represented by letters she wrote during the early nineteenth century; an October 1942 article from *American Mercury* about the Mercer girls' voyage around Cape Horn for matrimony in Puget Sound; political

radical Anna Louise Strong, "Red in the Ranks," with parts of her autobiography, *I Change Worlds*; Betty MacDonald's account of life on the Olympic Peninsula, *The Egg and I*; and two poems by Audrey May Wurdemann.

432. Leechman, J.D., and M.R. Harrington. *String Records of the Northwest.* No. 16 of *Indian Notes and Monographs,* ed. F.W. Hodge. New York: Museum of the American Indian/Heye Foundation, 1921. 64 pages. Notes. Photographs of string records kept in Yakima, Washington, and in Nicola Valley of Southern British Columbia.

J.D. Leechman, in "Some String Records of the Northwest," describes the Yakama women who kept a calendar by tying one knot per day in a long string. M.R. Harrington, in "Some String Records of the Yakima," explains that he bought a string calendar or "iti ta'mat," from "old Sally Jackson," a Yakama woman. It was thirty-five feet long and had 1,577 knots and 226 markers of colored yarns, beads, and shells.

433. Leighton, Caroline E. *Life at Puget Sound with Sketches of Travel in Washington Territory, British Columbia, Oregon and California, 1865-1881.* Boston: Lee and Shepard, 1884. ix, 258 pages.

In journal form, the author describes her travels throughout the Pacific Northwest (1865-1879), making many observations about weddings of Native Americans, births, funerals, burial customs, and the Goose-Dance of Gros Ventres women. She notes the Jesuit missionary efforts with the Coeur d'Alene tribe.

434. Leonard, John William, ed. *Woman's Who's Who of America. A Biographical Dictionary of Contemporary Women of the United States and Canada, 1914-1915.* New York: The American Commonwealth Company, 1914. Index, 961 pages.

Here is an alphabetical listing of prominent women in the second decade of the twentieth century. The entries consist of brief paragraphs that include birthdate, education, marriage, children, parents, address, organizational affiliations, religion, and stance on woman suffrage.

435. LeWarne, Charles P. "Imogen Cunningham in Utopia." *Pacific Northwest Quarterly* 74 (April 1983): 88-89. Footnotes. One photograph of Cunningham's father and one of the Puget Sound Cooperative Colony kindergarten.

In memory of the hundredth anniversary of Cunningham's birth, this brief account surveys her life, with emphasis on her stay at the Puget Sound

Cooperative Colony near Port Angeles, Washington. In 1887, at the age of four, she moved there with her family and they stayed for three years.

436. ———. *Utopias on Puget Sound, 1885-1915.* Seattle: University of Washington Press, 1975. xiv, 325 pages. Notes, bibliography, index. Photographs include women at the five colonies.

This surveys five utopian communities: Puget Sound Cooperative Colony, Equality Colony, Freeland, Burley Colony, and Home. In the photographs, women are evident everywhere. In the text, they are seen as spouses, teachers, cooks, writers, seamstresses, and cooperative store managers. There is mention of traveling speakers like Emma Goldman and of residents who supported the radical ideology of free love.

437. ———. *Washington State.* Seattle: University of Washington Press, 1986. 411 pages. Bibliography, index. Photographs: Colville woman digging for butterroot; Wishram bride; Nez Perce mother and child on horseback; Cowlitz coiled basket by Mary Kiona; Makah mother Mary Butler with baby in cradle; diorama at Fort Vancouver National Monument of the Whitmans and Spaldings being welcomed by Dr. John McLoughlin; McLoughlin and his half-Cree wife, Marguerite; missionaries Narcissa Whitman and Mary Walker; Robert and Julia Jefferson Espy, founders of Oysterville; Okanogan women on prairies of the Colville Reservation; girls at the Alaska-Yukon-Pacific Exposition in 1909 with Prince Albert, "The Educated Horse"; Elizabeth Gurley Flynn speaking to a free speech rally in June, 1913; Anna Louise Strong, political activist; two girls on skates wearing pro-union ribbons, "Don't be a Scab"; woman pumping gas at a service station during World War II; wedding portrait of banker Joshua and Laura Green; fish cannery workers at the turn of the century; women workers sewing wings for Boeing planes in the early twentieth century; group of Japanese picture brides at the Japanese Methodist Episcopal Mission; Delores Sibonga, Seattle city councilwoman in 1979, the highest elected Filipino official; Hmong woman; Mother Joseph; women plastering suffrage posters on fence; Mayor Bertha Landes; Rep. Lorraine Hine, Democratic Caucus chairperson, speaking on the floor of the House; Centennial Hall of Fame list of 100 distinguished citizens, including these women—Mother Joseph of the Sacred Heart, Pearl Wanamaker, Nellie Cornish, Julia Butler Hansen, Emma Smith DeVoe, Dr. Dora S. Lewis, Professor Erna Gunther, Thea Foss, May Awkwright Hutton, Patrice Munsell, Bertha Knight Landes, and Anna Louise Strong.

Among the women mentioned in this survey text are Representative Frances Axtel, Ramona Bennett, Alice Franklin Bryant, Dorothy Stimson Bullitt, Mary Butler, Anne Cochran, Nena Croake, Emma Smith DeVoe, Abigail Scott Duniway, Cora Eaton, the supporters of the Equal Rights Amendment, Julia Ann Jefferson Espy, Elizabeth Gurley Flynn, anthropologist Erna Gunther, Rep. Julia Butler Hansen, Laura Green, Lorraine Hine, May Arkwright Hutton, Native American women, Mother Joseph, Mary Kiona, poet Carolyn Kizer, Amelia Stewart Knight, Mayor Bertha Landes, writer Betty MacDonald, Catherine May, writer Mary McCarthy, Eliza Jane Meeker, Mercer girls, Governor Dixie Lee Ray, Rosie the Riveter, Sacajawea, Delores Sibonga, missionaries Mary Richardson Walker and Eliza Spalding, and ice skater Rosalynn Sumners.

438. Liestman, Daniel. "'To Win Redeemed Souls from Heathen Darkness': Protestant Response to the Chinese of the Pacific Northwest in the Late Nineteenth Century." *Western Historical Quarterly* 24 (May 1993): 179-202. Notes.

Although most of this essay deals with male missionaries to Chinese men, there is reference to Mrs. H.E. Pankhurst, who started a Chinese school at Seattle's First Methodist Episcopal Church in 1881; Kate Holt, who founded the Chinese Home in Portland's Presbyterian mission; and Baptist Aline Voss, who began a gospel school for Portland's Chinese children in 1858.

439. Lind, Anna M. "Women in Early Logging Camps: A Personal Reminiscence." *Journal of Forest History* 19 (1975): 128-135. Five photographs of cooks.

This reminiscence describes the working life of a woman cook in four Northwest logging camps, three in Washington: the Weyerhaeuser Camp in Wail in 1928; Simpson Camp near Shelton in 1929; and the Charles R. McCormick Camp near Port Townsend in 1931. The fourth camp was in Nehalem, Oregon, in 1935. It is a positive view of the experience, dealing with duties, rules, accommodations, slang, and free time.

440. Lind, Hope Kauffman. *Apart and Together: Mennonites in Oregon and Neighboring States, 1878-1976.* Scottdale, Pennsylvania: Herald Press, 1990. 415 pages. Notes, bibliography, index. Photographs of women, children, and families.

This volume describes the Zion Sewing Circle in 1945, identifying the names of twenty-one participants, all quilters. There is mention of Anna M. Snyder, women's missionary societies, girls' sewing circles, and women who canned fruits and vegetables for World War II relief.

441. *Little Known Tales from Oregon History.* Bend, Oregon: Sun Publishers, 1988. Vols. I and 2: 88 pages each. Photographs of women featured in the essays.

These two publications reprinted stories from *Cascades East Magazine* from 1982 to 1988, including these about women: "Missionary Mom" by Joanne McCubrey about Narcissa Whitman's life; "A Flight to Freedom," by George W. Linn about Maggie Wewa, Paiute Indian; "Whitman Museum, Cradle of Northwest History," by Vernon Selde about Narcissa Whitman's household and domestic life; "Bethenia Owens: Post-Mortem Pioneer," by Robert W. Pelton, about the physician's first autopsy; "Klondike Kate in Central Oregon," by Lucia Ellis about Kate Rockwell Dunn, a notorious gold rush entertainer from Dawson, in the Canadian Yukon; and "Sacajawea, Move Over," by Janet Mandaville about Marie Dorion, Iowa Indian who traveled in the William Price Hunt expedition to John Jacob Astor's Pacific fur trading post in 1811.

442. Locke, Mary Lou. "Out of the Shadows and into the Western Sun: Working Women of the Late Nineteenth-Century Urban Far West." *Journal of Urban History* 16 (February 1990): 175-204. Notes.

These case studies of four women, one from Oregon and three from California, are used to represent demographic trends in sex, age, marital status, birth, composition of households, and occupation in this era.

443. Lockley, Fred. *Conversations with Pioneer Women.* Vol. I in Oregon Country Library Series. Eugene, Oregon: Rainy Day Press, 1981. Comp. and ed. Mike Helm. x, 310 pages. Index.

This is the first volume in a series of oral histories with Oregon women, sponsored by the Oregon Country Library. It compiles ninety-nine articles based on interviews Fred Lockley conducted for the *Oregon Journal* in the 1920s and 1930s. Each portrait varies in length from a half page

to six pages. Each story is told in the first person with occasional brief narrative added by Lockley, and it chronicles the pioneer experience, courtship, social life, and Indian Wars of the 1850s.

444. ———. *History of the Columbia River Valley From The Dalles to the Sea.* 3 vols. Chicago: S. J. Clarke Publishing Co., 1928. Vol. I: xxiv, 1,105 pages. Index. Vol. 2: 941 pages. Index. Photographs of Mrs. Marcia M. Nicholson, Mrs. Alma L. Lowe, Mrs. William H. Gray, the residence of Mrs. Caroline A. Kamm, Mrs. Jacob Kamm, Mrs. Charles H. Dye, Mrs. Dennis A. Walters, Mrs. William J. Robinson. Vol. 3: 994 pages. Index. Photographs of Mrs. Ida May Doane, Mrs. Mary E. Stanley, Mrs. Chris Ebsen.

Vol. 1 contains an interview with Mrs. Mary Stewart, whose family crossed the plains in 1845. Mrs. Kate Morris tells of the early days of the Old Oregon Trail. Mrs. James Hembree remembers long gone days. In Vol. 2, there is mention of writer Eva Emery Dye; Alma L. Howe, who founded the Hood River Hotel; Mrs. Jacob Kamm, daughter of William Gray; Matilda C. Preston, the first white child born in Idaho; Mrs. J. S. Schenck; Portland dentist Maude Tanner; and Henrietta E. Wingard. Vol. 3 includes information about Sarah F. Abernethy, from an early family of Forest Grove; Ella Wilson Burt; Portland x-ray operator Edna E. Christofferson; medical laboratory owner Emma Howe Cole; Elizabeth Cosgreff of La Grande; physiotherapist Dr. Mabel B. Easter; Virginia Gray; Mrs. J G. Hustler; Genevieve E. Kidd who opened the Portland Doctors Exchange and Nurses Registry in 1917; and pharmacists Lillian D. and Mary Kyllonen, sisters who owned and ran the Highway Drug Store.

445. ———. *Oregon's Yesterdays.* New York: Knickerbocker Press, 1928. v, 350 pages.

One chapter in this volume is entirely devoted to the remembrances of Mrs. Catherine ("Kate") Thomas Morris, aged eighty-seven. Born in 1841, she crossed the plains in 1851 when Native Americans, who expected to trade twenty horses for a young woman in the wagon train, disrupted their progress. "Kate" married at age sixteen, raised eight children, and held many offices in the Oregon Grange. Other brief references to women are made throughout the rest of the book.

446. ———. "Reminiscences of Mrs. Frank Collins, nee Martha Elizabeth Gilliam." *Oregon Historical Quarterly* 17 (1916): 358-372.

Here are reminiscences of a girlhood in The Dalles, by Martha Gilliam. Her family arrived in The Dalles in 1844 and her father was Oregon's first postal agent and a militia leader. She discusses relations with the Native Americans and pioneer justice.

447. ———. *Visionaries, Mountain Men and Empire Builders: They Made a Difference.* Vol. 3 in Oregon Country Library series. Eugene, Oregon: Rainy Day Press, 1982. Comp. and ed. Mike Helm. x, 396 pages. Index.

This is the third in a series of volumes sponsored by the "Oregon Country Library." Based on columns Lockley wrote for the *Oregon Journal*, it compiles thirty biographies, one of which is about a woman. Reprinting the March 3, 1928, and October 21, 1934, articles, the Abigail Scott Duniway stories tell about the suffragists' involvement in founding women's clubs and of Duniway's tour of the Pacific Northwest with Susan B. Anthony on behalf of the enfranchisement of women. The volume also contains an interview with Miss Leila McKay of Portland who recounts the story of the McKay family fur trades and Indian fights.

448. Lord, Mrs. Elizabeth. *Reminiscences of Eastern Oregon.* Portland: Irwin-Hodson Company, 1903. 255 pages. Two photographs of women—Elizabeth Lord and Mary Laughlin.

This book is actually Elizabeth Lord's diary of her family's travels from Missouri to Oregon and their dealings with Native Americans during the mid-1800s.

449. Lorenz, Richard. *Imogen Cunningham: Ideas Without End.* San Francisco: Chronicle Books, 1993. 180 pages. Notes, bibliography, index. Photographs of Imogen Cunningham and those taken by her.

Here is a biography of Portland-born photographer Imogen Cunningham (1883-1976), who Lorenz praises "for creating commercial portraiture and pictorialist imagery often based on poetic and allegorical themes." It details her Seattle youth, adolescence, and early career and marriage. In 1917, she and her family moved to California.

450. Love, Helen Marnie Stewart. *Diary of Helen Stewart, 1853.* Eugene, Oregon: Reproduced by Lane County Pioneer-Historical Society, 1961. 27 pages.

Helen Stewart, born in Pennsylvania in 1835, came to Oregon with her parents in 1853. They tried a new route from Fort Boise to the Willamette Valley and were part of the 1,000 people lost near the present site of Eugene, Oregon. They suffered from lack of food and traveled with exhausted oxen and horses before they finally arrived in the Willamette Valley in fall of 1853.

451. Lovejoy, Esther C.P. "My Medical School, 1890-1894." Introduction by Bertha Hallom, *Oregon Historical Quarterly* 75 (March 1974): 7-35. Notes. Photographs of Esther Lovejoy alone and with her son.

The second woman graduate of the University of Oregon Medical School, the first to devote her lifetime to medicine, reminisces about her education.

452. Lowenstein, Steven. *The Jews of Oregon, 1850-1950.* Portland: Jewish History Society of Oregon, 1987. xv, 236 pages. Bibliography, index. Photographs of Neighborhood House, well baby clinic, kindergarten, cooking class of 1914, citizenship class of 1920, and Ida Loewenberg with her family.

This account identifies Ida Loewenberg as president of the Portland chapter of the National Council of Jewish Women in its early years. Her daughter Zerlina became its librarian and Ida served as an executive director of Neighborhood House (a settlement house) from 1912 to 1945. The work surveys prominent women from the pioneer era through the 1960s.

453. Luchetti, Cathy Lee in collaboration with Carol Olwell. *Women of the West.* Oakland, California: Antelope Island Press, 1982. 240 pages. Bibliography. One hundred forty large black and white photographs of frontier women from Arizona to Alaska in a variety of poses—as mothers, hunters, herders, and mountain climbers. They are also making soap, bathing babies, teaching, processing canned foods, and playing in a cowgirl band.

The text consists of excerpts from memoirs, diaries, and correspondence, both published and unpublished, of eleven individuals. In addition, there is one chapter on "Minority Women" which surveys African Americans, Native Americans, Jewish, Chinese, and Japanese experiences. The Northwest is represented by two people. Physician Bethenia Owens-Adair (1840-1926) contributes a memoir spanning birth to retirement. Missionary Mary Richardson Walker (1811-1897) is illuminated via her diary excerpts from 1833-1847 describing her westward journey from Maine to Oregon.

454. Lucia, Ellis. *Klondike Kate: The Life and Legend of Kitty Rockwell. The Queen of the Yukon.* New York: Ballantine Books, 1962. ix, 243 pages. Notes, bibliography, index.

Here is an account of Kansas-born Kathleen Eloisa Rockwell (1876-1957), notorious Yukon dance hall entertainer, who grew up in Spokane Falls.

455. ———. *Seattle's Sisters of Providence: The Story of Providence Medical Center—Seattle's First Hospital.* Seattle: Providence Medical Center, 1978. 61 pages. Bibliography.

This recounts the work of Mother Joseph (1823-1902) and other Sisters of Providence who established Seattle's Providence Medical Center in 1877. Background on earlier Northwest work of the sisters is provided, but emphasis is on the growth of the Seattle institution in 1887, 1888, 1893, and 1901, due to the impact of the great fire of 1886, the gold rush, and a growing population. There are many details on the numbers of patients and their illnesses.

456. Luthy, Dorothy Beckley. "Memoirs of Delia Beckley, 1888-1898." *Oregon Historical Quarterly* 83 (Spring 1982): 5-23. Photographs of Delia Beckley.

Delia Beckley (1858-1962) was born in Wisconsin, four years after her family migrated to the United States from Prussia. She grew up in Minnesota, married in 1876, and with her husband moved to the Pacific Northwest. Her account, as compiled by her granddaughter, Dorothy Beckley Luthy, narrates her catching a twenty-pound salmon and establishing a church in Milwaukie, Oregon.

457. Lyman, William Denison. *History of the Yakima Valley Washington: Comprising Yakima, Kittitas and Benton Counties.* The S. J. Clarke Publishing Company, 1919. xii, 954 pages. Index. Photographs of Ka-Ya-Ta-Ni, daughter of Chief Kamiakin; DAR monument at Union Gap to U.S. troops' victory against the Yakamas in 1855; Yes-to-Lah-Lemy, wife of Lu-Pah-Hin; schoolhouses.

This study draws on Narcissa Whitman's diary for its examination of the missionary period. It provides a directory of teachers in Yakima County during 1917 and 1918 in dozens of schools. Mrs. Anna R. Nichols was county superintendent. Teachers at the normal school in Ellensburg are named. Women's clubs are described, including the Woman's Club of Yakima, PEO, Daughters of the American Revolution, Ladies Musical Club, Twentieth Century Club, Mother's Congress, Portia Club, Home Economics Club, Coterie Club, and Yakima Valley District Federation of Women's Clubs, founded in 1911.

458. ———. *Lyman's History of Old Walla Walla County.* 2 vols. Chicago: S. J. Clarke Publishing Company, 1918. Vol. 1: 716 pages; vol. 2: 836 pages. Indices for vols. 1 and 2. Many drawings and photographs of important local places and of prominent early men and women settlers.

These two volumes, embracing Walla Walla, Columbia, Garfield, and Asotin counties, constitute a detailed and comprehensive but conventional history of Walla Walla County and surrounding areas from the early nineteenth century until 1918. Vol. 1 offers a general history of the area and some biographies of prominent settlers. Vol. 2 consists entirely of biographies. No sources are listed, and women are mentioned mainly in connection with their husbands. However, some accounts in the section of vol. 1 entitled "Pioneer Reminiscences" were written by women. These include "A Woman's Experience Crossing the Plains," by Mrs. Brewster Ferrel; "Beginnings of Schools in Asotin County," by Mrs. Lillian Clemans Merchant, and "Recollections of the First Woman in Columbia County," by Mrs. Margaret Gilbreath. Biographies include Mrs. Ida May Wolfe and Mrs. Mary Long in vol. 1; Mary A. Kimmerly, Mary C. Nichols, and Mary J. Thomas in vol. 2.

459. McArthur, Lewis A. *Oregon Geographic Names.* Portland: Western Imprints, Press of Oregon Historical Society, 1982. ix, 839 pages. Index.

The fifth edition of this work expands on editions from 1928, 1944, 1952, and 1974. The lengthiest entry on a woman relates the biography of Josephine Rollins, for whom Josephine County is named. Many additional women are catalogued for inspiring the naming of the towns of Marylhurst, Susanville, Luda, Mabel, Maud, Idaville, Ella, Ada, Elmonica, Mount Emily, Mount Fanny, Annie Creek, Marys Creek, Ana River, Jessie M. Honeyman Memorial State Park, and Bosley Butte. The guide is also a gold mine for those collecting the names of early women postmasters, for it lists those who selected the names for their pioneer communities.

460. McBeth, Kate C. *The Nez Perces Since Lewis and Clark.* New York: Fleming H. Revell Company, 1908. 272 pages. Photograph of Miss S.L. McBeth, sister of the author and her school/home in Kamiah, and Rev. James Hayes and family.

The bulk of this text memorializes the Presbyterian missionary work of Scotland-born Sue McBeth, educator to the Nez Perces at the government school in Lapwai in 1873. Since the Lapwai area of Washington Territory became part of Idaho in the 1860s, only Kate McBeth's overview of early missionary activity in the Pacific Northwest is pertinent to our survey of Washington and Oregon histories.

461. McCall, Dorothy Lawson. *Copper King's Daughter: From Cape Cod to Crooked River.* Portland: Binfords and Mort, 1972. xii, 190 pages. Photographs of Jeannie Goodwillie, wife of the "Copper King" Tom Lawson; the Copper King's sister Mary in 1875; and his daughters Bunny and Dorothy.

Following an introduction by Governor Tom Lawson McCall is an account by his mother, Dorothy Lawson McCall, who came to Oregon as a bride and pioneer in 1911. Her first novel, *Ranch Under the Rimrock*, described the family ranch near Prineville and Redmond, where she lived from 1910 to 1930 with her husband Hal and raised five children. This volume, however, features her father, who organized Amalgamated Copper Company with John D. Rockefeller and Henry Rogers of Standard Oil.

462. McCarthy, Mary. *Memories of a Catholic Girlhood.* New York: Harcourt, Brace, 1957. 245 pages. Photographs of the author and her relatives.

This autobiography discusses the author's childhood, including the death of her parents in the 1918 influenza epidemic, her unhappy years with her Minneapolis grandparents, and her happier home and school experiences in Seattle with her maternal grandparents, Harold and August Preston. McCarthy writes a loving portrait of her grandmother's sister, Rose Morganstern Gottstein, the impresario for the Seattle Ladies Musical Club and volunteer in Jewish organizations.

463. McCoy, Genevieve. "The Women of the ABCFM Oregon Mission and the Conflicted Language of Calvinism." *Church History* 64 (March 1995): 62-82. Notes.

The American Board of Commissioners for Foreign Missions, founded in 1810, sponsored the Pacific Northwest missionary work of Mary Richardson Walker, Eliza Spalding, and Narcissa Whitman. This essay dissects their writings to evaluate their revision of the complex doctrines of Calvinist theology and suggests they feminized it by challenging the ideals of women's meekness and self-denial.

464. McCrosson, Sister Mary of the Blessed Sacrament. *The Bell and the River.* Palo Alto: Pacific Books, 1956. xvii, 268 pages. One sketch of Mother Joseph of the Sacred Heart.

This is a biography of French-Canadian nun and architect Mother Joseph of the Sacred Heart, from her early childhood until her death in 1902. It was written to commemorate the establishment of the Sisters of Charity of Providence in Vancouver, Washington, the first mission in the Northwest. In addition, the book records the settlement and development of the Oregon Territory, notably the dozens of schools, hospitals, orphanages, rest homes, and poorhouses her order created.

465. Mc Donald, Lucile. *A Foot in the Door: the Reminiscences of Lucile Mc Donald.* Pullman: Washington State University Press, 1995. Twenty-five photographs of Mc Donald. xvii, 295 pages.

This is one of several autobiographies written by Lucile Mc Donald (1898-1992), Northwest journalist and novelist. She wrote this version in 1975 and 1980, describing her seventy-five year career writing for newspapers in Bend, Coos Bay, Salem, and Portland, Oregon; the *Seattle Times* (1946-1966); and, beginning at the age of seventy-nine, the *Bellevue Journal-American* (1977-1984). Not only did she produce twelve hundred feature articles about the Pacific Northwest, but she also wrote thirty-four books, mostly juvenile fiction and popular history. She collaborated with Zola Helen Ross on eleven of her works. Her remarks emphasize her career, locally and internationally, rather than her marriage and her private life. Her son Richard has provided a preface and historian Lorraine McConaghy has written a foreword which outlines Mc Donald's life.

466. Mc Donald, Lucile. *Where the Washingtonians Lived: Interesting Early Homes and the People Who Built and Lived in Them.* 224 pages. Seattle: Superior Publishing Company, 1969. Index. Photographs on nearly every page of homes, only two with women and men in forefront.

This study of early homes surveys log cabins of the 1850s to turn-of-the-century Victorian homes. Photographs illustrate every home mentioned. Women are noted in relation to the homes as owners, inheritors of furniture, or wives of owners. The book is divided into city and county sections of Washington homes.

467. Mc Donald, Lucile, and Werner Lenggenhager. *The Look of Old Time Washington.* Seattle: Superior Publishing Company, 1971. 159 pages. Index. Photographs of buildings which were women's spaces.

Supplementing marvelous photographs of buildings, signs, fences, hitching posts, schools, and lumber flumes remaining from old Washington are details about women as teachers and nuns. Mary Ann Boyer (alias Madame Damnable) established the Felker House, a hotel in downtown Seattle. Aunt Becky Howard founded the Pacific House in Olympia, a popular meeting place of legislators. She was a fine cook and a former slave. Miss Sarah Lorette Denny bequeathed money for a Pioneer Association Hall. Women on the advisory board for Pioneer Hall raised additional funds and supervised the building of its cobblestone fireplace.

468. McGiffin, Joy. *Home Town Heritage: A Remembered History of 1910 in Kittitas County, Washington.* Ellensburg, Washington: *Daily Record,* 1979. 108 pages. Index. Photographs of 1910 dormitory at normal school.

Here is a collection of 177 reminiscences from the Ellensburg *Daily Record,* collected from bi-weekly accounts from 1975 to 1979. Topics discussed include the history of food, clothing, relations with Native Americans, homesteading, marriage, home activities, jobs in town, downtown Ellensburg, life in Cle Elum, Roslyn, and Ronald, coal mining, making a living, social life, railroad jobs, children's chores, schools, college, and Christmas.

469. McHenry, Robert. *Liberty's Women.* Springfield, Massachusetts: G.&C. Merriam Company, 1980. xi, 482 pages. Index.

McHenry's brief biographies of one thousand American women include Seattle Mayor Bertha Knight Landes, suffragist Abigail Scott Duniway, journalist Anna Louise Strong, and author Mary McCarthy.

470. McKee, Ruth Karr. *Mary Richardson Walker: Her Book.* Caldwell, Idaho: The Caxton Printers, Ltd., 1945. 357 pages. Six photographs of women.

This is the history of Mary Richardson, who came west from New England to marry Elkanah Walker. The couple served as missionaries, traveling to Oregon Territory to work with the Indian tribes near Colville. The account uses excerpts from her diary, meditations, and letters.

471. McKenzie, Barbara. *Mary McCarthy.* New Haven: College and University Press, 1966. 191 pages. Notes, bibliography, index. Photo of Mary McCarthy on front cover.

This book is a literary biography of Mary McCarthy. Published in 1966, it precedes by one year a comparable biography by Doris Grumbach. McKenzie's book provides much less about Mary McCarthy's Seattle years, but has the virtue of footnotes over Grumbach's work. The first two chapters of McKenzie's biography analyze Mary McCarthy's early years by drawing on her memoirs and novels to gain the meaning of her childhood experience.

472. McLellan, Sara J., ed. "Chronicles of Sacred Heart Academy, Salem, 1863-73, Part I." *Oregon Historical Quarterly* 80 (1979): 341-364. Notes. Photographs of Sister Mary of the Visitation, Sister Mary of Calvary, Sister Mary Margaret and Sister Mary Florence, Julia Wilson, Mary D'Arcy, and the graduating class of 1876.

This piece catalogs the history of the Sacred Heart Academy of Salem, founded by the Sisters of the Holy Names of Jesus and Mary in 1863. They recorded a daily chronicle in English and the 1863-1873 entries reveal details about the administration, the building, expenses, personnel, the convent, the growth of the student population, Christmas entertainments by the pupils, graduation ceremonies, acquisition of land, the festival of St. Theresa, and the curriculum.

473. ———. "Chronicles of Sacred Heart Academy, Salem, 1863-73, Part II." *Oregon Historical Quarterly* 81 (1980): 75-95. Notes. Photograph of Jane Kelly, the first Academy graduate.

This continuation of Part 1 explores such aspects of Sacred Heart Academy history as the St. John's Church Fair, quarterly exams, Christmas vacation, a smallpox epidemic, death of one of the sisters, a fund-raising festival, and the laying of the cornerstone for a new convent in 1872.

474. "Mabel Zoe Wilson, First Librarian." *Imprint: Western Washington University Libraries* 3 (Fall 1990): 1-2, 4. Photographs of Mabel Zoe Wilson and the state normal school Building in New Whatcom, Washington.

Here is a biography of Ohio-born Mabel Zoe Wilson, who came to the Northwest in 1902 and spent forty-three years as the librarian at the normal school in Bellingham. The achievements of her long career are catalogued.

475. Mainiero, Lina, ed. *American Women Writers, A Critical Reference Guide from Colonial Times to the*

Present. New York: Frederick Ungar Publishing Company, 1979. Vol. 1: xlviii, 601 pages. Bibiography, index. Vol. 2: xlii, 582 pages. Bibiography, index. Vol. 3: xliii, 522 pages. Bibiography, index. Vol. 4: xv, 544 pages. Bibiography, index.

This biographical work studies the writing of several Northwest women. Included here are essays about Abigail Scott Duniway, Ella Rhoades Higginson, Mary McCarthy, Anna Louise Strong, Frances Fuller Victor, and Narcissa Prentiss Whitman.

476. Maquire, Jean Shepard. *Beside the Point.* New York: George W. Stewart, Inc., 1944. viii, 190 pages.

Here is a story told through Jean Shepard Maguire's eyes of how she grew up and met her husband. They settled near Three Tree Point on Puget Sound, a short distance from Seattle. Her short anecdotes include remembrances which reflect a rather romantic view of life.

477. Mansfield, Dorothy M. "Abigail S. Duniway: Suffragette With Not So Common Sense." *Western Speech* 35-36 (1971-72): 24-29. Notes.

The essay uses generous quotations from the suffragist's writing to argue that Duniway possessed good humor and common sense. She has been unfairly painted as an unreasonable separatist for her opposition to Prohibition, but she subscribed to moral views.

478. Marshall, John R. and Project Committee Authors. *A History of the Vancouver Public Schools.* Dallas, Texas: Taylor Publishing Co., 1975. 296 pages. Photographs of women teachers.

This study surveys the growth of the Vancouver Public School System, the histories of the present twenty-eight Vancouver schools, the history of the Vancouver Council of Parent-Teacher Associations, a history of Clark College from 1933 to 1975, and histories of the Washington state schools for the deaf and blind. It includes material on Clark County School district superintendents M. Ella Whipple (1884-1887), Elizabeth Sterling (1913-1915), and Ada Gill Holliday (1947-1955). The register of staff lists more women employed than men. PTA past presidents from 1931 to 1975 and winners of the Elsie M. Johnson Community Service Award show strong representation by women.

479. Marshall, William I. *Acquisition of Oregon and the Long Suppressed Evidence About Marcus Whitman. Part I, Part II* 2 vols. Seattle: Lowman and Handford Company, 1911. Vol. 1: vi, 450 pages. Vol. 2: vii, 368 pages. Index.

The study relies heavily on the letters and diaries of Narcissa Whitman. Vol. 1 provides a history of the Oregon Territory, including its maritime story, the Lewis and Clark expedition, the trading company at Astoria, and the early government. Vol. 2 emphasizes the missionary work of the Whitmans and discounts the theory that he was a government scout.

480. Martin, Grace Brandt. *An Oregon School Ma'am: From Rimrocks to Tidelands* and *An Oregon School Ma'am: Book Two, The Depression Years.* Brownsville, Oregon: Calapooia Publications, 1981. 143 pages each. Seventeen photographs of the author with her students, friends, and colleagues.

This author, born in 1906, provides a memoir of her education (Franklin High School, Oregon normal school, University of Oregon, and Oregon State University) and her experiences teaching in one-room schoolhouses in isolated cattle ranching communities. Her account details the friends she made, the courses she took, the students she remembers, recreation, and her philosophy of education.

481. Martin, Jim. *A Bit of Blue: The Life and Work of Frances Fuller Victor.* Salem, Oregon: Deep Well Publishing, 1992. xiv, 280 pages. Notes, bibliography. Three photographs of Victor.

Frances Fuller Victor (1826-1902) was born in Rome, New York, and grew up in Ohio. She began to publish her writing at the age of fourteen, for newspapers. In her lifetime, she wrote eleven books about life and history in the Pacific Northwest, among them *Women's War with Whiskey, All Over Oregon and Washington, Early Indian Wars of Oregon,* and essays on such topics as women's roles. The author provides extensive quotations from her writings.

482. Matsuda, Mari J. "The West and the Legal State of Women: Explanations of Frontier Feminism." *Journal of The West* 24 (January 1985): 47-56. Notes.

While this article is concerned with western women in general, the author uses Abigail Scott Duniway's experiences as a young wife, subjected to the devastating consequences of her husband's financial irresponsibility, as an example of the vulnerability of a typical American wife in the nineteenth century. The author relates a list of unrealized rights of women of the day, but points out that the western United States led the way in granting equal rights to women. She cites the 1850 Oregon Donation Act which gave land ownership rights to women. The author argues that unique conditions in the West contributed to the receptive attitude of legislators to requests for removing legal barriers to equality for women.

483. Maxwell, Ben. "A Hundred Years of Salem Theatrical History." *Marion Country History* 4 (1958): 25-29. Photographs of three structures.

This essay uses newspaper accounts to provide descriptions of early Salem theaters. Maxwell offers the names of leading ladies who toured in Salem, mentions an 1865 theater benefit for the women's Civil War Sanitary Aid Society, and includes a long list of local men and women who appeared at Reed's Opera House.

484. Mays, Theodore, ed. *100 Years, 100 Women: 1889-1989; Yakima County, Washington.* Yakima: Print Masters, 1989. viii, 209 pages. Photographs of all 102 women profiled in the text.

Two women's clubs, the Woman's Century Club of Yakima and Athenaeum Club of Wapato, initiated a project to profile thirty pioneer women of the region, thirty-three settlers from the turn of the century, and thirty-nine modern women. Eighteen authors, most of them women, detail the lives of educators, clubwomen, and others with distinguished public careers. The biographies include: Myra Wiggins, artist; Sue Lombard Horsley, educator, YWCA president, and member of the board of regents at the state normal school at Ellensburg; Ruth Parton, the first woman to receive a thoroughbred training license; Kara Kondo, a Japanese American who was interned during World War II; Sister Kathleen Ross, the president of Heritage College at the Yakama Reservation; and Genevieve Hooper, the first woman ever elected to the Yakama Indian Tribal Council.

485. Meacham, A.B. *Wi-Ne-Ma (The Woman Chief) and Her People.* Hartford: American Publishing Company, 1876. 172 pages. Drawing of Winema with husband Frank Riddle.

The biographer was an ex-superintendent of Indian affairs, chairman of the Late Modoc Peace Commission, and author of *Wigwam and Warpath*. He wrote this account to honor the Native American woman who interpreted her Modoc language into English and "who at the peril of her life sought to save the ill-fated Peace Commission to the Modoc Indians in 1873." He provides considerable biography and some detail about Modoc life in Oregon.

486. Merriam, Dr. H.G. *Northwest Books: Report of the Committee on Books of the Inland Empire Council of Teachers of English.* Portland: Binfords and Mort, 1942. 356 pages. Notes, bibliography, author index according to residence.

This volume contains reviews of 1,100 Northwest authors of fiction and non-fiction. The annotations are arranged in alphabetical order, according to the author's last name. Many titles have been written by women. It is possible to locate titles pertaining to Oregon (pp. 252-254) and Washington (pp. 254-256), in the location index. It is also possible to locate authors from Oregon (pp. 260-262) and Washington (pp. 262-264) in the author index. A Northwest magazine bibliography lists authors and titles from periodicals dated 1932-1942.

487. Mickey, Melissa Brisley. "Cornelia Marvin Pierce." In *Dictionary of American Library Biography*, ed. B. S. Wynar, pp. 395-398. Littleton, Colorado: Libraries Unlimited, Inc., 1978. Bibliography.

Here is the biography of Cornelia Marvin Pierce (1873-1957), who served as Oregon State Librarian from 1913 to 1928. Her administration created 706 traveling public library stations and 82 public libraries. She resigned in 1928 to marry the former Oregon governor Walter M. Pierce. She served on the Oregon State Board of Higher Education from 1931 to 1935 and served as her husband's advisor and speechwriter while he was U.S. congressman from 1935 to 1942.

488. Miles, Charles, and O. B. Sperlin. *Building a State: WA, 1889-1939* vol. 3. Tacoma: Washington State Historical Society Publication, 1940. xi, 607 pages. Photograph of officers of the Washington State Historical Society, including Secretary of State Mrs. Belle Reeves, Mrs. J. B. Davidson, and Mrs. Sarah S. Patton; couple on Yakima farm; curators Mrs. Lena Lewis and Mrs. Cora Matthews; Kate Stevens Bates, daughter of the first territorial governor.

This work contains an essay entitled "The Flag" by Emma P. Chadwick, which describes the effort of the Daughters of the American Revolution to deliver a Washington state flag to Washington, D.C. It also includes a biography of "Kate Stevens Bates, Daughter of Our First Territorial Governor," by Ethel B. Nelson. The text documents painters Ella Shephard Bush, Mary G. Allen, Harriet Fletcher Beecher, Mrs. Alcorn, Mrs. Hardwich, Kathleen Houlahan, Elizabeth Warhanik, Anna Stone, Louise Williams, Helen Loggie, Dorothy Dolph Jensen, Julia Caskey; the organization Women Painters of Washington; sculptor Virginia Pratt; pioneer music teacher Mrs. David Kellogg; Ladies Musical Club of Tacoma; Ladies Musical Club of Seattle; St. Cecilia Chorus; Washington State Federation of Music Clubs; musicians Pearl McDonald, Helen Crowe Snelling, Mary I. Short, Clara M. Bundy, Coralie Flaskett, Anna Rollins Johnson, Nellie Cornish, Mrs. Silvio Risegari, and Clara Moyer Hartle; and women writers Minnie Myrtle Miller, Audrey Wurdemann, Mary Carolyn Davies, Genevieve Taggard, Babette Hughes, Nora Burglon, Rhoda Nelson, and Delia Stevenson. For the theater are included popular actresses Henriette Crossman, Annie Russell, Leslie Carter, Viola Allen, and Ethel Barrymore. Ellen Van Volkenberg was a director. Mother Ryther is identified as founder of the Seattle Children's Home. Noted curators at the Washington State Historical Society include Sarah S. McM. Patton, Mrs. J. B. Davidson, and Elizabeth Ferry Leary.

489. Miller, Emma Gene. *Clatsop County, Oregon: A History*. Portland: Binfords and Mort, 1958. 291 pages. Bibliography, index. Photographs of teachers, pioneer women, and Mrs. William H. Gray, the wife of a Presbyterian minister.

Women are not central to this history, but brief mention is made of several individuals, including Helen Latty, the widow who established the Seaside Hotel in 1850.

490. Miller, Helen Markley. *Woman Doctor of the West, Bethenia Owens-Adair*. New York: Julian Messner, Inc., 1960. 191 pages. Bibliography, index.

This is a biography for young people, recounting the life of early Oregon physician and social reformer Bethenia Owens-Adair (1840-1926). Dialogue is reconstructed in this story, illustrating her independence in youth and throughout adulthood.

491. Miller, Jay. *Mourning Dove: A Salishan Autobiography*. Lincoln: University of Nebraska Press,

1990. xxxix, 274 pages. Notes, bibliography, index, and glossary of Colville-Okanogan terms. Photographs of the author and of Colville Reservation women.

Christine Quintasket (1886-1936), of the Confederated Tribes of Eastern Washington state, wrote under the pen-name Mourning Dove and was the first Native American woman to publish a novel. She authored *Co-Ge-We-A, the Half Blood* (1927 and reprinted in 1981); *Coyote Stories* (1933); and *Tales of the Okanogans* (posthumously published in 1976). The author of this book has assembled the drafts of her writings to outline three topics: a woman's world, seasonal activities, and Okanogan history.

492. Mills, Hazel E., ed. *Who's Who Among Pacific Northwest Authors*. Salem, Oregon: Pacific Northwest Library Association, 1957. 114 pages. Bibliography, index.

This is a biographical dictionary of living Northwest authors, including many women. Each biography lists occupation, education, organizational affiliations, awards, marriage, children, and published works. Two supplements have also been published: one in 1961, edited by Phoebe Harris, and the other in 1970, edited by Frances V. Wright.

493. Minority History Committee of Bainbridge Island School District No. 303, Brian Roberts, ed. *They Cast a Long Shadow: A History of the Non White Races on Bainbridge Island*. Bainbridge Island, Washington: Minority History Committee of Bainbridge Island School District no. 303, 1975. iii, 118 pages. Many photographs of minority women.

This account includes mention of women as individuals and as wives and family members in the Japanese, Native American, and Filipino communities. It mentions Mrs. Yoshida, the first child born to a Japanese family on Bainbridge Island; the work of women housekeepers; Lena Hillaire, a Suquamish Indian; the internment of Japanese Americans during World War II; courtship; Dorothy Almojueca, a Canadian Indian; and the first Filipina wives who came to Bainbridge Island in 1948.

494. Mohler, Samuel R. *The First Seventy-Five Years: A History of Central Washington State College, 1890-1966*. Spokane: C. W. Hill Printers, 1967. ix, 374 pages. Notes, bibliography, index.

Women students and teachers receive occasional attention alongside the history of campus sports, expansion of property, and program development at the institution known as Ellensburg normal school and, after 1937, Central Washington State College. References to women's athletics, social activities, dormitory life, and extracurricular activities are sparse, but biographical detail on leading women teachers such as Sue Lombard Horsley, Amanda Hebeler, Margaret Randall, Elizabeth Spurgeon, and Dorothy Dean, is rich.

495. Monroe, Anne Shannon. *Happy Valley*. Chicago: A. C. McClurg, 1916. Corvallis, Oregon: Oregon State University Press, 1991. xxxiii, 347 pages. Notes, bibliography.

Anne Shannon Monroe's 1916 novel, *Happy Valley*, is an account of eastern Oregon homesteaders in Harney County, Oregon. Included with the novel is an introductory biography by Karen Blair. Monroe (1877-1942) wrote twelve books of fiction and non-fiction (including the 1912 *Making a Business Woman*, which fictionalizes her real-life advertising office in Portland), and their plots are summarized here.

496. Montgomery, James W. *Liberated Woman: A Life of May Arkwright Hutton*. Spokane: Gingko Publishers, 1974. 134 pages. Bibliography. Several photographs of May Arkwright Hutton, the places where she lived, and influential people in her life.

The chief virtue of this survey of May Arkwright Hutton's life, childhood to grave, is its liberal use of primary material. It quotes great chunks from newspaper clippings by and about her, uses her *Coeur d'Alenes or a Tale of the Modern Inquisition in Idaho* and Lucille Fayo's unpublished "Mrs. Hercules" from the Spokane Public Library. It describes Hutton's work as a cook and restaurant proprietor in Idaho, her marriage, the silver strike that made her fortune, and her life as a millionaire in Spokane, Washington. Full attention is given to May Arkwright Hutton's friendship with Abigail Scott Duniway and their work for the Washington state suffrage campaign.

497. Moore, Lucia W., Nina W. McCornack, and Gladys W. McCready. *The Story of Eugene*. New York: Stratford House, 1949. xii, 271 pages. Index. The photograph of the University of Oregon graduating class of 1896 contains eight women students and ten men.

While men dominate this story of the development of Eugene, Oregon, women appear in a section on women's organizations. The clubs discussed include the Sunshine Club, Woman's Republican Patriotic League, Fortnightly Club, Charity Club, Welfare League, Daughters of the American Revolution, National League of American Pen Women, Business and Professional Women's Club, Quota Club, Zonta, American Association of University Women, and Hospitality Club. Among the biographies of University of Oregon professors is an account of Luella Clay, instructor.

498. Moreland, J.C. "Pioneer Seat of Learning: the Portland Academy and Female Seminary." *Oregon Native Sons and Historical Magazine* 2 (1900): 286-304. Photographs of 1865 building; Annie Pope; Josie DeVore; Kate Shaw.

Founded in 1851, the Portland Academy and Female Seminary employed women teachers to instruct boys and girls. By 1863, there were 250 students in the institution. This account provides the maiden name of female students along with the married name, adult hometown, and whether they pursued careers.

499. Morgan, Murray. *Skid Row: An Informal Portrait of Seattle*. Seattle: University of Washington Press, 1951. vii, 288 pages. Index. Image of A.B. Waud's sketch of the Mercer girls from the January 1866 *Harper's Weekly*; the Little Egypt troupe of female dancers in costume; showgirls in Seattle in a 1916 performance of *Robinson Crusoe*; and two women who packed medicines in a pharmacy during World War I.

This text provides only brief mention of women. "Mercer's Maidens" are described for their journey to marry Northwest bachelors and 1880s suffragist Mary Kenworthy is profiled.

500. ———. *Puget's Sound: A Narrative of Early Tacoma and the Southern Sound*. Seattle: University of Washington Press, 1979. x, 360 pages. Bibliography, index. Photographs of Annie Wright, Alice Blackwell, the Foss family, Rev. John P. Richmond and his wife America, Lt. William A. Slaughter and Mary Wells Slaughter, Gertrude and Nicholas Delin, Marietta Carr, Mary Ann McCarver, Janet Elder Steele.

Women are peripheral, mentioned chiefly as wives and sisters in this text.

501. Morrison, Dorothy Nafus. *Chief Sarah: Sarah Winnemucca's Fight for Indian Rights*. New York: Atheneum, 1980. 170 pages. Bibliography. Several photographs of Winnemucca, her relatives.

This biography of Paiute scout, interpreter, author, lecturer, educator, and lobbyist Sarah Winnemucca provides details about her life and work in Nevada, California, Oregon, and Washington. It employs fictionalized dialogue to tell the tale.

502. ———. *Ladies Were Not Expected: Abigail Scott Duniway and Women's Rights.* New York: Atheneum, 1977. ix, 147 pages. Bibliography, index. Photographs of Abigail Scott Duniway, her parents, sisters and brothers, her journal, map of overland journey, husband, children, Albany and Portland residences, and title pages of some of her books.

This is a young adult biography of pioneer Abigail Scott Duniway (1834-1915) and her fight for woman suffrage.

503. Mott, Frank Luther. *A History of American Magazines.* 5 vols. Cambridge, Massachusetts: The Belknap Press of Harvard University Press, 1930-1968. Notes, index. Vol. 1: 848 pages; volume 2: xi, 608 pages; vol. 3: xiii, 649 pages; vol. 4: xvii, 858 pages; vol. 5: xvii, 595 pages.

This massive survey of American magazines devotes a chapter in each volume to women's issues and women's magazines. Vol. 3 mentions Abigail Duniway's publication *The New Northwest.* Vol. 4 mentions that Duniway was the first editor of the *Pacific Empire* and wrote suffrage editorials for it. These two entries are the only ones concerning Northwest women specifically. Naturally, however, Northwest women read publications that were published elsewhere and are documented in this massive reference work.

504. Moynihan, Ruth Barnes. "Children and Young People on the Overland Trail." *Western Historical Quarterly* 6 (July 1975): 279-294. Notes.

This well-written and researched article is based on the diaries and memories of young pioneers on the trail west. None of it deals specifically with life in Oregon and Washington, although the Pacific Northwest was the destination of many adventurers. The diaries of several girls and young women are drawn on, including that of Narcissa Whitman. Daily activities, food, chores, play, and relationships with Native Americans are described.

505. ———. "Of Women's Rights and Freedom: Abigail Scott Duniway." In *Women in Pacific*

Northwest History: An Anthology, ed. Karen J. Blair, pp. 9-24. Seattle: University of Washington Press, 1988. Notes.

Reprinted from "Abigail Scott Duniway: Pioneer Suffragist of the Pacific Northwest," Linfield College *Casements* 4 (Spring 1984), Moynihan provides a short account of Duniway's life.

506. ———. *Rebel for Rights: Abigail Scott Duniway.* New Haven: Yale University Press, 1983. xv, 273 pages. Notes, bibliography, index; three appendices of family tree. Several photographs of Abigail Scott Duniway.

Here is the strongest, most serious scholarly work on Duniway's life and work. Moynihan illuminates her subject's story with sensitive use of an exhaustive array of resources. Duniway's seventeen novels, serialized in her newspaper *The New Northwest,* are mined for their relationship to her personal life. There is close attention to the impact of her parents and marriage, her labors on the farm and millinery shop, her views and contributions on sex and marriage, Prohibition, economics, politics, finance, and woman suffrage. Succinct background is provided on an impressive range of topics. Not only does this biography put a turn-of-the-century feminist in perspective, but it also creates a lively portrait of life in early Oregon.

507. Mumford, Esther. *Calabash: A Guide to the History, Culture, and Art of African Americans in Seattle and King County, Washington.* Seattle: Ananse Press. xii, 158 pages. Bibliography. Photographs of the author; Sherry Harris, first African American woman elected to the Seattle City Council; Sara Oliver Jackson in 1936 production of "Noah" at Seattle Negro Federal Theater; Zoe Dusanne's art gallery; Lora Chiora Dye and the Sukutai Marimba Ensemble; Denise Johnson Hunt, urban designer for the city of Seattle; Cheryl Glass, fashion designer; 1950 Seafair parade float with women from East Union/East Madison neighborhood; Edna Daigre, dancer and teacher at Ewajo Studio; Woodson Apartments owned by Irene and Zacharias Woodson; Barbara and John Pool, owners of Seaway Construction; Louise Gayton at Hazelwood School in 1912; Minisee family in Franklin, Washington, in 1907; churches in which women have been active.

This gazetteer divides Seattle and King County into eleven neighborhoods and provides considerable detail about the contemporary scene. For historians, there are brief biographies of government officials, actors, playwrights, business women, church founders, educators, and the choreographer Mildred Fort. Readers are introduced to Emma Ray, who founded the local Women's Christian Temperance Union; the Dorcas Charity Club which donated beds to Children's Orthopedic Hospital; and camp directors and Sunday school teachers.

508. ———. "Group Portrait: My Mother, My Grandmother, and I." *Backbone* 3 (1981): 33-37. Five photographs of African American women of the Northwest.

Here are excerpts from interviews conducted by Esther Mumford with nine black women of the Northwest: Louise Gayton Adams, Arlie Chappell, Willetta Riddle Gayton, Mattie Vinyerd Harris, Fern Johnson Proctor, Juanita Warfield Proctor, Emma Hunter Saunders, Ina Burnside Toney, and Isabella Smith. Among the topics briefly noted are family life, daily life in the Northwest, and the restaurant business.

509. ———. *Seattle's Black Victorians, 1852-1901.* Seattle: Ananse Press, 1980. 235 pages. Notes, bibliography, index. Photographs of black women throughout the text including: Mrs. Sara Elizabeth Heights Maunder and children; Mrs. Elizabeth Thorne and Mrs. Jennie Clark, restaurant owners; Susie Revels Cayton, associate editor of the *Seattle Republican*; Mrs. Therese Brown Dixon; Mrs. Sarah Grose; members of the First American Methodist Episcopal Church, 1900 conference; members of Frances Harper Woman's Christian Temperance Union; Mrs. Nettie J. Asberry, musician; Mrs. Olivia Washington; Mrs. May B. Mason, first black woman to go to the Yukon.

The population of African American women, according to the 1891 Seattle City Directory, numbered twenty-four. Mumford's chap. 6, "Women and Social Life," examines their contributions. It surveys women's efforts as wives, mothers, nurses, educators, music teachers, church founders, temperance supporters, restaurant owners, laundresses, hops pickers in King and Pierce county fields, charwomen, clerical workers, singers, and officers in the Seattle chapter of the National Afro-American Council.

510. ———. *Seven Stars and Orion: Reflections of the Past.* Seattle: Ananse Press, 1986. v, 104 pages. Notes, bibliography, index. Photographs of each of the seven subjects Mumford interviewed.

Here is the result of an oral history project conducted with seven African American women and one African American man from the Pacific Northwest. The introduction provides the historical context for the senior citizens Mumford interviewed in 1975. The life experiences of these women are included: LeEtta Sanders King, who lived in Yakima at the turn of the century but moved to Seattle later in life; Elva Moore Nicholas, from a mining family in Roslyn, Franklin, and Ravensdale, Washington; Marguerite Carroll Johnson of Seattle; Juanita Warfield Proctor; Muriel Maxwell Pollard; Sara Oliver Jackson, who describes Seattle's Negro Repertory Theater from the 1930s WPA Project; and Betty Collins Shellman, who was born in Wenatchee in 1917 and moved to Seattle in in 1936.

511. Munger, Asahel, and Eliza Munger. "Diary of Asahel Munger and Wife." *Quarterly of the Oregon Historical Society* 8 (December 1907): 387-405. Notes.

This diary by Asahel Munger relates his journey west in 1839. The only references he makes to his wife Eliza concern her health and her teaching of Native American children with Narcissa Whitman in Walla Walla.

512. Museum of History and Industry of Seattle, Washington. *Fidelity to Nature: Puget Sound Pioneer Artists, 1870-1915.* Seattle: Museum of History and Industry, 1986. 56 pages. Fifty-six images of oil paintings, water colors, and pencil drawings, many by women artists, and photographs of Harriet Foster Beecher and Emily Inez Denny.

This catalog accompanied a 1986 exhibition of 100 local art works at the Museum of History and Industry in Seattle. It contains biographical material about Harriet Foster Beecher and illustrates several of her paintings, including two portraits of Ezra Meeker, *Puget Sound near Port Townsend, Expanse of Beach and Point Wilson Lighthouse, Alameda,* and *Cliffs and Steamer.* Emily Inez Denny's biography is supplemented with illustrations of her works. Among them are *The Battle of Seattle* (January 26, 1856), *Panoramic View of Olympic Mountains, Indian Basket Weaver, Port Townsend, Mount Rainier, Three Bear Cubs,* and *Forest Scene.* Other women artists are also represented, such as Mary Fletcher, Jessie M. Elliott, Gertrude Willison, Mary Bes Lewis, and Ella Shephard Bush.

513. Myall, Carolynne. "Mabel East and Mabel West— Early Innovators in Washington Libraries." *ALKI, The Washington Library Association Journal* 8 (July 1992): 20-22. Notes. Photographs of Mabel M.

Reynolds, Mabel Zoe Wilson Library in Bellingham, cartoon about Miss Reynolds, 1912 fire in Cheney library.

Here are two biographies of Washington state normal school librarians. Mabel M. Reynolds was educated in the Midwest and became the first trained librarian at Cheney state normal school. She served from 1903 to 1924. Mabel Zoe Wilson came to New Whatcom (now Bellingham) normal school in 1902. The study examines the growth of both libraries under the administrations of these librarians.

514. Nathan, Maud. *The Story of an Epoch-Making Movement.* Garden City: Doubleday Publishers and Company, 1926, 245 pages.

Included in this general history of the National Consumer's League is a portrait of the origins and early achievements of the Oregon Consumer's League, which was formed in 1903 to address health issues at the workplace, the minimum wage, child labor, and the Ten-Hour Law protecting women workers.

515. Nelson, Herbert B. "First True Confession Story Lectures Oregon 'Moral.'" *Oregon Historical Quarterly* 45 (June 1944): 168-176. Notes.

This essay discusses Margaret Jewett Bailey's 1854 Oregon novel, *Grains, or Passages in the Life of Ruth Rover.* This semi-autobiographical account of the author's divorce received negative reviews when it was published, due to public disapproval of divorce as immoral.

516. ———. *The Literary Impulse in Pioneer Oregon.* Corvallis: Oregon State College Press, 1948. 86 pages. Notes, bibliography.

This book delves into literature and its authors in early Oregon. Only two women are mentioned: Margaret J. Smith [Margaret Jewett Bailey], a missionary who wrote an autobiography under the title of *Ruth Rover*, and Abigail Scott Duniway, pioneer and author of the novel *Captain Gray's Company.*

517. ———. "Ruth Rover's Cup of Sorrow." *Pacific Northwest Quarterly* 50 (July 1959): 91-98. Notes. Photograph of title page of novel *Ruth Rover.*

This essay compares the biography of Oregon author Margaret Jewett Bailey with the life of the heroine in her novel, *The Grains, or Passages in the Life of Ruth Rover.* The author used the novel to tell the public her side of the scandal which led to her marriage and divorce from Dr. William J. Bailey.

518. Nesbit, Virginia. "Sarah Helmick and Helmick Park." *The Quarterly of the Oregon Historical Society* 26 (December 1925): 444-447. One portrait of Sarah Helmick.

This short essay is a superficial account of the overland trip of Henry and Sarah Helmick in 1845, and of their first years in Oregon. There are few details here. The purpose of the essay is to laud Sarah Helmick (1823-1924) for giving part of her land to the state for Helmick Park in 1924.

519. Newell, Gordon. *Rogues, Buffoons, and Statesmen: The Inside Story of Washington's Capitol City.* Seattle: Superior Publishing Company, 1975. 512 pages. Index. Photographs.

Newell surveys capital city Olympia, Washington, and Washington state politics from 1845 to 1973. This book covers early miscegenation laws and bills introduced in the legislature concerning women's right to vote in the late nineteenth century. Specific women or groups of women discussed include Mrs. Hamm (1855), teacher in Olympia; Rebecca Howard, owner of the Pacific Hotel, a meeting place for legislators; Mercer girls from New England, imported to help solve the woman shortage in the Pacific Northwest; Sisters of Charity, who erected St. Peters Hospital; Mrs. McGraw, the governor's wife; Ina Forrest (1897), first female page in Olympia; Margaret McKenny, early ecologist; Emma DeVoe, president of the Washington Woman Suffrage Association in 1909; women legislators in the early twentieth century; Mrs. Mowell, head of Minute Women (1918), a group devoted to war service; and Josephine Corliss Preston (1918), first woman state superintendent of public instruction.

520. ———. *Westward to Alki: The Story of David and Louisa Denny.* Seattle: Superior Publishing Company, 1977. 122 pages. Index. Photographs of Sarah Denny, Margaret Lenora Denny, Anna Louisa Denny, and Louisa Denny.

Chap. 9, "Sweetbriar Bride," describes the 1853 marriage of David Denny to Louisa Denny, drawing on Roberta Frye Watt's reminiscences of pioneer Seattle. Despite its title, the work concentrates on David Denny's story.

521. Nichols, Ellen. *Images of Oregon Women.* Salem, Oregon: The Madison Press, 1985.

208 pages. One photograph of each woman described.

Here are fifty biographies of women, including Judge Betty Cantrell Roberts of Portland; Violet Balcomb Orr of Cottage Grove, an activist for the American Civil Liberties Union and Women's International League for Peace and Freedom; Shirley Douglass Patton, an actress at the Ashland, Oregon, Shakespeare Festival; Genera Banks Jones, author of "Mary Cullin's Cottage," a food column for the *Oregon Journal*; historical preservationist Barbara Barker Sprouse; and Nellie Batman Fox, a lobbyist for the AFL-CIO.

522. Nies, Judith. *Seven Women: Portraits from the American Radical Tradition*. New York: Viking Press, 1977. xvi, 238 pages. Bibliography and index.

Among these literary portraits, Nies includes Anna Louise Strong (1885-1970), radical journalist, editor, and author who grew up in Seattle and went on to publicize the advent of Communism in the U.S.S.R. and People's Republic of China.

523. Nixon, O.W. *How Marcus Whitman Saved Oregon*. Chicago: Star Publishing Company, 1895. 346 pages. Illustration of Narcissa Whitman.

In its account of the overland journey, mission life, and the Whitman massacre, this work quotes from the diaries and letters of missionary Narcissa Whitman.

524. Nomura, Gail M. "Tsugiki, a Grafting: A History of a Japanese Pioneer Woman in Washington State." *Women's Studies* 14, No. 1 (1987): 15-37. Notes. (See also Blair, Karen J., *Women in Pacific Northwest History*.)

This article provides a biography of Japanese-born poet, Teiko Tomita (b. 1896), and translates forty-two of her poems. Much of her poetry reflects the twentieth-century experiences of Japanese American settlers in the Northwest and documents their contributions to the economy and culture.

525. Northport Over Forty Club, comps. *Northport Pioneers...Echoes of the Past From the Upper Columbia County*. Colville, Washington: *Statesman-Examiner*, Inc., 1981. x, 294 pages.

This local history includes biographies of pioneer settlers, provided by descendants. Anna Beusan Paparich and Louisa Margaret Rivers relate turn-of-the-century experiences, including working as schoolteachers at Fort Colville, gardening, employment in a hotel, waitressing, marrying, childraising, and the advent of electricity in 1920.

526. Oberdeck, Kathryn J. "'Not Pink Teas': The Seattle Working-Class Women's Movement, 1905-1918." *Labor History* 32 (Spring 1991): 193-230. Notes.

During the 1910s, the Women's Union Label League united with other women's organizations to form a municipal lodging house for girls and publicize the value of purchasing goods with a union label.

527. Ochsner, Jeffrey Darl, ed. *Shaping Seattle Architecture: A Historical Guide to the Architects*. Seattle: University of Washington Press, 1994. 416 pages. Bibliography. Photographs of architects Mother Joseph (Esther Pariseau) and Elizabeth Ayer, and several of the buildings Ayer designed.

This survey of significant Seattle architects includes the 750-word biography of Elizabeth Ayer, the first woman to join the American Institute of Architects in Washington state. A gazetteer at the back of the collection provides capsule descriptions of additional architects and includes Mother Joseph (Esther Pariseau), often credited with being the earliest woman architect in the region.

528. Ogburn, William F., and Inez Gottra. "How Women Vote: A Study of an Election in Portland, Oregon." *Public Science Quarterly* 34 (September 1919): 413-433. Notes, five tables.

This is a statistical analysis of the 1914 general election in Oregon. It attempts to measure how women voted on twenty-four initiatives.

529. O'Hara, Edwin V. *Pioneer Catholic History of Oregon*. Portland: Press of Glass and Prudhomme Company, 1911. xii, 236 pages. Bibliography, index.

This work explores Catholic pioneer contributions to the Northwest. It covers the role of pioneer missionaries, their defeats and accomplishments from 1810 through 1885. Attention is devoted to the educational and social service institutions founded by nuns.

530. O'Harra, Marjorie. *Ashland: The First 130 Years*. Jacksonville, Oregon: Southern Oregon Historical Society, 1981. 201 pages. Notes, bibliography, and index. Photographs of women in

music class, at social gatherings, picking berries, in Lithia Park, Alice Applegate, Kay Atwood, Nan Franklin, Marjorie O'Harra.

This work credits the Ladies Chautauqua Park Club, the Ashland Study Club, and the Woman's Civic Club of Ashland with many civic improvements. The account addresses the closing of the normal school in 1910 and the fifteen-year struggle to re-open the institution for teacher training.

531. *Okanogan Independent. Glimpses of Pioneer Life, a Series of Biographies, Experiences and Events Intimately Concerned with the Settlement of Okanogan County, Washington.* Okanogan: Okanogan Independent, 1924. 137 pages.

This volume compiles articles that appeared in the *Okanogan Independent* during 1923 and 1924. Most of these articles are short biographies full of anecdotes and colorful details about the early settlers in Okanogan County. The remaining accounts are personal reminiscences. The women featured include Mrs. Mary F. Malott; Virginia M. Hermann—one of the original owners of the townsite of Okanogan, post-mistress of Okanogan, and student at the University of Washington during the early 1880s; Mrs. Sarah Jones—operator of a roadhouse for travelers; and Mary E. Carpenter.

532. Oliphant, J. Orin. *History of the State Normal School at Cheney, Washington.* Spokane: Inland-American Printing Company, 1924. vi, 175 pages. Bibliography, index.

Although women dominated the teaching profession in the early twentieth century, they are peripheral to Oliphant's administrative history of a teacher training institute, from the year of its founding in 1890 through 1923. However, he includes names of women founders, early teachers in the academy, and the early graduates, mostly young women. Women's names appear as officers in early student organizations and there is an account of the woman's dormitory, constructed in 1919. A woman physician ran the student infirmary. Curriculum and degree requirements, which future teachers met, are catalogued.

533. Olson, Ronald L. *The Quinault Indians.* University of Washington Series of Publications in Anthropology, vol. 6. Seattle: University of Washington Press, 1936. 194 pages. Notes, bibliography, index. Photographs of women's clothing and baskets.

Based on visits in 1925 and 1927 to the Olympic Peninsula of Washington's coast, this anthropologist recounts Quinault women's responsibilities for collecting camas roots and describes women's clothing, face painting, tatoos, hair dressing, jewelry, toys, games, puberty, marriage, pregnancy, and the absence of taboos against lesbianism.

534. O'Meara, Walter. *Daughters of the Country: The Women of the Fur Traders and Mountain Men.* New York: Harcourt, Brace and World, 1968. 368 pages. Notes, bibliography, index.

In this broad survey, the only Northwest Native Americans to receive attention are the Chinook on the Columbia River. Quoted here are observations about the women's hard work by Captain William Clark of the Lewis and Clark expedition, Ross Cox on Chinook prostitution and venereal disease at Astoria, and the elaborate ritual of Koale-zoa, when the daughter of Chinook Chief Comcomly married Archibald McDonald on the beach.

535. Oregon Pioneer Association. *Transactions of the Oregon Pioneer Association (1873-1928).* Portland: Oregon Pioneer Association, 1875-1933.

This publication routinely included memoirs of pioneer women. Among its entries are several described in this volume, including those by Cecilia E. M. Adams, Susan P. Angell, Eva Emery Dye, Elizabeth Dixon Smith Geer, J.D. Kellogg, Mrs. Emelia Knight, Inez E.A. Parker, and Cornelia Sharp. The 1897 membership list for the Woman's Auxiliary of the Oregon Pioneer Association can be found on page six of the twenty-fifth volume (1897), where there is also a list of those members who actually attended the twenty-fifth annual reunion.

536. Oregon Writers' Program. *Oregon, End of the Trail.* Portland: Binfords and Mort, 1940. xxxii, 549 pages. Bibliography, index. Photographs of family of settlers on Owyhee Project, Basque Girls in Malheur County.

Brief references are made, throughout the text, to such Oregon women as poet Anna Marie Pittman, poet Minnie Myrtle Miller, children's author Mary Jane Carr, Oregon Tuberculosis Association officer and 1940 General Federation of Women's Clubs President Saidie Orr Dunbar. Mentions of women's groups, too, are sprinkled throughout: YWCA, Girl Scouts, Campfire Girls, and Oregon State Music Teachers' Association among them.

537. Owens-Adair, Dr. Bethenia A. "Mrs. Sarah Damron Adair, Pioneer of 1843." *Transactions of the Oregon Pioneer Association* (1900), 28th annual reunion, pp. 65-82. Portland: Oregon Pioneer Association, 1900.

Dr. Bethenia Owens-Adair writes about her mother Sarah, and quotes extensively from Sarah's narratives about her life. The essay covers the pioneer trip across the country in 1843 and follows the family history during its first decade in Oregon. It deals with contacts between Sarah and Native Americans and her domestic and income-producing industries of growing and spinning flax, making butter, and selling wool and sheep.

538. Owens-Adair, Dr. B. A. *Dr. Owens-Adair: Some of Her Life Experiences.* Portland: Mann and Beech, 1906. 537 pages.

This work seeks both to describe the life of Oregon physician Bethenia Owens-Adair and to document the history of some of the issues she supported. The first hundred pages consist of an autobiographical account. Later chapters, written by an unnamed longtime friend, tell the Owens-Adair story in the third person. Among the primary sources scattered throughout are letters she wrote to newspapers, to her son, and to famous individuals like Susan B. Anthony, some Valentine poems she received, temperance song lyrics she collected, articles and speeches she wrote on temperance, women physicians, and divorce, and dozens of biographies of early men and women who settled Oregon.

539. Parker, Adella A. "The Woman Voter of the West, A New Force in Politics." *The Westerner* 16 (August 1912): 3-6, 37-39. Ten photographs of suffragists in portrait, five group photos, three political cartoons, one map of the extent of the suffrage movement.

This is a state-of-the-movement report by an active Washington suffragist. She records the political chronology of woman suffrage in the English-speaking world, with special attention given to Washington state and other western states.

540. Parker, Inez Eugenia Adams. "Early Recollections of Oregon Pioneer Life." *Transactions of the Oregon Pioneer Association* (1928), 56th annual reunion, pp. 17-36. Portland: Oregon Pioneer Association, 1933.

This is a detailed childhood reminiscence. It begins with stories of the trip west and then relates numerous stories of Parker's childhood in the Willamette Valley, schooling, Indian relations, family, and friends.

541. Paul, Rodman Wilson, and Richard W. Etulian, eds. *The Frontier and the American West.* Arlington: AHM Publishing Company, 1977. xviii, 174 pages. Bibliography, index.

Essentially this is a bibliographical index listing works on the early American West frontier. Sample chapters cover such topics as the army, frontier hypothesis, "Indians," scientists, immigrants, and transportation. Chap. 30 (p. 130) is entitled "Women, The Family, and Women's Rights in the West," with seventy-five entries.

542. Pearce, Stella E. "Suffrage in the Pacific Northwest; Old Oregon and Washington." *Washington Historical Quarterly* 3 (1912): 106-114. Notes.

Stella Pearce recounts the struggle of women to gain the vote in the Pacific Northwest before statehood. Washington Territory instituted woman suffrage in 1883, based on a provision in the law that stated that all citizens were eligible to vote. In 1887, however, after hot debate, women were denied the right to vote and they did not regain it in Washington state until 1910 and Oregon in 1914.

543. Peltier, Jerome. *Madame Dorion.* Fairfield, Washington: Ye Galleon Press, 1980. Bibliography, index.

Marie Aioe Dorion Venier Toupin (1786-1850), an Iowa Indian, and her children traveled west with her interpreter husband Pierre Dorion on Wilson Price Hunt's 1814 overland expedition for John Jacob Astor's Pacific Fur Company. Madam Dorion's part in the journey and her subsequent marriages to Louis Venier and John Toupin are narrated.

544. Pelz, Ruth. *The Washington Story: A History of Our State.* Seattle: Seattle Public Schools, 1979. 302 pages. Index. Photos: group shots of Native American women.

Pelz's textbook was the first to consider seriously contemporary issues such as the natural environment, Native Americans, and women, although she also treats such traditional topics as explorations and claims, fur traders and missionaries, government, treaties and war, and the industrializing twentieth century. Among the many women included are: Mrs. Barkley, the first woman to visit Pacific Northwest; Mother Joseph (Esther Pariseau); missionaries Narcissa Whitman, Mrs. Cushing Eells, Mary Walker, and Eliza Spalding; pioneer diarists Charlotte Stearns Pengra and Helen Stewart; suffragists Lizzie Ordway and May Arkwright Hutton; and prohibitionist Bertha Landes, first woman mayor of Seattle. Pelz describes how Washington women got the vote and provides a list of women who were prominent activists.

545. Peterson, David. "Physically Violent Husbands of the 1890s and Their Resources." *Journal of Family Violence* 6, no. 1 (1991): 1-15. Notes.

Using court records, Peterson located fifty-six women (out of a total of 232 dissolution petitions) in Lane County, Oregon, who appeared in divorce suits between the years 1891-1900, claiming that their husbands had abused them. The author traces the low economic and social resources of the husbands.

546. ———. "Wife Beating: An American Tradition." *Journal of Interdisciplinary History* 23 (Summer 1992): 97-118. Notes.

Peterson analyzes fifty-six divorce cases filed between 1891-1900 in white, rural, largely middle-class Lane County, Oregon. Eighty-five percent of the couples won their cases. The essay explores the social context, including women's fight for the vote, support from friends and family, and men's and women's attitudes about abuse.

547. Peterson, Emil R., and Alfred Powers. *A Century of Coos and Curry: History of Southwest Oregon.* Portland: Binfords and Mort, 1952. 599 pages. Index. Photographs of Ellen Tichenor, first white child in southwest Oregon; Minnie Myrtle Miller, poet; and Coquille Women's Band in 1894.

Men dominate the tale, but women appear in the chapters on education, literature, libraries, and the pioneer association. Maude Liddell Barry contributed an essay on education since 1854, which names the women and men who taught in the early schools in Empire. Ruth McBride Powers provided brief biographies, excerpts from publications, and bibliographies for several women writers, including Agnes Ruth Sengstacken, Minnie B. Tower, Minnie Myrtle Miller, Alice Bay Maloney, Grace McCormac French, Ruth McBride Powers, Beatrice K. Noon, Mary Lucile McLain, and Olive Barber. She also quotes Amuel Stillman Mann's essay, "The Paucity of Females" concerning Native American wives of early nineteenth-century trappers. A chapter on folk literature recounts "The Mermaid of the Rogue," preserved by Arthur Dorn. The chapter on libraries lists the names of town librarians, and the chapter on the Pioneer Association lists early settlers, many women among them. The final section of the work is devoted to biographies. They include Harriet J. Brando, who operated Brando Apartments; Daisy Codding, trained nurse; Alonza Davis, in the sawmill business; Florinda Fahy, dressmaker; Emily Fitzhugh, teacher; Lyda A. Horsfall, founder of the Chaminade (Music) Club; May Rees Keizer, superintendent of the Keizer Hospital; Mancy Belle Laird, telegraph operator; Clare Lehmanowsky, civil engineer for the Coos Bay Lumber Company; Frances S. Elrod McLeod, who ran a credit organization; Maryette Morse, justice of the peace and real estate agent; Martha E. Mulkey Purdy, teacher and county school superintendent; Georgia Richmond, nurse and superintendent of Southwest Oregon General Hospital; Ellen Rudnas, clerk; Clara Stauff, musician and county treasurer; and Zenie Strang, farmer.

548. Peterson, Martin. "Swedes of Yam Hill." *Oregon History Quarterly* 76 (1975): 5-27. Notes. Photographs of Anne and Matilda Collinson, Christine Lindberg and family, the Jernstedt family, Agnes Johnson's wedding party, and a group of hops pickers.

This account traces Oregon Swedes in the last quarter of the nineteenth century, residing near Carlton. The author provides the life stories of several of the men and women in the community.

549. Peterson-del Mar, David. "Intermarriage and Agency: A Chinookan Case Study," *Ethnohistory* 42 (Winter 1995): 1-30. Notes. Photographs of Celiast and Solomon Smith and Charlotte and Silas Smith.

This biography of Celiast Smith, Chinookan woman born at the mouth of the Columbia River in the early nineteenth century, challenges studies which assert that white contact and colonization undermined Native American women's power. Smith used intermarriage to French-Canadian baker Basile Poirier for her own ends and to the advantage of both partners.

550. Pflieger, Pat. *Beverly Cleary.* Boston: Twayne Publisher, G.K. Hall, 1991. xi, 208 pages. Notes, bibliography, index. Photograph of Cleary.

This is a study of prize-winning children's book author, Beverly Cleary (1916-), her life and work. While most of the study examines her writing, chap. 1 explores Cleary's youth in McMinnville and Portland, Oregon, her training as a librarian at the University of Washington, and her post as a children's librarian in the Yakima Public Library (1939-1940). The biography does not offer the details that Cleary's two autobiographies, *A Girl from Yamhill,* (1988) and *My Own Two Feet* (1995) do.

551. Pi Lambda Theta Research Committee, Washington Alumnae Chapter (National Education Association for Women). *Women of the Pacific Northwest: A Study of Their Status Today, Their Emotional Adjustment, Their Thinking on the Post-War Period.* Seattle: Pi Lambda Theta, 1945. 51 pages. Bibliography.

Here is the result of a three-and-a-half-year study undertaken by the Pi Lambda Theta chapter of the National Education Association for Women. It is based on a questionnaire completed by 125 members and their neighbors, and addresses problems facing professional women and women's attitudes toward the post-war period.

552. Pierce County Library and Tacoma Public Library. *All My Somedays: A Living History Project.* Tacoma: Pierce County and Tacoma Public Library, 1982. Photograph of each subject.

This extensive collection of oral histories contains dozens of contributions by Pierce County women. Among them is an interview of Alice Elizabeth Yates (*My Irish Connection*, 72 pages), who traces her grandfather's origins and discusses her own childhood in Los Angeles, her first date, graduation, the Great Depression and World War II. Lydia Netsch (*Our Family: Sunshine in Our Souls*, 148 pages) provides a genealogy of her Mennonite grandparents and her youth in Portland during the Great Depression. Julie Ann Peterson Hebert (*First Taste: My Celebration of the Good Life*, 134 pages) describes her father's occupation as forest ranger at Upson Ranger Station.

553. Pieroth, Doris H. "Bertha Knight Landes: The Woman Who Was Mayor." *Pacific Northwest Quarterly* 75 (July 1984): 117-127. (See also Blair, Karen J., *Women in Pacific Northwest History*.) Notes. Photographs of the mayor, her house, a handbill from her campaign.

This biography of Mayor Landes describes her campaign and analyzes the strengths and weaknesses of her "Municipal Housekeeping" platform and two-year administration (1926-1928). The forces which shaped her thought are studied, especially her childhood, education, supportive husband, role models and prominence in the woman's club movement of the era. This article won the journal's prize for best contribution of the year.

554. Pioneer Ladies Club, comps. *Reminiscences of Oregon Pioneers.* Pendleton: *The East Oregonian* Publishing Company, 1937. 257 pages.

Here is a collection of ninety-seven essays by different authors, many of them women. The project was sponsored by the Pioneer Ladies Club, a group organized in 1919 "to renew and extend acquaintance, promote sociability and collect from living witnesses such history of Pendleton and Umatilla County as the club may deem worthy of preservation." They have included an 1873 "prohibition against colored girls from attending public schools," biographies of WCTU leader Esther A. F. May, teacher Anna Storie, club member Nettie Kenney Boylen, autobiographies of Mrs. O. F. Thomson, Anna Mendenhall, and Mrs. Lee Moorhouse, and an account of pioneer school teachers. There is a list of the 103 charter members of the club and a list of past presidents.

555. Pitzer, Paul C. "Dorothy McCullough Lee: The Successes and Failures of 'Dottie-Do-Good.'" *Oregon Historical Quarterly* 91 (Spring 1990): 5-42. Notes. Six photographs of Dorothy McCullough Lee and one of a demonstration by victims of the 1948 Vanport flood.

This provides a biography of Dorothy "Dauntless Dottie" McCullough Lee (1901-1981), first woman mayor of Portland, Oregon. She was elected to office in 1948 after a long career as attorney, Oregon state legislator, chair of the Oregon Crime Commission, state senator, and Portland city councilperson. Her vigorous attack on crime brought her supporters from the Women's Christian Temperance Union, Oregon Presbytery, and Portland Retail Trade Bureau.

556. Pollard, Lancaster. "A Checklist of Washington Authors." *Pacific Northwest Review* 31 (January 1940): 3-96.

This lists authors and book titles from Washington writers up through January 1940. Approximately 1,000 authors are mentioned, one quarter of whom are women.

557. ———. "A Checklist of Washington Authors: Additions and Corrections." *Pacific Northwest Quarterly* 35 (July 1944): 233-266.

Approximately 500 additions and corrections are provided for the period up to January 1, 1943. Again, about one quarter of these are women authors.

558. ———. *A History of the State of Washington.* Ed. Lloyd Spencer. 4 vols. New York: American Historical Society, 1937. Vol. 1: 516 pages; vol. 2: 374 pages; vol. 3: 408 pages; vol. 4: 358 pages. Bibliography at the end of each chapter in vols. 1 and 2, indices at the end of vols. 2 and 4.

This is an academic four-volume history of Washington state from the sixteenth century until 1937.

Vol. 1 presents the history of Washington state, including letters written by Narcissa Whitman in chap. 7 and a brief discussion of the suffrage movement in Washington in chap. 9. Vol. 2 examines industrial history, e.g., lumber, fishing, agriculture. The works of women writers are discussed in chap. 24, "Cultural Development." Biographies include Jessie A. Knight, Eliza Farnham Van Fleet, Maria Childs Watkinson, Mrs. Philip Henry Schnebly, Mrs. Sadie Marie Siverling Cadwork, Mrs. Zelda (Skinner) Ellis, Julia Waldrip Ker, Dr. Edna Valeria Dale, and Charlotte Algier in (volume 3); and Cecelia B. Krudwig, Laura Shragg, Bertha Knight Landes, Mrs. Frances Clarinda (Loomis) Knox, Mary Van Wilson Marion, Hazel M. Surber, Verna Cook Salomonsky, Margaret Cenia Splawn, Viola Moore, and Clydene Lauretta Morris (in vol. 4).

559. Porter, Kenneth W. "Jane Barnes, First White Woman in Oregon." *Oregon Historical Quarterly* 31 (June 1930): 125-135. Notes.

Jane Barnes lived on the Columbia River at Astoria in 1814. This describes her interactions with the Chinook Indians and reviews her origins as a bar maid in England and her adventures between England and Oregon.

560. Potter, Elizabeth Walton. "The Missionary and Immigrant Experience as Portrayed in Commemorative Works of Art." *Idaho Yesterdays* 31 (Spring/Summer 1987): 85-117. Notes. Washington photographs: monument to Marcus and Narcissa Whitman, and Great Grave and monument to William and Mary Gray, both in Walla Walla; and Avard Fairbanks' Pioneer Mother statue at Esther Short Park in Vancouver. Oregon photos: Alice Cooper's statue of Sacajawea in Washington Park, Portland; Pioneer Mother statue on the University of Oregon campus, Eugene; and the Barry Faulkner mural in Oregon's capitol rotunda in Salem depicting the Whitmans' and Spaldings' arrival at Fort Vancouver. Wyoming photograph: the Narcissa Whitman-Eliza Spalding Monument in South Pass.

This essay discusses individuals and organizations who sponsored memorials to Mary Gray, Narcissa Whitman, Eliza Spalding, Sacajawea, the pioneer woman, and two of the wives of missionary Jason Lee. Sponsors included the Sons and Daughters of the Oregon Pioneers, General Federation of Women's Clubs, Oregon Trail Memorial Association, American Association of University Women, Daughters of the American Revolution, and Mrs. Smith French.

561. Potts, Ralph Bushnell. *Seattle Heritage.* Seattle: Superior Publishing Company, 1955. 192 pages.

Chap. 13, entitled "The Women," provides rich detail about women's organizations, including Daughters of the Nile, Spastic Aid Council, and the guilds of Children's Orthopedic Hospital.

562. Powers, Alfred. *History of Oregon Literature.* Portland: Metropolitan Press, 1935. 809 pages. Index. Photographs of women: sketch of Indian women, Abigail Scott Duniway, Sacajawea monuments, Minnie Myrtle Miller, Frances Fuller Victor, and Opal Whiteley.

In exploring the history of Oregon literature, women are included in sections of contemporary poets; novelists, dramatists, and short story writers; literary magazines and book publishers; minor poets from 1850-1900; song writers and songs since 1860; college songs of the Willamette Valley; historians; Oregon authors about each other; and "squaw" wives and "squaw" men. The work includes Katherine Berry Judson on American Indian legends; Laura B. Downey on Chinook jargon; Elizabeth Dixon Smith Geer's diary; the poetry of Minnie Myrtle Miller, Belle W. Cooke, Elizabeth Markham, Lulu Piper Aiken, Frances Gill, and Queene B. Lister; Frances Fuller Victor on temperance; Abigail Scott Duniway's suffrage campaign songs; lyrics by Sarah Fisher Hadeson and Ella Higginson; Opal Whiteley's diary; college pledge song to Oregon normal school; writings of missionary women; pioneer accounts; and editors Lischen Miller, Catherine Cogswell, and Frances E. Gotshell. Dozens of other women authors are mentioned in passing.

563. Priestley, Marilyn, comp. *Comprehensive Guide to the Manuscript Collection and to the Personal Papers in the University Archives.* Seattle: University of Washington Libraries, 1980. 600 pages. Bibliography, index.

Access to papers and manuscripts about women is limited because "woman," "women," "suffrage," "feminism," or other likely access points are not used in the subject index. The personal name index includes the names of many women, and also of the following organizations whose name begins with "woman," or "women's." *Woman Citizen* (periodical); Women in Community Service; Women Painters of Washington; Women's American ORT, Seattle chapter; Women's Christian Temperance Union; Women's Defense League; Women's International League for Peace and Freedom; and Women's Legislative League of Washington.

564. Pringle, Catherine Sager. *Across the Plains in 1844*. Fairfield, Oregon: Ye Galleon Press, 1989. 41 pages. Index.

This is a reprint of the 1905 memoir by an adopted daughter of Marcus and Narcissa Whitman, probably written between 1860 and 1866. One of seven Sager children who were orphaned on the Overland trail in 1844, she recounts her journey across the plains, life at the Whitman mission, the 1847 massacre at Waiilatpu when she was thirteen, and her captivity by the Indians.

565. Prosch, Thomas W. *David S. Maynard and Catherine T. Maynard. Biographies of Two of the Oregon Immigrants of 1850*. Seattle: Lowman and Hanford Stationary and Printing Company, 1906. 83 pages. Illustration of Catherine T. Maynard in 1865 and photo of her in 1906.

Prosch chronicles the life of Kentucky-born Catherine T. Maynard (1816-1906), who came west with her first husband in 1849 and later married Seattle pioneer Doc Maynard. They operated a dry goods store and developed friendly relations with Chief Sealth and his daughter Angeline. Fearful of attack by eastern Washington Klickitats in 1856 and 1857, she lived on the Port Madison Reservation for a year and a half.

566. ———. *McCarver and Tacoma*. Seattle: Lowman and Hanford Stationary and Printing Company, 1906. viii, 198 pages. Photograph of Julia A. McCarver.

Here is an account of Missouri-born Julia A. McCarver (1825-1897), who in 1847 journeyed to the Pacific Coast and later joined the "Washingtonians," Oregon's first temperance society.

567. Putnam, Roselle. "The Letters of Roselle Putnam." Transcript and Notes by Sheba Hargreaves, *Oregon Historical Quarterly* 29 (September 1928): 242-264. Notes.

This article is comprised of the engaging and detailed letters by Roselle Putnam to her in-laws, written between 1849 and 1852. She writes compellingly about her environment in the Umpqua Valley, her family's economic condition, her children, and her emotional well being. Sheba Hargreaves's notes are explanatory, rather than analytical. Hargreaves considers this collection to be representative of the pioneer experience in Oregon but emphasizes the clarity of expression in these as the "mark of a genius" in Roselle Putnam.

568. Quackenbush, Marian Lowe. *Air, Sunlight and a Bit of Land*. Fairfield, Washington: Ye Galleon Press, 1982. 80 pages. Photographs of the author.

This short work is an autobiographical account of an early resident of the Pacific Northwest who grew up in Owyhee River region of eastern Oregon. She attended Whitman College in 1923 and raised her family in Spokane. She describes family life and her activity in the PTA, American Association of University Women, PEO, St. Andrew's Episcopal Church, and the Grange.

569. Queener-Shaw, Janice. *Fidelity to Nature: Puget Sound Painters*. Seattle: Museum of History and Industry, 1986.

See Museum of History and Industry.

570. Quimby, George I. "The Wife of Portsmouth's Tale, 1813-1818: An Apology to Miss Jane Barnes." *Pacific Northwest Quarterly* 71 (July 1980): 127-130. Notes.

Miss Jane Barnes was a barmaid in Portsmouth, England, when John McDonald, fur trader, invited her to accompany him to Astoria. Excerpts from the diary of Ross Cox, a company clerk, describe her 1814 arrival, her clothes, and her marriage proposal from the son of Comcomly, the principal chief of the Chinook Indians.

571. Rakestraw, L., ed. "Documents: Gifford Pinchot, Agnes V. Scannell, and the Early Years of the U.S. Forest Service." *Oregon Historical Quarterly* 92 (Spring 1991): 60-75. Notes. Photographs of Adolf Ashoff's "Mt. Home" in Marmot, Oregon, and *Tahn*, a launch Scannell encountered.

This biography of Agnes V. Scannell, hired in January 1907 in Washington, D.C. as a clerk/stenographer for the U.S. Forest Service, describes a train trip to Portland, brief work at the YWCA, timber preservation work, meeting Gifford Pinchot, visiting the ranger station at Mt. Hood, the Alaska-Yukon- Pacific Exposition in Seattle in 1909, and Skagway and Sitka, Alaska.

572. Ransom, Lucy Sophia. "Country Schoolma'am." Ed. Jay Ellis Ransom. *Oregon Historical Quarterly* 86 (Winter 1985): 419-434 and (Summer 1985): 117-152. Photographs of Lucy S.A. Ransom.

In several issues of the *Oregon Historical Quarterly*, Jay Ellis Ransom provides excerpts from his mother's writings. Lucy Ransom was born in upstate New York in 1875, attended Pennsylvania normal school in 1893, and moved to Portland, Oregon, in 1903. The summer issue describes her 1903 trip to the Pacific Northwest, through Spokane and Yakima, Washington. Her impressions of Portland's saloons, red-light district, Chinatown, her apartment, teaching, shops, Methodist Church, Meier and Frank department store shopping, and recreation are detailed. The winter issue contains descriptions of 1907 teaching experiences in Baker County, Malheur, Clatsop County, Durkee, and in Skamokawa, Lyle, and Snowden, Washington. She offers her impressions of the 1905 Lewis and Clark Exposition in Portland.

573. ———. "Country School Ma'am." Ed. Jay Ellis Ransom. *Oregon Historical Quarterly* 87 (Spring 1986): 67-87. Two photographs of Lucy Sophia Ransom in 1907-1908.

This account relates Lucy Sophia Ransom's trip to Malheur County, Oregon after completing the Idaho teacher's exam in Boise, Idaho, in 1907. She comments on the landscape and boarding at the Hotel Westfall.

574. Raufer, Sister Maria Ilma. *Black Robes and Indians on the Last Frontier: A Story of Heroism.* Milwaukee: Bruce Publishing Company, 1966. xvi, 496 pages. Notes, bibliography, index. Twenty photographs of women—Native Americans and Roman Catholic nuns.

This history of St. Mary's Mission on the Colville Reservation in Omak, Washington, from 1885 through the 1960s, includes a chapter on "Lady Catechists," or lay women who were recruited to teach Native American and Caucasian boys and girls to clean, cook, and wash. Sources include a rich correspondence between Father Etienne de Rouge, S.J., the mission's founder, and his donors.

575. Ray, Lloyd, and Emma Ray. *Twice Sold, Twice Ransomed.* Seattle: Emma Ray, 1926. 320 pages. Photographs of the Rays and their community, members of the Colored Women's Christian Temperance Union of Seattle.

An introduction by Rev. C. E. McReynolds, from the First Free Methodist Church in Seattle, sets the context for Emma Ray's autobiography. Born in 1859 in Springfield, Missouri, to slave parents, she married Lloyd P. Ray, an alcoholic, in 1887. She became involved in the Colored Women's Christian Temperance Union in Seattle, the Olive Branch Mission, the county hospital and with Mother Ryther, of the Mission and Rescue Mis-

sion. She participated in the revival at the African Methodist Episcopal Church in Seattle and later joined Rev. McReynolds's Free Methodist Church.

576. Ray, Verne F. *Cultural Relations in the Plateau of Northwestern America.* Los Angeles: Southwest Museum and Frederick Webb Hodge Anniversary Publication Fund, 1939. xii, 308 pages. Notes, bibliography.

In this study, the author includes considerable detail about girls' puberty observances among Wenatchi, Okanogan, Sanpoil, Spokane, Coeur D'Alene, Cayuse, Yakama, Klickitat, Kittitas, Tenino, Molale, Umatilla, Palus, and Nez Perce adolescents.

577. ———. *Lower Chinook Ethnographic Notes.* University of Washington Publications in Anthropology, vol. 7. Seattle: University of Washington, 1938. 136 pages. Two photographs—Emma Millet Luscier and an unnamed Cowlitz woman—and seven images of baskets.

The author collected data from Lower Chinook informants in the summers of 1931 and 1936, notably from Mrs. Bertrand, born in 1843. Among the topics covered are pregnancy and birth, puberty, marriage, domestic life including cooking and weaving, dress and ornamentation, mythology, diversions, and feasting.

578. ———. *The Sanpoil and Nespelem: Salishan Peoples of Northeastern Washington.* University of Washington Publications in Anthropology, vol. 5. Seattle: University of Washington Press, 1933. 240 pages. Notes, bibliography, and index. Twenty-one figures, of women's sewing bag, rawhide carrying bag, saddle, bone dice for women's dice game.

Ray describes women's dress, hair, tools for sewing, basketry, food gathering, puberty, spirit quest, courtship, marriage, pregnancy, labor, post-natal care, rape, adultery, lesbianism, and masturbation.

579. Reed, Georgia Willis. "Women and Children on the Oregon-California Trail in the Gold-Rush Years." *Missouri Historical Review* 39 (October 1944): 1-23. Notes.

This piece begins with statistics on the numbers of people traveling on the Oregon-California trail in 1848-1849. The numbers of women and children and their respective roles in the parties are emphasized. Great losses of young children through disease, starvation, and exhaustion are described.

580. Reid, Russell. "Sakakawea." *North Dakota History* 30 (1963): 101-113. Photograph of statue of Sakakawea by Leonard Crunelle, dedicated by the North Dakota Federation of Women's Clubs in 1910.

This is an account of Sakakawea, Shoshone Indian captured at the age of twelve in 1800 by a war party of Hidatsa or Minnetarees. Reid discusses the debate over the spelling and meaning of her name and the date and place of her death. He extracts many references to her usefulness on the Lewis and Clark expedition of 1804-1806 by citing accounts from diaries of expedition members.

581. Reiff, Janice L. "Scandinavian Women in Seattle, 1888-1900: Domestication and Americanization." In *Women in Pacific Northwest History: Essays*, ed. Karen J. Blair. Seattle: University of Washington Press, 1988. Notes. This is a reprint of an essay which appeared in the *Journal of Urban History* 4 (1978): 275-290.

This article researches the Americanization of domestic servants in Seattle, focusing on the period around 1900. Most Scandinavian emigrants arrived in the Pacific Northwest single and lived as boarders until marriage. They worked primarily as domestic servants. While retaining some patterns of their homeland, most women adopted American patterns when they married, dropping out of the labor force and interacting with non-Scandinavians in their neighborhoods. By the second generation, the daughters spoke English as their first language, left home later, and no longer worked as domestic servants. Thus, their Americanization was nearly complete.

582. Remley, David. "Sacajawea of Myth and History," In *Women in Western American Literature*, ed. Helen Winter Stauffer and Susan J. Rosowski, pp. 70-89. Troy, New York: Whitson Press, 1982. Notes.

Remley compares fictional accounts of Sacajawea with historical sources, labeling biographers Ella E. Clark, Margot Edmonds, and Grace Hebard as more temperate in their assessment than the romantic novelists: Eva Emery Dye (*Noah Brooks—First Across the Continent);* William R. Lighton (*Lewis and Clark*); Thomas Bulfinch (*Oregon and Eldorado; a Romance of the Rivers*); Jerry Seibert (*Sacajawea: Guide to Lewis and Clark*); Della Gould Emmons (*Sacajawea of the Shoshones*); Anna Lee Waldo (*Sacajawea*); Frances Joyce Farnsworth (*Winged Moccasins*); Anna Wolfrom's play (*Sacajawea, the Indian Princess*); Will Henry—pseud. Henry Wilson Allen (*Gates of the Mountains*); and Vardis Fisher (*Tale of Valor*).

583. Richards, Kent D. *Washington: Readings in the History of the Evergreen State.* Lawrence, Kansas: Coronado Press, 1978. 299 pages.

This book is a collection of primary accounts of the people, places, and events of Washington state. Richards covers regional geography, fur trade, missionaries, provisional and territorial government, Indians, railroads, statehood, populists, progressivism, law and order, immigrants, labor, cities, natural resources, agriculture, depression politics, Washington in World War II, and the future of Washington. Richards mentions briefly a few pioneer women in the mid-1800s. There is a complete letter to the *Puget Sound Courier* about woman suffrage written by Mary Olney Brown (1878). There is also a description of prostitution in Seattle in its crib houses, red light district, maiden's parlor houses, and dance halls.

584. Richardson, Marvin M. *The Whitman Mission: The Third Station on the Old Oregon Trail.* Walla Walla, Washington: Whitman Publishing Company, 1940. 160 pages. Notes, bibliography, index. Photographs of the Whitman monument, Whitman grave, and Marcus and Narcissa Whitman.

Richardson has assembled the details of the physical space, including the houseplan, of the Whitman compound during the years 1836-1847. The work describes construction, catalogues the farm and household inventory, and explores home life using memoirs of Eliza Spalding, letters of Narcissa Whitman, and Catherine Sager Pringle's journal. Subsequent tenants of the facility are enumerated. Richardson also recounts the Oregon Pioneer Historical Society's efforts to acquire the grave sites, and with the Daughters of the American Revolution and Kiwanis Club, to create in 1936 a Whitman National Monument.

585. Richey, Elinor. *Eminent Women of the West.* Berkeley, California: Howell-North Books, 1975. 276 pages. Bibliography, index. Photographs of Abigail Scott Duniway, Imogen Cunningham, and Sarah Winnemucca.

Richey gives brief biographies of suffragist Abigail Scott Duniway, photographer Imogen Cunningham, and Piute Indian translator Sarah Winnemucca.

586. ———. "Sagebrush Princess with a Cause: Sarah Winnemucca," *American West* 12 (November 1975): 30-33, 57-63. Two photographs of Sarah Winnemucca.

This is an excerpt from *Eminent Women of the West* by Richey which takes liberties interpreting Winnemucca's feelings about the events in her life as a Piute interpreter, educator, and lecturer.

587. ———. "The Unsinkable Abigail." *American Heritage* 26 (February 1975): 72-75, 86-89. Three portraits of Abigail Scott Duniway, 1862, 1867, 1871; one photo of Ben Duniway with two of their children, 1858; one snapshot of Abigail voting for suffrage in 1912; and celebrating her seventy-eighth birthday with other feminists in 1912.

The purpose of this popular article is to introduce a general readership to Duniway's life and political activism. Richey succeeds very well. There are not new interpretations in this work, but Richey summarizes Abigail Duniway's life in an educational and entertaining style.

588. Roberts, Mildred, comp. *Women: Their Struggle for Equality: A Selected Bibliography.* 2nd ed. Olympia: Washington State Library, 1977. 18 pages. Bibliography.

This bibliography covers three subject areas: economic and legal discrimination, sex discrimination in education, and women in government. It lists important books and documents on a national scale, but, more importantly, Washington state documents and articles. There are some brief annotations. Most citations are dated in the early 1970s.

589. Robinson, William G. "Sa Ka Ka Wea—Sa Ca Ja Wea: Where and When did Sa Ka Ka Wea, the Indian Bird Woman Die and Where Was She Buried?" *Wi - iyohi: Bulletin of South Dakota Historical Society* 10 (September 1, 1956): 1-8. Notes.

This essay dissects the debates over the woman Indian guide who participated in the Lewis and Clark expedition. Historians do not agree on the spelling and meaning of her name and the place and time of her death.

590. Rohrer, Mary Katherine. *The History of Seattle Stock Companies from Their Beginnings to 1934.* Seattle: University of Washington Press, 1945. xiii, 76 pages. Notes, bibliography, index. Photographs of actors, actresses, theatres.

This study describes the rise of Seattle stock companies (1890-1902), the height (1902-1915), and the slow decline (1915-1934). To do so, it makes liberal use of quotations from newspapers. Women, as actors, playwrights, and protagonists of plays, appear with frequency. Three appendices are provided: stock companies, theatres, dates; plays, authors, dates; and location and name changes of theatres.

591. Ross, Nancy Wilson. *Heroines of the Early West.* New York: Random House, 1944. 178 pages. Index. Photographs of Northwest women.

This is a young adult biography in the Landmark Book Series on U.S. history. It is not strictly a work of history, insofar as it fictionalizes events and conversations from the past. Among the Northwest women it includes are missionaries Mary Richardson Walker, Anna Maria Pittman Lee and Narcissa Whitman; suffragist Abigail Scott Duniway; Catharine Blaine; member of the Lewis and Clark expedition Sacajawea; six Roman Catholic sisters; and the Mercer girls. There is mention of the formation of the Columbia Maternal Association.

592. Roth, Lottie Roeder, ed. *History of Whatcom County.* Chicago: Pioneer Historical Publishing Company, 1926. Vol. 1: xiv, 984 pages, index; vol. 2: 955 pages, index. Photographs of wives of leading founding fathers.

Vol. 1 contains histories of pioneer families and pays attention to the experiences of Teresa Eldridge, Elizabeth Roeder, Mrs. Charles E. Roberts; teachers in the Whatcom Schools; the Woman's Sewing Society of 1876; social life; journalist Mrs. H.A. Judson—"The Mother of Lynden"; and school inspector Mrs. Ellie S. Coupe. There is discussion of the Mercer girls, Children's Home, Carrie E. Kalloch, and the Young People's Bible Institute, library founders, writer Mrs. Ella Higginson, the state normal school, and performing artists who appeared in Whatcom. Women's clubs are treated, with background, projects undertaken, and officers. The Monday Club, Ladies Cooperative, Aftermath, music clubs, Business and Professional Woman's Organization, Twentieth Century Club, Daughters of the American Revolution, PEO, Women of Rotary, Young Women's Christian Association, Women's Christian Temperance Union, Grand Army of the Republic Auxiliary, Mothers Club, Parent-Teachers Association, and Progressive Literary and Fraternal Club are among those detailed.

Vol. 2 consists of thumbnail biographies of hundreds of men. Twenty-nine women receive attention, often as wives of prominent husbands. Those included are educator Mary D. C. Anderson, beautician Therese Bevans, Bernice F. Bryant, Minnie Clark, Maria M. Clark, Ella M. Collett, Alice K. Goodwin, Margaret N. Grant, Ragla Hawkinson, Martha D.A. Hawthorne, Agnes Hinckley, Lena M.

Holman, Feronia Y. Johnson, Meredith Jones, Florence E. Lees, Mary O. Lindberg, Ethel H. Lindstrom, Ethel Mathews, Mrs. Thomas Nelson, Eva C. Piper, Abbie H. Raymond, Maria E.A. Richard, Dr. Frances B. Ripley, M.D.; Katherine M. Ryan, Mary A. Serl, Mollie O. Trezise, Ellen M. Wright, Minnie H. Yates, and Margaret C. Young.

593. Rowley, Nancy J. "Red Cross Quilts for the Great War." *Uncoverings: Research Papers of the American Quilt Study Group* 3 (1982): 43-51. Notes, bibliography. Photographs of three quilts, including a portion of the 1918 Oregon Red Cross quilt.

The author, a textile conservator, explains that Northwest women raised money for the Red Cross during World War I by producing quilts to sell. The author features Alma Lauder Keeling, who produced one quilt near Arlington, Oregon.

594. Ruby, Robert H., and John A. Brown. *The Cayuse Indians: Imperial Tribesmen of Old Oregon.* Norman, Oklahoma: University of Oklahoma Press, 1972. xix, 350 pages. Notes, bibliography, index.

This account of the Whitman massacre reminds readers that Narcissa Whitman was the only woman killed on November 29, 1847. Two children died in the aftermath. The account of three woman captives, Mrs. Nathan Kimball, Helen Meek, and Esther Lorinda Bewley, are included.

595. Ruby, Robert H. and John A. Brown. *Indians of the Pacific Northwest: A History.* Norman, Oklahoma: University of Oklahoma Press, 1981. 294 pages. Notes, bibliography, index. One hundred-twenty photographs, many of women: wife of Makah Chief Tatooche; Indian woman sorting reeds; Nehalem woman in 1915; Molly Carmichael and her mother, Tututni Indians; Princess Oscharwasha, a Rogue River Indian; Annie Rock, Chitco oyster gatherer; George and Jennie, Methow Indians; Kutenai Chief David and his wife; Tillie Atkins, a Chehalis Indian; Skagit woman working on a mat; Old Polly, a Nootsack; Paiute Chief Paulina; Nettie Wright, a Klamath Indian, and her daughter; a Columbia Plateau woman, painted by William F. Reese; Cayuse woman and children in 1900; boys and girls at Fort Spokane boarding school; Paiute woman, 1872; and Indian basket seller on Seattle street in 1900. Women also appear in group photographs.

The text mentions women only incidentally. The emphasis is on male fur traders, Protestant and Catholic missionaries, medicine, and treaties.

596. Russell, Jervis. *Jimmie Come Lately, History of Clallam County.* Port Angeles: Publishers Printing Company, 1971. xxvi, 631 pages. Bibliography, index. One hundred-eighteen photos, five of women: Native American mother and child, nurses, pioneer, Miss Sophia Coleman, and switchboard operators.

This book records the history of Clallam County through the eyes of the people who lived there. The book covers the beginnings of government services, agencies, industry, and societies. A few women are mentioned, such as Sue Smith, postmistress from 1932 to 1935.

597. Ryesky, Diana. "Blanche Payne, Scholar and Teacher: Her Career in Costume History." *Pacific Northwest Quarterly* 77 (January 1986): 21-30. (See also Blair, Karen J., *Women in Pacific Northwest History.*)

Ryesky writes about the career of Blanche Payne (1896-1972), who taught costume history and apparel design at the University of Washington from 1927 to 1966.

598. Sager, Catherine, Elizabeth Sager, and Matilda Sager. *The Whitman Massacre of 1847.* Fairfield, Washington: Ye Galleon Press, 1981. 208 pages. Notes, index. Photographs of the three sisters, together and alone, and Henrietta Sager Sterling.

This is a series of three autobiographical accounts of the Whitman massacre by three survivors. The seven Sager children, orphaned on the journey west, were adopted by Marcus and Narcissa Whitman. They saw their foster parents and two brothers, John and Frank, killed during the massacre. There are slight differences between the Catherine Sager Pringle account, recorded in 1905, and that of Elizabeth in 1855 and of Matilda in 1920.

599. Sagiv, Clair. *Notable Women in the History of Oregon.* Portland: Oregon Lung Association, 1983. 15 pages. Photograph of 1923 meeting of Multnomah County Public Health Association, of Eliza Barchus's painting of Multnomah Falls, and of twenty-two women in Oregon history.

Here are twenty-two brief biographies of women in art, business, community service, education, law, medicine, science, and politics. They include: Saidie Orr Dunbar, an early officer of the Oregon Lung

Association; Eliza R. Barchus, painter; Gretchen Hoyt Corbett, volunteer in music and art activities, as well as social worker; Julia E. Hoffman, arts patron and artist; Tabitha Moffett Brown, businesswoman in merchandizing and real estate; Mary L. Muir, first U.S. woman licensed as a customs broker (1930); Marguerite Tilden Stasek, Tillamook County treasurer (1935-1959); Sarah A. Evans, volunteer worker; Marie Norris, Klamath Indian Tribal services; Ethlyn O'Neal Whitney, volunteer worker; Margaret Zwickel Bondurant, volunteer worker; Beatrice Morrow Cannady, first black female attorney to practice in Oregon, with involvement in NAACP and Oregon Prison Association; Sister Miriam Theresa Gleason, educator who created the significant Consumer League survey on working women; Zula Griswold, of Free Time School; Claire Angevin Argow, lawyer and executive director of Oregon Prison Association, 1945-1960; Lola G. Baldwin, first American woman to be appointed under civil service to the police department; Dorothy McCullough Lee, lawyer who served in Oregon state legislature (1929-1943); Dr. Ester Pohl Lovejoy, physician; Dr. Bethenia Owens-Adair, physician; Grace Phelps, nurse; Abigail Scott Duniway, suffragist; and Narcissa Whitman, missionary.

600. Saltvig, Robert. "The Tragic Legend of Laura Law." *Pacific Northwest Quarterly* 78 (July 1987): 91-99. Notes. One photograph of Laura Law.

This article details the January 5, 1940, murder of Laura Law, wife of a prominent labor leader, Dick Law. While her assailant was never caught, her spouse claimed her death was retaliation for his efforts to unionize lumber workers in an anti-radical era.

601. Sapir, Edward. "Notes on the Takelma Indians of Southwestern Oregon." *American Anthropologist* 9 (April-June 1907): 251-275.

In 1906, Sapir conducted research among Rogue or Upper Rogue River Indians just north of the California border. His results include extensive material on women's work at food preparation, clothing, entertainment, facial decoration and tatoos, puberty rituals, and marriage.

602. Schaeffer, Claude E. "The Kutenai Female Berdache: Courier, Guide, Prophetess, and Warrior," *Ethnohistory* 12 (Summer 1965): 193-236. Notes, bibliography.

This study of cross-dressing and transvestism among western Native Americans includes a biography of British Columbia-born Qanqon, a woman who dressed like a man and engaged in men's work activities. Fur trappers have left observations of this woman who had two conventional and unsuccessful marriages and then presented herself as a male, taking female partners, working as a letter carrier to Fort Astoria in 1811, mediating between Northwest residents, disseminating the Prophet Dance doctrine among Athapascan tribes of the Mackenzie area of Canada, and raiding enemy horses near Cusick, Washington. Qanqon died in 1837, killed by a Blackfoot in trying to save a Flathead.

603. Schlick, Mary Dodds. "Art Treasures of the Columbia Plateau Indians." *American Indian Basketry* 1 (1980): 12-20. Notes, bibliography. Photographs of Yakama cornhusk bag, Julia Pimms Sohappy weaving a hat, beaded bags, Umatilla and Nez Perce women with bags.

Schlick studied 203 bags and baskets woven by Sahaptin-Chinook women weavers. She explores their uses and training, materials, design, and color.

604. ———. "A Columbia River Indian Basket Collected by Lewis and Clark in 1805," *American Indian Basketry Magazine* 1 (1979): 10-13. Photograph of Wasco bag of Lewis and Clark at Harvard University.

Challenging the idea that Wasco-Wishram basketry was initiated for tourist trade in 1900, Schlick argues that hemp fiber baskets enjoyed a long history among Native American women weavers and were elaborately decorated with twisted grass into human and animal forms. As proof, she claims that the Lewis and Clark expedition acquired one of these in 1805 and it is now held by the Peabody Museum at Harvard University.

605. ———. *Columbia River Basketry: Gift of the Ancestors, Gift of the Earth.* Seattle: University of Washington Press, 1994. xvi, 234 pages. Notes, bibliography, index and glossary. Photographs of Native American women and their basketry, including Nettie Jackson of White Swan, Washington.

Native American women basketmakers of the mid-Columbia River area have produced several types of utilitarian objects. These are hats, flat bags, root-digging bags, coiled cedar-root baskets, folded cedar-bark baskets, and full-twined bags. Drawing on objects from art collectors, museums, and dealers, Schlick explores the history, evolution, materials, technique, and design, as well as outstanding Wasco, Klickitat, Yakama, and Cowlitz makers, notably Marie Slockish, Elsie Thomas, Nettie Jackson, Cecilia Totus,

Wash-us-etan-way, Patricia Courtney Gold, Elsie Pistolhead, Susie Walsey Billy, and Edythe Burt Jermak.

606. Schlicke, Carl P. "Nun in Statuary Hall." *Pacific Northwesterner* 24, no. 3 (1980): 41-45. Bibliography. Photo of Mother Joseph.

Here is a biography of Esther Pariseau (Mother Joseph), the Sister of Providence whose statue was dedicated in the U.S. capitol building in 1980. She established seventeen hospitals, seven academies, four Indian schools, and one orphanage in the Pacific Northwest, serving as architect, master builder, and financier of all of them.

607. Schlissel, Lillian. "Family on the Western Frontier." In *Western Women: Their Land, Their Lives*, ed. Lillian Schlissel, Vicki L. Ruiz, and Janice Monk, pp. 81-91. Albuquerque: University of New Mexico Press, 1988. Notes.

This essay describes and analyzes the frontier experiences of the Malick family, who settled in Vancouver, Washington Territory, in 1848. Schlissel draws on correspondence between family members between 1848-1867, examining family patterns and problems, including the pain of separating from Illinois family members, the accidental death of a son en route to Washington Territory by overland trail, infant and maternal mortality, rebellious adolescents, flooding by the Columbia River, divorce, the demands of homesteading, and insanity.

608. ———. "Women's Diaries on the Western Frontier." *American Studies* 18 (Spring 1977): 87-100. Notes.

While Schlissel draws on diaries of many women heading for Washington and Oregon, her purpose is to explore themes surrounding women's dislocation in moving west from 1840-1860. Traditional work patterns were overturned, women now doing "men's" work. Long-standing friendships in the East were severed. Women's inner lives and social selves were altered by the westward migrations.

609. Schlissel, Lillian, Byrd Gibbens, and Elizabeth Hampsten. *Far From Home: Families of the Westward Journey*. New York: Schocken Books, 1989. xviii, 264 pages. Notes, index. Photograph of Mary Ann Malick Albright and her husband.

This volume contains accounts of four western families. One of these, written by historian Lillian Schlissel, explores "The Malick Family in Oregon Territory, 1848-1867," drawing on seventeen years of letters Abigail Malick wrote from Vancouver (now Washington) to her daughter in Illinois. Schlissel has pieced together a detailed pioneer family history which includes farming, a Native American uprising, floods, behavior problems among children, madness, death, and generational conflict.

610. Schoenberg, Wilfred P., S.J. *A History of the Catholic Church in the Pacific Northwest, 1743-1983*. Washington, D.C.: Pastoral Press, 1987. xi, 883 pages. Notes, index. Photographs of Mother Joseph of the Sacred Heart on horseback, Providence Sisters at a reservation, Sister Bertha Granez, Sister Mary Andre Campan, Mother Johanna Zumstein, Mother Katherine Drexel, St. Frances Cabrini visiting Seattle in 1903, St. Elizabeth Hospital and Cathedral in Baker City in 1906, and nuns at groundbreaking of College of Sister Formation, Issaquah in 1959.

Bishop Blanchet first called French Canadian nuns in Montreal to Oregon in 1852. In 1856, Mother Joseph of the Sisters of Providence was among the next wave of Roman Catholic sisters in the region. Sisters of the Holy Names, Sisters of St. Mary, Dominican Sisters, Sisters of St. Francis, and Sisters of St. Joseph came west to establish great numbers of schools, hospitals, and orphanages. The founding and maintenance of numerous of these institutions is documented here.

611. ———. *Gonzaga University: Seventy-Five Years, 1887-1962*. Spokane: Gonzaga University, 1963. xii, 612 pages. Notes, index. Three photographs of campus women.

Chap. 50 deals with coeducation at Gonzaga University, which began in 1948. At that time, seventy women were enrolled in a student body numbering two thousand. No campus residence was built for two years. The deans of women and deans of the School of Nursing are listed.

612. ———. *These Valiant Women: History of the Sisters of St. Mary of Oregon, 1886-1986*. Portland: Sisters of St. Mary in Oregon, 1986. x, 373 pages. Notes, index. Photographs of the motherhouse in Beaverton, Oregon, its chapel, schools, children posed with teachers, portraits of many superior generals and nuns.

This is a survey of the Roman Catholic order of the Sisters of St. Mary of Oregon from 1886 through its centennial year, including the European and U.S. roots of the order. Schoenberg catalogs the growth of the facilities, biographies of leading administrators in the order, mission work with Native Americans, and the development of St. Mary's Home for Boys.

613. Schuddakopf, Jean Wheeler, ed. *Women of Washington: Women's Involvement in Community Concerns: A Washington State History.* Comp. American Association of University Women, Washington State Division. Gig Harbor, 1977. 24 pages. Bibliography, index.

This pamphlet is a condensed fact book about women in Washington state. Brief vignettes appear about individuals in the fields of literature, journalism, teaching, counseling, health services, social work, performing arts, visual art, business, agribusiness, administration, research, environmental and historic preservation, law, the church, peace, and political action. There is a section on pioneers and settlers, and a list of all the women who have served in the U.S. House of Representatives and the Washington state legislature up through 1976.

614. Schwabacher, Emilie B. *A Place for the Children: A Personal History of Children's Orthopedic Hospital and Medical Center.* Seattle: Children's Orthopedic Hospital, 1977. 97 pages. Notes. Dozens of photographs of women and children using the facility.

Anna Clise called twenty-three friends together in 1907 to establish a children's hospital in Seattle, the first of its kind on the West Coast. A survey of the fund-raising and the growth of facilities, volunteers, and services is provided up to 1982. Lists of the original trustees, the presidents, and chairmen of the board supplement portraits of sick children.

615. Schwantes, Carlos A. *The Pacific Northwest: An Interpretive History.* Lincoln: University of Nebraska Press, 1996. xxiii, 568 pages. Bibliography, index. Photographs of Abigail Scott Duniway, May Arkwright Hutton, and women apple sorters.

This survey of Washington, Oregon, and Idaho history emphasizes male occupations and activities. It covers fur-trading, lumbering, railroads, mining, salmon fishing, farming, missions, and shipyards. There is mention of missionaries Eliza Hart Spalding and Narcissa Prentiss Whitman, labor agitator May Arkwright Hutton, and journalist Abigail Scott Duniway and the suffrage campaign, Washington Governor Dixie Lee Ray and women legislators, wartime contributions of women workers, and distinguished writers and historians.

616. Schwantes, Carlos, Katherine Morrissey, David Nicandri, and Susan Strasser. *Washington: Images of a State's Heritage.* Spokane: Melior Publications, 1988. xi, 198 pages. Index. Photographs of Washington women.

This survey of Washington history deals with women telephone operators, laundresses, cannery workers, and clam diggers. It also examines their efforts to win the vote by recounting strategies suffragists employed to win enfranchisement.

617. Schwartz, Gerald. "Walter M. Pierce and the Birth Control Movement." *Oregon Historical Quarterly* 88 (Winter 1987): 371-384. Notes. Photograph of birth control advocate Margaret Sanger.

Walter M. Pierce, influenced by his suffragist wife Cornelia Marvin Pierce, was a strong supporter of the eugenics movement. As an Oregon state senator in 1917 and 1929, he supported a bill for sterilization of the unfit. As governor of Oregon, he signed the nation's second bill allowing sterilization of the feeble-minded and criminally insane in state institutions. As the eastern Oregon congressman from the second congressional district, he introduced legislation in the early 1930s to allow dissemination of informartion on birth control. Many women activists supported him in his efforts, including nationally known birth control advocate Margaret Sanger. His legislation failed, but he raised public awareness of this issue.

618. Scott, Leslie M. "Indian Women as Food Providers and Tribal Counselors," *Oregon Historical Quarterly* 42 (September 1941): 208-219. Notes.

Women's key role in food preparation, digging roots, weaving, dressing skins, and making clothing gave them influence, independence, and authority among Okanogan, Spokane, Flathead, Nez Perce, Chinook, Clatsop, and Chehalis Indians. Scott provides a long list of edible roots, seeds, nuts, and berries women collected for medicine, basket-making, and meals.

619. Searcey, Mildred. "The Little Brown Jug." *Historical Magazine of the Protestant Episcopal Church* 43 (1974): 57-64.

Searcey wrote this account of the beginnings of the Episcopal Church in Pendleton, Oregon, in 1971, the institution's centennial year. She credits Mrs. Aura Goodwin Raley and Mrs. W. H. Marshall as the original Sunday school teachers, Miss Katie Webb as first organist, and lists members of the 1875 choir and Parish Aid Society (later the Women's Auxiliary).

620. Seller, Maxine Schwartz, ed. *Women Educators in the United States, 1820-1993: A Bio-Bibliographical Sourcebook.* Westport, Connecticut: Greenwood Press, 1994. Notes, bibliography.

One essay, by Margaret Connell Szasz, provides a biography of educator Martha Beulah Mann Yallup (1942-), founder in 1981 of Heritage College on the Yakama Indian Reservation in Washington state.

621. Sengstacken, Agnes Ruth. *Destination, West!* Portland: Binfords and Mort, 1942. 219 pages.

Sengstacken has written an introduction to her mother's memoir of life in Coos County in Oregon Territory. There is lively detail about her youth in New York State and Ohio, the overland journey to Oregon in 1851, the early marriages of western girls, her teaching career, friendships with Native Americans, social life, and parties.

622. Seymour, Flora Warren. *Women of Trail and Wigwam.* New York: Woman's Press of YWCA, 1930. 6, 114 pages.

Written for girls, this study provides short biographies with fictionalized dialogue for six Northwest Native American women. These are Julia of the Flatheads of Puget Sound, who was the wife of fur trappers; Holy Rainbow or Bright Spirit, Pierre Dorion's Dakota partner; Bird Woman or Sacajawea, guide on the Lewis and Clark expedition; Sarah Winnemucca, Piute interpreter and lecturer and author of *Life Among the Piutes;* the Modoc Woman Chief, "Toby Riddle," who interpreted for the commission to sign a treaty with the Modocs in 1873; and Mary McLoughlin, from an eastern Canadian tribe, who was raised in a Quebec Catholic orphanage, came west to Astoria with her husband Alexander McKay, and married John McLoughlin, the "Father of Oregon," after McKay's death.

623. Sharbach, Sarah E. "A Woman Acting Alone: Louise Olivereau and the First World War." *Pacific Northwest Quarterly* 78 (January/April 1987): 32-40. Notes. Photographs of Louise Olivereau and Minnie Parkhurst, images of correspondence between them, and newspaper clippings reporting their story.

The Socialist stenographer Louise Olivereau (1884-1963) was convicted and sentenced to prison during World War I for advising young men to consider avoiding the draft. The focus here is on the friendship between Olivereau and Minnie Parkhurst.

624. Sharp, Cornelia. "Diary of Mrs. Cornelia A. Sharp. Crossing the Plains from Missouri to Oregon in 1852." *Transactions of the Oregon Pioneer Association* (1903), pp. 171-188. Portland: Oregon Pioneer Association, 1904.

The diary of Cornelia Sharp covers every day of her journey from Missouri to Oregon in the summer and fall of 1852. Her entries are brief, mentioning chiefly the weather, road conditions, and supply of grass.

625. Sheldon, Henry D. *History of the University of Oregon.* Portland: Binfords and Mort, 1940. Notes, index. Photographs of Luella Clay Carson, the English composition and elocution professor of 1888 and the dean of women in 1895; men and women in the classes of 1879, 1882, 1883, and 1893.

This survey of campus history from 1876-1937 stresses the curriculum, donors, board of regents, presidents, new buildings, and male professors. There is little material on women, except as instructors in the preparatory department. President Charles Chapman's wife Alice Hall Chapman founded the Women's Fortnightly Club in 1895, which pressed for a free public library in the city of Eugene. Women created the Treble Clef Club at the school of music in 1900. Mrs. George Gerlinger served on the board of regents and led a drive which raised $50,000 to build the Woman's Building in 1919, containing an elegant reception parlor and woman's gymnasium. The original woman's dormitory was Susan Campbell Hall.

626. Sicherman, Barbara, et al. *Notable American Women: The Modern Period: A Biographical Dictionary.* Cambridge, Massachusetts: The Belknap Press of the Harvard University Press, 1980. xxii, 773 pages. Bibliography, index.

Four hundred and forty-two American women who died between 1951 and 1971 are included in this biographical dictionary. Entries range from one to two pages. A few Northwest women are represented, including "Anna Louise Strong" by Stephanie F. Ogle.

627. Sisters of the Holy Names of Jesus and Mary. Province of Oregon. *Gleanings of Fifty Years, 1859-1909.* Portland: Glass and Prudhomme, 1909. xvi, 230 pages. Photographs of St. Frances Academy for Orphan Girls, Academy of the Holy Names in Astoria, St. Rose's Academy of Seattle, the Mother House of the Sisters of the Holy Names in Montreal, and the first two graduates of St. Mary's Academy in Portland (1867)—Irene Smith and Amanda Mann.

Twelve Roman Catholic nuns, from Montreal, Canada, started the Oregon effort which grew into the establishment of a multitude of educational and social service institutions throughout the Northwest. The context of western life and clerical bureaucracy is woven throughout the story of the work of the Sisters of the Holy Names of Jesus and Mary.

628. Skold, Karen Beck. "The Job He Left Behind: American Women in the Shipyards During World War II." In *Women, War and Revolution,* ed. Carol Berkin, et al., pp. 55-88. New York: Holmes and Meier Publishers, 1980. Notes, annotated bibliography.

This is a statistical and analytical article discussing women's work in the Portland shipyards during World War II.

629. Slickpoo, Allen P., Senior. *Noon Nee-Me-Poo (We, The Nez Perces): Volume One, Culture and History of the Nez Perces.* No city: Nez Perce Tribe of Idaho, 1973. viii, 318 pages. Bibliography. Fourteen photographs include women in regalia; Tolo, a Nez Perce woman; missionary Sue McBeth; early day dress; modern dress; female students at Chemawa School, Oregon; early Nez Perce home with woman in rocking chair; women on horseback; a feast; Tsoets-Ya-Yuht (Agnes Moses), daughter of Tolo; and Hattie Enos at one hundred years of age.

This is a comprehensive study of Nez Perce society of north central Idaho, southeastern Washington, and northeastern Oregon, including its history from the pre-contact period through 1934. Chap. 4, on social life, contains extensive information on the girls' puberty ceremony, marriage preparation and the wedding ceremony, child-bearing, and child-raising.

630. Smith, Charles Wesley. *Pacific Northwest Americana: A Check List of Books and Pamphlets Relating to the History of the Pacific Northwest.* Portland: Binfords and Mort, 1950. 381 pages. Bibliography.

Smith offers a list of books and pamphlets, but no articles, dealing with the history of Idaho, Montana, Oregon, Washington, British Columbia, Alaska, and the Yukon. The listings are arranged alphabetically by author only. This potentially valuable resource is limited in its usefulness by its lack of a subject index or subject headings. It includes many women authors and the titles of their works.

631. Smith, Helen Krebs. *The Presumptuous Dreamers: A Sociological Listing of the Life and Times of Abigail Scott Duniway, 1834-1915.* Lake Oswego, Oregon: Smith, Smith and Smith Publishing Company, 1974. xiii; 303 pages. Notes, bibliography, index.

This history of Oregon suffragist and pioneer Abigail Scott Duniway draws on personal letters, diaries, and family correspondence. It excerpts Duniway's writings about her private life, her opinions on women's work and women's rights, and her view of the 1871 lecture circuit of Susan B. Anthony in the Northwest. Smith also mentions other Northwest women, including Mercer's Belles, the unmarried women who were brought west for the men, and Belle W. Cook, who was a suffragist and wrote *Tears and Victory,* a book of poems.

632. ———. *With Her Own Wings: Historical Sketches, Reminiscences, and Anecdotes of Pioneer Women.* Portland: Beattie and Company, 1948. 248 pages.

Out of seventy-five sketches, sixty-three contributions were made by women. These pieces come from diaries, letters, articles, and books. Among the featured topics are Mary Ann Royal, first president of the Oregon Women's Christian Temperance Union and founder of the Juvenile Templars for children; Mary Drain Albro's tale about the only darning needle in Pass Creek Canyon; Lucretia Ann Wilber, who with her husband built Taylor Street Church and the Portland Academy and Female Seminary; Mary Leonard, the first woman to practice law in Oregon, 1886; Sarah Evans, founder of the Portland Woman's Club in 1895 and supporter of free public libraries; Lola Baldwin, the first woman in police service in the United States; the Columbia Maternal Association, an early woman's club established by Narcissa Whitman and Eliza Spalding; and the Women's Christian Temperance Union of Oregon.

633. Smith, Leta May. *The End of the Trail.* Hicksville, New York: Exposition Press, 1976. x, 290 pages. Photos: one of author, six portraits of Native American and white women.

This book is about pioneer families during the late 1800s who settled in the Kittitas Valley in central Washington. Smith covers women postmasters in Liberty, Washington; women teachers and their students, including Mrs. Letitia Haines, who taught in the first school in Yakima County; women's work during threshing, such as feeding the male crew; the county fair exhibitors and a list of handmade goods displayed such as silk mitts, quilts, and lace; women's work at making soap, washing and drying fruits and vegetables, and sewing; nurse Catherine Troutman Maynard; cosmetics used by women, e.g., buttermilk for skin bleach and cornstarch for face powder; pioneer and dressmaker Mrs. Elizabeth Steele of Seattle; restaurant owner Mrs. Jacob Durr; Native American women's work and their relationship with the whites.

634. Snowden, Clinton A. *History of Washington: The Rise and Progress of an American State.* 6 vols. New York: Century History Company, 1909. Notes, illustrations. Vol. 1: ix, 497 pages; vol. 2: 499 pages; vol. 3: 511 pages; vol. 4: 499 pages; vol. 5: 425 pages: vol. 6: 230 pages.

Women enjoy only sporadic attention in this gigantic history. The duties of the farmer's wife, the aid of Sacajawea to the Lewis and Clark expedition, the missionary work of Narcissa Whitman and Eliza Spalding, the presence of Native American women in the Northwest, and the teaching career of Mrs. Delesca J. Eldridge in Lynden, Washington, in 1888, are the most concrete examples provided of women's contributions.

635. Solinger, Rickie. *The Abortionist: A Woman Against the Law.* New York: Macmillan, 1994. xi, 253 pages. Bibliography. Ten photographs of Ruth Barnett, her family and friends.

Ruth Barnett (1895-1969) was a Portland abortionist from 1918-1968, performing 40,000 abortions, without a loss of a mother's life, during the years when it was illegal. This biography details her upbringing, her training, her procedures, her arrests in 1951 and 1966, her huge fortune, and her network of friends and colleagues. The author presents Barnett as she presented herself, as a useful healthcare professional, not as a lawbreaker.

636. Soltow, Martha Jane, and Mary K. Wery. *American Women and the Labor Movement, 1825-1974: An Annotated Bibliography.* Metuchen, New Jersey: The Scarecrow Press, 1976. viii, 247 pages. Index.

This reference work offers no access by geographic region. There are references to published and archival material about journalist and radical Anna Louise Strong and Spokane free speech advocate Elizabeth Gurley Flynn.

637. Somerville, Mollie D. *Historic and Memorial Buildings of the Daughters of the American Revolution.* Washington, D.C.: The National Society, Daughters of the American Revolution, 1979. 339 pages. Photographs of five buildings preserved by members of this women's organization.

Here is a description of five properties owned and maintained by the Daughters of the American Revolution (D.A.R.) in Washington and Oregon: the Seattle, Washington, Rainier Chapter House (1924); the Columbia, Oregon, Caples House (1870); the Champoeg State Park Robert Newell House (1852) and Pioneer Mothers' Memorial Cabin (1931); and the Lakeview, Oregon, Schminck Memorial Museum (1921). Somerville provides the history of each house and garden, its original owners and furnishings, and the role of the local D.A.R. in preserving the property.

638. Sone, Monica. *Nisei Daughter.* Seattle: University of Washington Press, 1953. xvii, 238 pages. One photo of author on cover.

An introduction by S. Frank Miyamoto provides the context for this engaging memoir. Sone's story tells of growing up in a Japanese American family in Seattle in the 1930s, when her parents ran a hotel. She describes racism before and during World War II and paints the picture of her family's internment in wartime. The autobiography is rich in detail about life from a growing girl's perspective.

639. Speidel, William C. *Sons of the Profits; or, There's No Business Like Grow Business: the Seattle Story, 1851-1901.* Seattle: Nettle Creek Company, 1967. 345 pages. Bibliography, index.

Women are incidental to this gossipy tale. Carson Denny is labeled "henpecked" by his wife and mother. Henry Yesler is notable for marrying Minnie Gagle, fifty-five years his junior. There is brief attention to the woman suffrage issue during territorial days.

640. Sperlin, O. B. "Two Kootenay Women Masquerading as Men? Or Were They One?" *Washington Historical Quarterly* 21 (1930): 120-130. Notes.

The author has collected five historical memoirs and two historical accounts describing a Native American woman who dressed and behaved as a man in Astoria, Oregon, from 1811 until her death in 1837. He analyzes the commonalities in the accounts and the discrepancies among them.

641. Sprague, William Forrest. *Women and the West*. Boston: Christopher Publishing House, 1940. Reprint, New York: *New York Times* Company, 1972. 240 pages. Notes, bibliography, index.

Here are extracts from the diary kept by Narcissa Whitman en route to Oregon Territory in 1836. There is mention of Abigail Scott Duniway's role in founding suffrage organizations and escorting Susan B. Anthony through her speaking tour in 1871, and of the brief suffrage women of Washington Territory enjoyed from 1883 to 1887.

642. Starbuck, Susan. "The Washington Women's Heritage Project: The Next Stage." *Pacific Northwest Forum* 7 (Summer-Fall 1982): 3-9. Notes.

This essay describes the Washington Women's Heritage Project, a three-year effort to seek "historical materials which document the presence, the roles, and the experiences of women in Washington State History." A fourteen-panel exhibit, "Working and Caring," toured the state in 1981 and 1982, and reflected the search by exhibiting photographs collected and quotations from women interviewed by participants. One oral history, with Peggy Cook of Seattle, is quoted at length.

643. Steeves, Sarah Hunt. *Book of Remembrance of Marion County, Oregon, Pioneers, 1840-1860*. Portland: Berncliff Press, 1927. 348 pages. Index.

This is a compilation of biographies of pioneers, both male and female, by their descendants. Each biography divulges the historical sources used and provides information about the birthplace, family, overland journey to Oregon, life in the West, and descendants.

644. Steilacoom Historical Museum Association. *Town on the Sound: Stories of Steilacoom*. Tacoma: Media Production Associates, 1988. iii, 200 pages. Notes, index. Thirty-four photographs including images of women.

This volume features material about four Steilacoom pioneer women, including Luzena Brazelton Wallace, who wrote an account of coming to Steilacoom in 1854 to join her husband. Extracts from her reminiscences are included. There is a portrait of the Sisters of Providence and Mother Joseph, who founded thirty schools and hospitals in the West, including a school in Steilacoom, in 1863. Laura Belle Downey Bartlett was a pioneer settler who arrived in 1853. Dr. Mary Fletcher Perkins received her medical training at the University of Michigan.

645. Stephens, Louise G. ("Katherine"). *Letters from an Oregon Ranch*. Chicago: A. C. McClurg and Company, 1905. 212 pages.

In a flowery literary style, the author, "Katherine," recounts to her friend Nell, back East, the details of establishing a new life on the Ranch of the Pointed Firs with her husband Tom, in late nineteenth-century Oregon. Anecdotes about baking bread, churning butter, gardening, raising cows and chickens, and celebrating the Christmas holidays dominate the narration.

646. Stern, Bernard. *The Lummi Indians of Northwest Washington*. New York: AMS Press, 1934. Reprint, New York: Columbia University Press, 1969. One photograph of a Native American woman.

This study of the Northwest coast of Washington near the Canadian border describes the Lummi household, women's work, girl's puberty rites, pregnancy, marriage, weaving, and spirit dances. The legends recounted here anthropomorphize the region's islands as women partners of the male Mt. Baker.

647. Stern, Susan. *With the Weathermen: The Personal Journey of a Revolutionary Woman*. New York: Doubleday and Company, 1975. xi, 376 pages. Chronology. Fifteen photographs of author in radical demonstrations.

Stern's autobiography explores her upbringing, education, membership in SDS (Students for a Democratic Society), her role as the only woman founder of the Seattle Weathermen in 1969, and her participation in political demonstrations. This memoir quotes clippings from the *Seattle Times* and *New York Times* and letters she wrote from Purdy State Prison, 1970-1972.

648. Stevens, Helen Norton. *Memorial Biography of Adele M. Fielde, Humanitarian*. New York: Fielde Memorial Committee, 1918. 377 pages. Two photographs of Adele M. Fielde.

Adele Marion Fielde (1839-1916) was a missionary in Asia who translated fifty religious tracts into Chinese, wrote the life of Jesus in Chinese, and compiled a dictionary of Swatow dialect with English equivalents. After a full career in China, the New York State-born woman retired to Seattle in 1907 and spent the last six years of her life engaged in reform activism. She supported woman suffrage, the eugenics movement, public health and sanitation reforms, Prohibition, direct legislation, workmen's compensation, widow's pensions, and a minimum wage for women, and campaigned against the white slave traffic. She participated in the Equal Suffrage League, Rainy Day Club, and organized good government clubs for political study.

649. Stewart, Agnes. "The Journey to Oregon—A Pioneer Girl's Diary." Ed. Claire Warner Church. *Oregon Historical Quarterly* 29 (March 1928): 77-98.

This is partly a diary and partly a recounting by her grandson of the pioneer journey of Agnes Stewart from Pennsylvania to Oregon in 1853. Some diary entries were very brief, others full and expressive. Stewart wrote extensively about her beloved friend, Martha Hay, who remained in Pennsylvania.

650. Stewart, Anne B. "A Woman's Baton." *Woman Citizen* 8 (December 15, 1923): 8, 27, 28. One photograph of Madame Davenport Engberg.

This is a story of Madame Davenport Engberg, founder of a volunteer civic orchestra in Bellingham, Washington, the only woman-conducted orchestra in the country. She moved to Seattle after World War I and conducted Seattle's Civic Symphony Orchestra.

651. Stewart, Edgar I. *Washington: Northwest Frontier.* 4 vols. New York: Lewis Historical Publishing Company, Inc., 1957. Vol. 1: xvi, 415 pages, notes; vol. 2: 444 pages, notes, index; vols. 3 and 4 numbered consecutively with 809 pages, index. Photographs of wives posed with famous husbands.

Hundreds of wives, mothers, and daughters are mentioned in passing in the biographies of men in vols. 3 and 4.

652. Stewart, Patricia. "Sarah Winnemucca." *Nevada Historical Society Quarterly* 14 (Winter 1971): 23-28. Notes.

This biography draws on extensive research, using a wide variety of sources and quoting historical materials generously to recount Native American Sarah Winnemucca's efforts "to publicize the plunder of her homeland."

653. Stimson, William L. *Going to Washington State: A Century of Student Life.* Pullman: Washington State University Press, 1989. xvi, 304 pages. Index. Numerous photographs of women as students in classes, dances, and commencement, and Jennie May Thomas Harold '44, the first female student body president.

With an emphasis on extracurricular life, Stimson offers information about curfews, housemothers, panty raids, sororities, women's dorm life, domination of the school newspaper while the men went to war in the 1940s, and career tracking in the 1950s toward teaching, nursing, secretarial work, and home economics.

654. Stowell, Cynthia D. *Faces of a Reservation: A Portrait of the Warm Springs Indian Reservation.* Portland: Oregon Historical Society Press, 1987. xxii, 202 pages. Notes, bibliography, and index. Fifty-two photographs of women accompany their oral histories.

Based on fifty-two interviews conducted in the 1980s, this volume provides reminiscences by C.R. Squiemphen, a prize-winning barrel-racer at the rodeo; Trudee Clements, who held the titles of Miss Warm Springs, Miss Indian North America, and Miss National Congress of American Indians; Masami Danzuka, child dancer and pow wow champion; Bernice Mitchell, Head Start teacher, council woman, and longhouse elder; Maxine Switzler, bead worker; and Mary Hote, the first person to own and drive a car on the Warm Springs Reservation.

655. Stratton, David H., and George A. Frykman, eds. *The Changing Pacific Northwest: Interpreting its Past.* Pullman: Washington State University Press, 1988. xii, 190 pages. Notes. Three photographs of women: Nez Perce woman, Card and Label League Building at Spokane Fair, and women on the 1920 assembly line for Sun Maid Raisins.

This collection includes an essay by Susan Armitage on "The Challenge of Women's History." See also Blair, Karen J. *Women in Pacific Northwest History: Essays.*

656. Stratton, David H., ed. *Washington Comes of Age: The State in the National Experience.* Pullman: Washington State University Press, 1992. xxxi, 174 pages. Notes.

This collection of nine essays by nine authors, delivered under the auspices of the Pettyjohn Distinguished Lecturers Series at Washington State University, includes "Let Women Vote: Abigail Scott Duniway in Washington Territory" by Ruth Barnes Moynihan.

657. Strong, Anna Louise. *I Change Worlds: The Remaking of an American.* New York: H. Holt and Co., 1935. Reprint, Seattle: Seal Press, 1979. xxvi, 450 pages. Bibliography of Anna Louise Strong's works, index. Photo of author.

Here is a reprint, with an introduction by Barbara Wilson, of Anna Louise Strong's 1935 autobiography. The Seattle-born journalist lived in the Soviet Union and then the People's Republic of China and wrote in support of their revolutions. In chap. 5 ("I Love My America") she describes her work on the Seattle school board. Chaps. 6 and 7 explore her growing involvement in radical politics in Washington state in 1918 and 1919.

658. Strong, Tracy B., and Helene Keysser. *Right in Her Soul: The Life of Anna Louise Strong.* New York: Random House, 1983. xiii, 399 pages. Notes, bibliography, index. Twelve photographs of Anna Louise Strong.

This readable and careful biography is written by Anna Louise Strong's great-nephew and his wife. The origins of her radicalism are explored, including the progressivism of her minister father, her Oberlin College experience, her volunteer work at Hull House, and her University of Chicago Ph.D. in 1908. Chap. 5 is devoted to her Seattle years and the experiences which channeled her energies into leftist causes. The study makes a strong case for the importance of her Seattle circle in drawing her to the Soviet Union and later China to make a life and build a career dedicated to radical politics.

659. Sunoo, Sonia S. "Korean Women Pioneers of the Pacific Northwest." *Oregon Historical Quarterly* 79 (Spring, 1978): 51-63. Notes. One photograph of an unidentified Korean family and one of a Korean woman.

Here are six portraits, of In-Sook, Ok-Ja, Myong-Soon, Soon-Hi, Bokki, and Bong-Nim, Korean picture brides who came from southern or central Korea to work on Oregon and Montana farms. Brief accounts of their lives in Korea and their American marriages are provided. The Chinmock-hoc (Friendship Club) is described, in which Korean families met socially in each other's homes.

660. Swan, James G. *The Northwest Coast; or, Three Years' Residence in Washington Territory.* New York: Harper and Brothers, 1857. 442 pages. Index.

James Swan was a government agent who spent a long career along the coast of Washington Territory. Chap. 10 of Swan's account describes the Native Americans north of the Columbia River. He discusses women's attire, games played by girls and women, puberty rituals, ornaments worn, and the position of women as "not so degraded as with the tribes of the Plains."

661. Swanson, Kimberly. "Eva Emery Dye and the Romance of Oregon History." *Pacific Historian* 29 (Winter 1985): 59-68. Notes. Photographs of Eva Emery Dye, the Dye family home in Oregon City, the National American Woman Suffrage Association conference at the 1905 Lewis and Clark Exposition in Portland, and Abigail Scott Duniway, Helen Miller Senn, and Josephine Wallis French voting at the polls.

Eva Emery Dye (1855-1947), a prominent literary figure and activist in the Oregon Woman Suffrage Association, wrote historical novels that were significant in launching myths from a romanticized view of Oregon history. Among her influential works are *Stories of Oregon* for children; *McLoughlin and Old Oregon* (1893); *The Conquest: The True Story of Lewis and Clark* (1902) which exaggerated the importance of Sacajawea; *McDonald of Oregon: A Tale of Two Shores* (1906); and *Soul of America: An Oregon Illiad* (1932).

662. Sweetman, Maude. *What Price Politics.* Seattle: White and Hitchcock Corporation, 1927. 136 pages. One photo of author.

In this book, Sweetman gives us an inside account of the working of politics in Washington state. Sweetman herself was a Washington state representative from 1923 to 1927. She covers such topics as: are women good politicians?; the organization of the legislature; and legislation during her terms in office. She wanted to be on the Rules Committee, but was told, "You know that 'Rules' Committees is a rough place. We swear and smoke, put our feet on the table, and call a spade a spade."

663. Taber, Ronald W. "Sacajawea and the Suffragettes: An Interpretation of a Myth." *Pacific Northwest Quarterly* 58 (April 1967): 7-13. Notes. One photo of Eva Emery Dye.

The point of this essay is that Oregon suffragists, especially Eva Emery Dye, inflated Sacajawea's importance on the Lewis and Clark expedition in order to use her as a propaganda figure for their cause. Dye, a novelist, publicized the role of the Native American interpreter in *The Conquest,* and, as president of the Portland Women's Club, formed the Sacajawea Statue Association. This group commissioned a $7,000 statue by Alice Cooper of Denver to be dedicated in 1905 at the Lewis and Clark Centennial Exposition in Portland during the annual convention of the National American Woman Suffrage Association. NAWSA president Anna Howard Shaw extolled the virtues and achievements of Sacajawea at the ceremonies, attended by major suffragists of the era. Historian Grace Raymond Hebard, also a suffragist, perpetuated a glorified image of Sacajawea's role in her 1933 work, *Sacajawea: A Guide and Interpreter of the Lewis and Clark Expedition.*

664. Tamura, Linda. *The Hood River Issei: An Oral History of Japanese Settlers in Oregon's Hood River Valley.* Urbana: University of Illinois Press, 1993. xxiii, 337 pages. Notes, bibliography, index. Family photographs of the fourteen men and women who were interviewed.

Pacific University professor Tamura, a third generation Japanese American, interviewed three men and eleven women in the 1980s. All were first-generation Japanese American octogenarians who shared their stories with the aid of a translator. Among those who agreed to assist Tamura was her maternal grandmother. The author provides brief biographies of her subjects and an overview of migration history from Japan to the United States. Forty short chapters excerpt the interviews, dealing with such topics as life in Japan, picture brides and marriage, family, Fujinkai (a woman's organization), churches, Girls' Day Celebrations, the bombing of Pearl Harbor, internment during World War II, the disposal of property in wartime, returning home to Hood River, Oregon, and attitudes about U.S. government efforts for redress in 1983.

665. Taylor, Lee. *Pend Oreille Profiles.* Fairfield, Washington: Ye Galleon Press, 1977. 344 pages. Photographs of women who were interviewed.

This collection of fifty biographies, which are drawn from interviews with older members of the Pend Oreille Valley, bare the origins, work, and voluntary efforts of Jeanne Bockemuehl, Freda Fox, Florence Graham, Jessie Hall, Sadie Halstead, Claire Howe, Althia Hutchins, Julia Johnson, Winifred Johnson, Loretta Leichner, Margaret McInturff, Sadie Overholt, Helen Roos, Madge Scott, Grace Sewell, May Sherman, and Eleanor Strayer. There is special attention to their experiences in Pend Oreille Valley.

666. Teit, James A. "The Salishan Tribes of the Western Plateaus." *Forty-fifth Annual Report of the Bureau of American Ethnology,* 1927-28, ed. Franz Boas, pp. 23-397. Washington, D.C.: Smithsonian Institution, 1930. Illustrations of Okanogan cradle-board, designs on front of Flathead women's leggings, designs from shoulders of Flathead women's dresses, beaded flaps for stirrings for Flathead women's saddles.

Using information he collected in the Pacific Northwest in 1904, 1908, and 1909, Teit examines Flathead customs in the Spokane area of eastern Washington, including household activity, clothing and ornaments, birth, childhood, puberty, and marriage. For the Okanogans in eastern Washington, he describes women's weaving, clothing, life cycle, baskets, and lodges, and provides biographies of leading chiefs, including women. Finally, he similarly investigates the Coeur D'Alenes.

667. *Ten Painters of the Pacific Northwest.* Utica, New York: Muson-Williams Proctor Institute, 1948. 20 pages. One image of a Margaret Tomkins painting.

This is a catalog to a 1947-1948 exhibition of the works of ten Pacific Northwest printers. The educational background of each artist is provided. Included is Margaret Tomkins, former assistant professor of art at the University of Washington.

668. *They Came to Puget Sound: Reminiscences of Seven Pioneer Women.* Tacoma: Tacoma Public Library, 1893. 105 pages.

In 1892, the *Tacoma Weekly Ledger* sponsored a contest inviting pioneers, forty years after the fact, to write accounts of their early settlement experiences. The following women's stories were reprinted: Sarah McAllister Hartman, Ellen Jane Mark Wallis, Esther Packwood Chambers, Nancy Russell Thomas, Mary Perry Frost, M.M. White Ruddell, and Luzana Brazelton Wallace.

669. Tinling, Marion. *Women Remembered: A Guide to Landmarks of Women's History in the U.S.* Westport, Connecticut: Greenwood Press, 1986. xiv, 796 pages. Bibliography, index.

This gazetteer traces women's landmarks in every state of the union. It identifies nineteen landmarks in fifteen cities of Oregon, including the monument in Astoria to Dr. Bethenia Owens-Adair; the Fort Clatsop National Memorial to Sacajawea, the Indian guide; and Tabitha Brown Hall at Pacific University in Forest Grove. For the state of Washington, Tinling located sixteen landmarks in twelve cities. These include Higginson Hall at Western Washington University in Bellingham, named for writer Ella Rhoads Higginson; the Washington State Federation of Women's Clubs Forest and the Catherine Montgomery Interpretive Center (named for a leading conservationist), both in Enumclaw;

the Sacajawea State Park and Museum in Pasco; the Cornish School of Seattle; the Hulda Klager Horticultural Center in Woodland; the Marcus and Narcissa Whitman mission site in Walla Walla; and the house of pioneer Eliza Leary in Seattle.

670. Toll, William. "The Female Life Cycle and the Measure of Jewish Social Change: Portland, Oregon, 1880-1930." *American Jewish History* 72 (March 1983): 309-332. Notes.

This study examines demographic patterns among Jewish women in late nineteenth-century Portland, identifying age at marriage, age differentials between wife and husband, and number of children born in the context of their family lives, businesses, and voluntary activities such as the Ladies Hebrew Benevolent Society.

671. ———. *The Making of an Ethnic Middle Class: Portland Jewery Over Four Generations.* Albany: State University of New York Press, 1982. xii, 242 pages. Notes, bibliography, index. Three photographs of women, including eight presidents of the Council of Jewish Women in 1905; teachers Ida and Zerlinda Lowenberg, Rose Loewenberg Goodman and Laddie Goodman Trachtenberg; and the Well Baby Clinic in 1920 at Neighborhood House, a settlement house the women sponsored.

Chap. 2, entitled "Jewish Women and Social Modernization, 1870-1930," examines the charitable endeavors of the first Ladies Hebrew Benevolent Society and the Council of Jewish Women. The latter offered Friendly Visitors to identify needy families and Kitchen Garden classes for children in home economics. In 1905, the group erected Neighborhood House, a settlement house offering social services to the community. The Council of Jewish Women affiliated with the Oregon Federation of Women's Clubs and lobbied for higher salaries for teachers and more women in education administration.

672. ———. *Women, Men and Ethnicity: Essays on the Structure and Thought of American Jewry.* Lanham, Maryland: University Press of America, 1991. xiv, 230 pages. Notes.

Chap. 7, "Maternal Surveillance and the Jewish Settlement Idea in the American West," compares settlement work by Jewish women in 1890s San Francisco, Seattle, and Portland. Women founded the settlements to offer relief, employment bureaus, sewing classes, Hebrew schools for boys, social clubs for working girls, Hanukkah and Purim celebrations and parties for children, campaigns for neighborhood services such as public baths, regular garbage collection and medical clinics, Travelers Aid for newcomers, visiting nurses, juvenile courts, and shelters.

673. Trachtenberg, Gladys G. "Neighborhood House—Its Evolution, Past, Present and Future." *Historical Scribe: Newsletter of the Jewish Historical Society of Oregon* (Winter/Spring 1978-79): 2-3. Photographs of the cast of a play in the 1920s and the 1910 facility at SW Second and Wood Street.

This is a survey of the social work of the National Council of Jewish Women's Portland chapter from 1896. Miss Ida Loewenberg was an influential director after 1912.

674. Tripp, Joseph F. "Toward an Efficient and Moral Society: Washington State Minimum Wage Law, 1913-1925." *Pacific Northwest Quarterly* 67 (July 1976): 97-112. Notes. Photographs of women telephone operators and clerical workers.

Washington state was early to enact both a minimum wage law and an eight-hour law for women. Members of the Washington State Federation of Women's Clubs lobbied for these laws and generated discussion about their importance.

675. Troxel, Kathryn. "Food of the Overland Emigrants." *Oregon Historical Quarterly* 56 (March 1955): 12-26. Notes.

Using the information in pioneer diaries, Kathryn Troxel describes the supplies that pioneers brought for their overland journey, the game and plants they found along the way, the methods of food preparation, and the types of medicine used. The essay has few specifics about individual pioneers.

676. Trusky, A. Thomas, ed. *Women Poets of the West: An Anthology, 1850-1950.* Boise, Idaho: Ahsahta Press, 1978. 95 pages. Bibliography.

Fourteen writers are identified, three of them from the Pacific Northwest. One biography treats Ella Mae Rhoads Higginson (1860-1941), who was born in Kansas, raised in La Grande, Oregon, and lived in Bellingham. She is represented with six poems from two collections. Hazel Hall (1886-1924), an invalid all her life, wrote poetry in Portland. Genevieve Taggard (1894-1948) was born and raised in Waitsburg, Washington. Seven of her poems are included.

677. Turnbull, George S. *History of Oregon Newspapers*. Portland: Binfords and Mort Publishers, 1939. 560 pages. Notes, index.

This book covers owners, publishers, and editors of Oregon newspapers with brief histories. Most of the material deals with men, but Catherine A. Scott Coburn is mentioned as editor and writer. Her sister, Abigail Scott Duniway, has her own section of three pages, surveying the *New Northwest*.

678. Turner, Russell M. *The First Forty-Five Years: A History of Cooperative Extension in Washington State*. Extension Miscellaneous Publication No. 55. Pullman: Washington State University, Institute of Agricultural Services (April 1961). 138 pages. Photos of: Pierce County staff in 1921 including Johanna Madsen (clerk), Hulda Heinke (club agent), Elmina White (home demonstration agent); farm homemaker stirring soap on her stove; Thurston County Canning Club in 1917; Eleanor Roosevelt with Washington state delegates to the 1933 National 4-H Club Camp in Washington, D.C.; young women arriving in Pullman for the 1931 state 4-H Club Camp at the college.

Turner served as assistant director of Cooperative Extension in Washington state from 1924 to 1954 and as director from 1954 to 1957. He surveys turn-of-the-century farmer's institutes and the official 1912-1914 formation of the extension service. The first woman hired was Mary C. Sutherland in October 1913, as extension specialist in home economics. She gave classes on canning food, cutting and fitting simple house dresses, cooking soup and meat substitutes, and making salads, soups, desserts, and milk bread. In 1913, the home demonstration train carried Miss Mary Anderson (Davis) and Agnes Crary to offer demonstrations in home economics. Early 4-H club work began with Mrs. Margaret Crews of Tieton, Yakima County, as leader in 1912. The first Home Economics Club began in 1914 in Wahkiakum County, the Seal River Canning Club. A list is provided of the first ten home agents:
Mabel Greene (1919-1920), Benton County
Della Delvin (1917-1920), Chelan County
Harriet D. Stowe (1918-1920), Clallam County
Ruth Kennedy (1918), Grant County
Catherine Bryden (1918), King County
Elmina White (1917-1922), Pierce County
Della Prell (1918), Spokane County
Myrtle Boone (1917-1920), Thurston County
Blanche Henry (1918), Whitman County
Josephine Arnquist (1916), Yakima County

A list of all 727 extension workers, from the founding through 1957, including 239 women, provides job histories for each.

679. Tyack, David. "The Tribe and the Common School." *Call Number* 27 (Spring, 1966): 13-23. Notes, copy of an irate parent's letter, first page of school newspaper.

This article concerns the district school in Ashland, Oregon, in the 1860s and its teacher, Oliver Cromwell Applegate. It describes what it was like to teach in a small frontier school, what was taught, and how a teacher was treated by the community. It also contains five letters by Herbert Hoover written to Miss Ney May Hill of Independence, Oregon, while they both studied in college.

680. Uhler, Margaret Anderson, ed. "Well and Strong and Fearless: Etta Anderson in Washington Territory, 1853-56." *Montana: the Magazine of Western History* 32 (Summer 1982): 32-39. Notes. Photograph of Henrietta Anderson.

Henrietta "Etta" Anderson (1834-1917) sent a letter to University of Washington professor Edmund S. Meany, describing her life in Washington Territory in 1853 through 1856. Her anecdotes describe the people and residences she saw in the West. Anderson's great-granddaughter edited this document.

681. Underhill, Ruth. *Indians of the Pacific Northwest*. Indian Life and Customs Series, no. 5. New York: AMS Press, 1944. 234 pages. Bibliography. Numerous illustrations of women—gathering wood, cooking, spinning and weaving, gathering clams, and in the fields. Pictured here is equipment for cooking, baskets for storage, and head flattening boards for children.

This is a textbook, with double columns of text and eighty illustrations for Cowlitz, Klickitat, Duwamish, Chinook, Makah, and Quinault people. Among the topics of concern to women are sections on gathering of roots and berries, cooking and housekeeping tools and tasks, women's work, and marriage to maturity, dealing with such topics as baby care, the wedding ceremony, and polygamy.

682. Van Horne, Bernard. "Mary Frances Isom: Creative Pioneer in Library Work in the Northwest." *Wilson Library Bulletin* 33 (February 1959): 409-416. Three photographs of Mary Frances Isom.

Here is a biography of a Portland librarian who took charge of the public library in 1901. Her home life and personality are included, but the focus is on her career, including her efforts to establish children's libraries, participate in professional organizations, and cooperate with county and state library systems. When her employee, pacifist M. Louise Hunt, refused to purchase war bonds during World War I, Isom refused to fire her and was herself viewed as disloyal to her country. She left her job to do war service in France in 1918 and returned to Portland to die of cancer in 1920.

683. Van Kirk, Sylvia. *Many Tender Ties: Women in Fur-Trade Society, 1670-1870*. Norman: University of Oklahoma Press, 1983. 300 pages. Notes, bibliography, index. Fifty-eight sketches and photographs of women.

Van Kirk's emphasis is on the late eighteenth-century and early nineteenth-century Native American wives of European fur-traders in western North America, including British Columbia and Hudson's Bay Company trading posts in the area now known as Washington state. The formality of the "custom of the country" or "marriage a la facon du pays," is examined between white fur-traders and Native American women, for its benefits and drawbacks to both parties. The change in relationships over time is discussed, due to company policy, the introduction of Roman Catholic and Protestant missionaries, and white women's arrival in the nineteenth century.

684. Victor, Frances Fuller. *The River of the West*. Hartford: R. W. Bliss and Company, 1870. 602 pages.

This book only mentions women in passing, as with "Sue Smith was the wife of the best fur trader in Oregon." Otherwise, the book covers Joseph L. Meek's life as a Rocky Mountain hunter and trapper.

685. ———. *Women's War with Whiskey*. Portland: George H. Himes, Steam Book and Job Printer, 1874. 60 pages.

This book deals with the founding and meetings of the temperance movement in Oregon. It describes the different tactics the women used to discourage alcohol consumption, such as praying in front of saloons and getting arrested for creating disturbances. For those women who were arrested, this book provides their trial's testimony, appeals, and verdict.

686. Vore, Elizabeth A. "A Successful Pacific Coast Writer: Ella Higginson." *Overland Monthly* 33 (May 1899): 434-436. One photographic portrait of Ella Higginson.

This article is a sympathetic review of the career of poetry- and short-story writer Ella Higginson of Bellingham.

687. Wagner, Henry R. and Charles L. Camp. *The Plains and the Rockies: A Bibliography of Original Narratives of Travel and Adventure, 1800-1865*. 4th ed. San Francisco: John Howell Books, 1982. 703 pages. Bibliography, index.

This large volume is arranged chronologically with each title listed under the year it was published. Many entries include explanatory notes or an abstract. Only sixteen out of 429 sources were authored by women.

688. Wagner, Laura Virginia. *Through Historic Years with Eliza Ferry Leary*. Introduction by Professor Edmond S. Meany. Seattle: Dogwood Press, 1934. xiii, 93 pages. Three photographs contain women.

The first half of this historical biography deals with Eliza Ferry Leary's life and the ways she assisted her father, a territorial govenor of Washington, her husband, and her community, through organizational work in the Ladies Relief Society, Children's Orthopedic Hospital Association, Red Cross, Y.W.C.A., and Sunset Club. She was most closely affiliated with the Daughters of the American Revolution, serving as state chairman for thirty years, but she was involved with a wide variety of national patriotic societies.

689. Wallace, Shelley Burtner. "Umatilla's 'Petticoat Government,' 1916-1920." *Oregon Historical Quarterly* 88 (Winter 1987): 385-402. Notes. Photograph of Laura Starcher, mayor of Umatilla.

Soon after suffrage was granted to Oregon women, Umatilla, Oregon, saw the election of several women. In 1916, Mayor Laura J. Starcher, four city council women, a recorder, and treasurer took office. Between 1916 and 1920, twelve women held council positions, including Anna Means, Mrs. H.T. Duncan, and Stella Pauly.

690. Walling, A. G. *History of Southern Oregon, Comprising Jackson, Josephine, Douglas, Curry and Coos Counties*. Portland: Walling, 1884. 545 pages. Photographs of Mrs. Joseph Lane and Mrs. Jacob Ish.

While most of the text deals with geography, economics, politics, journalism, legislators, transportation, and navigation, women are included in the lists of pioneers and members of lodges.

691. ———. *Illustrated History of Lane County.*
Portland: Walling, 1884. 508 pages. Index.

Half of this volume repeats material in Walling's *History of Southern Oregon.* There is reference to Mrs. Mary Skinner, the first white woman who made her permanent home within the boundaries of Lane County, Oregon. Walling also mentions the wives of reverends Jason Lee, Frost, Waller, Kone, Olley, Hines, Judson, Parish, and Richards.

692. Ward, Jean, and Elaine A. Maveety, eds. *Pacific Northwest Women, 1815-1915: Lives, Memories, and Writings.* Corvallis: Oregon State University Press, 1995. 349 pages. Bibliography, index. Photographs of women writers.

This volume excerpts fiction and non-fiction by thirty Washington and Oregon women, pieces written between 1815 and 1925. Not only does the collection offer tantalizing tidbits from short stories, essays, poems, letters, and memoirs, but it also includes concise biographies of the little-known authors, with substantial bibliographies for those who wish to do further reading on the women's lives and works. Among the writings sampled are those by Sui Sin Far, Mother Joseph, Mourning Dove, Abigail Scott Duniway, and Sarah Winnemucca (Hopkins). The themes deal with both private and public life.

693. Wardin, Albert W., Sr. *Baptists in Oregon.* Portland: Judson Baptist College, 1969. 635 pages. Bibliography, index.

While most of the text deals with male leadership, there is mention of women ministers (the earliest being Mrs. Mary C. Jones, Addie Williams [Mrs. C.E.] Short, Desdemona Smith, Miss Celia Pennington, Edith Hill, Minnie Oliphant, Mrs. Jack Frost, Mrs. A.W. DeLong); women delegates on the state convention board; and these women's organizations: Woman's Baptist Foreign Mission Society of Oregon, Woman's Baptist Foreign Missionary Society of the Pacific Coast, Woman's Baptist Missionary Society of the West, Women's Christian Temperance Union, WCTU Farm Home, Women's Mission Society of the Baptist Convention of the North Pacific Coast, Woman's Missionary Union, Ladies Aid of Baker First Baptist Church, Ladies Sewing Society of Oak Creek Church, and Ladies Benevolent Society of Salem Church. Some of the club projects are detailed.

694. Warren, Eliza Spalding. *Memoirs of the West: The Spaldings.* Portland: Marsh Printing Company, 1916. 153 pages. Photographs of the author, the grave of her father, her sister, and family members.

Warren's introduction reviews the story of her parents, missionaries Rev. H.H. Spalding and Eliza Hart Spalding. The author was a child, residing at the Whitman mission in 1847, when the famous massacre took place and she was taken captive. In addition to providing her family history from her own point of view, she has collected magazine and newspaper clippings, the memoirs of Mrs. Martha J. Wigle, youngest daughter of Dr. Spalding, the diary of Mrs. Henry Hart Spalding from 1836, letters from Henry H. Spalding, and a lecture by Dr. Spalding from the *Albany Democrat* in 1867.

695. Warren, Sidney. *Farthest Frontier: The Pacific Northwest.* New York: Macmillan Company, 1949. ix, 375 pages.

This book covers early exploration of the Northwest, Indians, missionaries, settlers in Oregon and Washington, social life of the pioneers, frontier politics, the growth and development of the region, and the literary frontier. Among the women mentioned are Indian women as slaves, prostitutes, and workers; Walla Walla missionary Narcissa Whitman; pioneer women on the trail and at home; newspaperwoman Roselle Applegate Putman; Abigail Scott Duniway; temperance advocate Mrs. Frances Fuller Victor; physician Bethenia Owens-Adair; actresses; writers Margaret Jewett Bailey, Belle W. Cooke, Mrs. Eva Emery Dye, Ada W. Anderson, and Caroline Chapman. There is a list of cosmetics used by pioneer women, including honey soap for softening skin and sage tea for hair coloring. Early marriages, enabling men to take advantage of the federal Donation Land Law of 1850, are mentioned. Late nineteenth-century social life, manner, clothing, and dances, are specified.

696. Washington Writers' Project. *Washington: A Guide to the Evergreen State.* Portland: Binfords and Mort, 1941. xxx, 687 pages. Bibliography, index. Photographs of women: Coast Indians weaving baskets, wife of farm immigrant, women and children clearing land, statue of Pioneer Mother, Japanese girls dancing on July 4th, WPA Nursery School, wrapping and packing apples in Yakima plant, forest homestead.

The text includes brief reference to individual women—Seattle Mayor Bertha Landes; missionary Narcissa Whitman; writers Mary Crawford Frazier and Ella Higginson; Moore Theater's impresario Cecilia Schultz; Nellie C. Cornish and her school for the arts; Mlle. Lucy Jeal's 1871 circus with "lady gymnasts"; Mrs. M.A. Synder's 1878 music class's performance of the juvenile opera "Little Red Riding Hood"; and Maggie Webb, the "colored nightingale" performing with the Kentucky Jubilee Singers in 1881. There is also reference to women suffragists, women painters of Washington, Ruth School for Girls, Red Cross Gray Ladies, and the founders of Seattle's Children's Orthopedic Hospital in 1907.

697. Watkins, Marilyn P. "Political Activism and Community-Building Among Alliance and Grange Women in Western Washington, 1892-1925," *Agricultural History* 67 (Spring 1993): 197-213. Notes.

Drawing from her doctoral dissertation on Lewis County (University of Michigan, 1991), Watkins examines a community midway between Seattle, Washington, and Portland, Oregon. She asserts that women in Lewis County transcended the limitations on activities generally present in a rural setting and gained a strong political voice. They balanced their traditional activities of providing food and entertainment for social functions by supporting woman suffrage and meeting with the men instead of separately. The author's sources include the *People's Advocate*, a newspaper of the Farmers' Alliance and Populist Party, and records of Grange organizations in which men and women were active: Alpha, Cougar Flat, Ethel, Hope, Silver Creek, and St. Urban Granges.

698. West, Leoti L. *The Wide Northwest: As Seen By A Pioneer Teacher*. Spokane: Shaw and Borden Company, 1927. viii, 286 pages.

Leoti West grew up in Illinois, but built a thirty-four-year teaching career (1877-1931) in Dubuque, Iowa, and Colfax and Walla Walla, Washington. Her book is full of her aspirations and encounters during her career as a highly motivated educator.

699. Western Writers of America. *The Women Who Made the West*. Garden City: Doubleday and Company, 1980. xi, 252 pages. Bibliography, index.

Twenty-one women members of the Western Writers of America wrote eighteen biographies on nineteenth-century figures, including: "Mother Joseph" by Lucile Mc Donald (pp. 120-129) and "From Rags to Riches" on May Arkwright Hutton by Roberta Cheney (pp. 220-239). The brevity of each makes these biographies quite general.

700. White, Sid, and S.E. Solberg, eds. *Peoples of Washington: Perspectives on Cultural Diversity*. Pullman: Washington State University Press, 1989. ix, 261 pages. Notes, bibliography. Photographs of Nettie J. Asberry, Chehalis Tribe basketmaker Hazel Pete with daughter and granddaughter, Makah women drumming, four generations baking, Senora Irene Casteneda, Lorena Seelatsee, and Mrs. Lippie Marks.

Women are mentioned throughout the text, which includes five essays: "Washington's Native American Communities" by Clifford E. Trafzer, "Washington's European American Communities" by Richard D. Scheuerman, "Washington's African American Communities" by Esther Hall Mumford, "Washington's Asian/Pacific American Communities" by Gail M. Nomura, and "Washington's Hispano American Communities" by Carlos B. Gil.

701. Whitfield, William, ed. *History of Snohomish County, Washington*. 2 vols. Chicago: Pioneer Historical Publishing Company, 1926. Vol. I: 838 pages, index. Vol. 2: 784 pages.

This is a two-volume history of Everett and Snohomish County from the sixteenth century until the mid-1920s. Vol. 1 offers a general history with the following chapters featuring the activities of women: Part 3, Chap. 3 ("Snohomish Institutions"); part 4, chap. 8 ("Arlington"); and part 7, chap. 2 ("County Schools"). Vol. 2 is comprised of biographies. Women whose biographies are featured include: Lydia T. Bedell, farmer; Sarah Cooke, first woman settler in the county; Marion E. Davis, osteopathic physician; Esther E. Ford, educator; Mathilda Reinstedt, dairy farmer; Josie K. Smith, farmer; Sarah Q. Smith, early settler; and Nora F. Wood, businesswoman who owned and operated a hotel.

702. Whitlow, Leonard A., and Catherine Cooper Whitlow, eds. "My Life as a Homesteader: Fannie Adams Cooper." *Oregon Historical Quarterly* 82 (Spring 1981): 65-84. Photograph of Fannie Adams Cooper.

This is an autobiographical account of Fannie Adams Cooper, born in 1867 in Pennsylvania. She traveled to the Northwest to homestead from 1889-1907. She and her husband lived in Tacoma, Washington, and Turner, Hood River, Junction City, Eugene, Grants Pass, Salem, Holley, and Fisher, Oregon. Her reminiscences provide details about neighbors, the weather, farm labor, and child-raising.

703. Whitman, Narcissa Prentiss. *My Journal, 1836*. Ed. Lawrence Dodd. Fairfield, Washington: Ye Galleon Press, 1982. 74 pages. Notes, index. Images of Northwest landscape and one page of Narcissa Whitman's journal.

This reprints the journal Narcissa Whitman kept from February 1836 to December 1836 as she travelled overland from New York state to the Pacific Northwest to establish a mission in Waiilatpu, now known as Walla Walla, Washington. The record provides details about the weather, food, services by Native Americans, and the school at Fort Vancouver.

704. ———. *The Letters of Narcissa Whitman.* Fairfield, Washington: Ye Galleon Press, 1986. 245 pages. Index. Illustration of Narcissa Whitman.

In the collection of letters offered here, Narcissa Whitman comments on her journey, the establishment of a Protestant mission, weather, the people she met, domestic duties, child-raising, and Bible study. Included also is the letter Henry Spalding wrote to her parents on April 6, 1848, informing them of her death on November 29, 1847.

705. Whitney, Marci. *Notable Women.* Tacoma: *Tacoma News Tribune,* 1977. iv, 59 pages. Index. Twenty-nine photographs.

Here are 25 short portraits of Northwest women in public roles. Among them are Lydia Ann Wright Bonney, teacher; Dr. Annie F. Reynolds; Myrtle Van Bevers, policewoman, captain, 1920; Dr. Nena Jolidon Croake, legislator; Alma Wagen, mountain guide; Ella Ryan, African American journalist; Mrs. H.N. Steele, hotel owner; Thea Foss of the Foss Launch and Tug Company, Inc.; Emma Smith DeVoe, president of the Washington Equal Suffrage Association; Mrs. Bertha Snell, first woman to be admitted to the Washington State Bar in 1899; Lillian McDonald, hospital manager; Blanche Funk Miller, Justice of the Peace.

706. Willard, Frances E., and Mary A. Livermore, eds. *A Woman of the Century: Fourteen Hundred Seventy Biographical Sketches Accompanied by Portraits of Leading American Women in All Walks of Life.* Detroit: Gale Research Company, 1893. Reprint, 1967. 812 pages. Portraits of nearly every woman mentioned.

Entries range from a paragraph to a page and provide valuable biographical information about each woman. Northwest women include Abigail Scott Duniway, Ella Higginson, and Emma Smith DeVoe.

707. Williams, Irena Dunn. *Reminiscences of Early Days in Eugene and Lane County, Oregon.* Eugene: Shelton-Turnbull-Fuller Co., 1941. 44 pages.

Williams relates family stories about her parents crossing the plains and settling and marrying in Eugene, Oregon. She recalls transportation and communications hardships as well as the problem of fields neglected after the California gold rush lured workers south. The roles of women as cooks, seamstresses, washers, spinners of wool, and family moral supporters are described. The author covers the main events of her youth in the 1860s, including floods, her encounters with Native Americans, her father's many businesses, her experiences in school and at the University of Oregon, the physicians who treated her family, the Pony Express, and the onset of the Civil War.

708. Williams, Jacqueline. *Wagon Wheel Kitchens: Food on the Oregon Trail.* Lawrence: University of Kansas Press, 1993. xxvi, 222 pages. Notes, bibliography, index. Seventeen photographs of cooking tools on the trail, such as rolling pins, cast-iron muffin tins, coffee grinder, interior of covered wagon, dough-mixing and kneading machine.

Williams has co-authored popular books on nutrition in modern America, but here she has lent her skills to examining pioneer diaries, letters, newspaper ads, and nineteenth-century cookbooks to consider the diet of pioneers on the overland trail. She discusses the 1840s guidebooks that advised on packing for the overland experience, details the essential equipment, catalogs ingredients the pioneers packed, and explains how women prepared beans, bacon, hard tack, and biscuits and acquired fresh foods that fortified the travelers.

709. Wilson, Joan Hoff, and Lynn Bonfield Donovan. "Women's History of West Coast Archival and Manuscript Sources." *California Historical Quarterly* Part 1 (Spring 1976): 74-83; Part 2 (Summer 1976): 170-185. Fourteen photographs of women from the late nineteenth and early twentieth centuries.

This is an annotated list of women's history sources in archives in California, Oregon, Washington, and British Columbia. The entries list the woman's or the organization's name, followed by the vital dates and profession or achievement. Following this is a description of the materials available to the researcher, the dates covered, and the amount of material. Forty-one institutions are surveyed, thirty in California, two in Oregon, five in Washington, and two in British Columbia. They include holdings in public and private universities, state archives and libraries, historical societies and private organizations and western branches of the federal archives. This study has now been superseded by Andrea Hinding, *Women's History Sources.*

710. Wilson, Maud. "Use of Time by Oregon Farm Homemakers." *Oregon Agricultural College Bulletin* 256 (November 1929). 71 pages. Notes, bibliography. Thirteen photographs of the Agricultural Experiment Station at Oregon State Agricultural College at Corvallis, Oregon.

Here is a survey of 513 women (288 farm homemakers, 71 non-farm country women, and 154 non-country and non-farming women), who worked an average of 63.7 hours/week. They spent 81 percent of their time on household tasks, 18 percent on farm work, and one percent on other tasks. Forty-three percent had no modern plumbing and electricity. Wilson considers their use of time and the factors that affect its distribution, including the presence of children, the age of the children, seasonal demands such as Christmas and midsummer, and whether or not the household was on a farm.

711. Wilson, Otto. *Fifty Years' Work with Girls, 1883-1933: A Story of the Florence Crittendon Homes.* Alexandria, Virginia: National Florence Crittendon Mission, 1933. 513 pages. Index. Photographs of Portland and Seattle missions.

The first Florence Crittendon Home to rescue outcast women and girls was founded in New York City in 1883, near houses of prostitution. This work studies the origins of the national network of maternity homes for unwed mothers and provides a history of each home, alphabetized by city. For each is listed the name and address of the facility, its capacity for women and babies, the number served in 1932, expenses and receipts, real estate value, invested funds, and officers. In Portland, Oregon, the E. Henry Wemme White Shield Home was at 955 East Glisan Street, named to honor the benefactor who provided the estate the mission occupied. The Portland mission had formerly been associated with the Portland Women's Christian Temperance Union, for the WCTU opened the institution in 1887 as the Industrial Home. Unable to afford its maintenance, the Oregon WCTU took it over. In 1889, it was reorganized as the Women's Refuge Home for Fallen Women and received financial support from the National WCTU. At that time, it embraced the Crittendon affiliation. Staff and improved sites are considered. The mission served the most young women in the years right after World War I.

In Seattle, Washington, the Florence Crittendon Home was located at 9236 Renton Avenue. It was founded in the 1890s by Mr. Crittendon. The state legislature, Seattle Community Fund, and Plymouth Congregational Church provided funding and Dr. Harriet J. Clark offered free medical services. A reorganization in the 1930s increased the capacity to serve women and invited auxiliaries of physicians' wives and YWCA members at the University of Washington to offer support. Lady Willie Forbus, the first woman attorney in Seattle, donated free legal advice.

In Spokane, Crittendon's 1899 speech inspired the First Methodist Episcopal Church to organize a Florence Crittendon Circle with sixty members. Mr. and Mrs. George W. Odell donated five lots at Ross Park to the new facility. Churches, Masons, Elks, The Ancient Order of Woodmen, Ladies Aid Society, and Christian Chinese raised money to build a structure on Crescent Avenus. It was destroyed by fire and the mission rebuilt at 707 N. Cedar Street.

712. Winsted, Jenifer P. "Tripping on the Light Fantastic Toe: Popular Dance of Early Portland, Oregon, 1800-1864." In *American Popular Entertainment: Papers and Proceedings of the Conference on the History of American Popular Entertainment*, ed. Myron Matlaw, pp. 231-240. Westport, Connecticut: Greenwood Press, 1979. Notes. Photograph of Lotta Crabtree.

The essay enumerates traveling performers who visited Portland, including Caroline Chapman (1857-60), Susan Robinson (1860), Lotta Crabtree (1855 and 1861), and dance hall waiter girls from San Francisco. Lively quotations are drawn from the local newspaper, *The Oregonian.*

713. Wittenmyer, Mrs. Annie. *History of the Women's Temperance Crusade.* Philadelphia: Women's Christian Temperance Union, 1878. 781 pages. Photographs of national leaders of the organization.

While no material about the Washington State Women's Christian Temperance Union appears in this volume, pages 699-715 are devoted to Oregon members. In 1874, several Prohibitionist women demonstrated against the Web Foot Saloon, praying and singing hymns outside to discourage drinking in the establishment. The chief of police arrested the women for inspiring a disturbance by an angry crowd. Court testimony is quoted here.

714. Woloch, Nancy. *Muller v. Oregon: A Brief History with Documents.* Boston: St. Martin's Press, 1996. xiii, 206 pages. Notes, bibliography, index. Photographs of reformers, including Curt Muller at his laundry with women employees.

In 1908, the Supreme Court unanimously upheld an Oregon law that set a ten-hour limit to the workday of women in factories and laundries. This decision set a key precedent for single-sex protective laws, which prevailed until the 1970s. This history of the case includes fourteen pertinent documents, from 1895 to 1941.

715. Wood, Elizabeth. "Journal of a Trip to Oregon, 1851." *Oregon Historical Society Quarterly* 27 (1926): 192-203.

These journal entries, from June to September 1851, cover Elizabeth Wood's pioneer journey between Wyoming and Oregon. The terrain, physical hardships, and Native Americans are the chief topics covered. In addition, Wood discusses purchasing goods in the East and selling them to Native Americans at exorbitant prices. For example, a faded dress, purchased new at ten cents a yard in Peoria, sold to a Native American for $3.50. She also alludes to constant theft by Native Americans.

716. Wright, Frances Valentine, ed. *Who's Who Among Pacific Northwest Authors.* Missoula: University of Montana Press, 1970. 105 pages. Index.

This book is divided into four sections: Idaho, Montana, Washington, and Oregon. Each section contains a list of authors from that state and provides a sketch of their lives, affiliations, and their work. For Oregon, fourteen women authors are listed. For Washington, forty-one women authors are listed.

717. Wright, Mary C. "Economic Development and Native American Women in the Early Nineteenth Century." *American Quarterly* 33 (Winter 1981): 525-536. Notes.

Native American women assisted in the success of fur trading in the Pacific Northwest in the 1830s and 1840s, serving as liaisons between the white and Native American cultures. On the Pacific seaboard, Chinook, Clatsop, and Chehelis women traded, gathered food, and manufactured crafts; they were customers, employees, mediators, prostitutes, and wives.

718. Writers' Program of the Work Projects Administration in the State of Oregon. *Oregon, End of the Trail.* American Guide Series. Portland: Binfords and Mort, 1940. xxxii, 549 pages. Index. Photograph of Basque Girls in Malheur County.

Women are mentioned in discussions of nursing, social services, Girl Scouts, Campfire Girls, YWCA, Oregon writers, and female actors on tour. Saidie Orr Dunbar is credited for her role as executive secretary of the Oregon Tuberculosis Association, Albertina Kerr for her Nursery Home, and Doris Smith as director of the Portland Labor College.

719. Yasui, Barbara. "The Nikkei in Oregon, 1834-1940." *Oregon Historical Quarterly* 76 (September 1975): 225-258. Notes. Photographs of Miyo Iwakoshi and Mrs. Shintaro Takaki and children; Japanese work camp in 1920 near Hood River; queen and princesses on 1929 Rose Festival float in Portland; evacuees of internment at livestock exposition.

This history of Japanese laborers from 1834-1940 deals mainly with working conditions, discrimination, churches, and community organizations in a general way, without focusing on women. However, the text mentions the Buddhist Women's Organization in Portland during the early twentieth century and discusses the rise in picture brides between 1910 and 1920.

720. Young, Nellie May. *An Oregon Idyll.* Glendale, California: The Arthur Clark Company, 1961. 111 pages. Bibliography. Photograph of Young family home in Pennsylvania and Presbyterian Churches in Gervais and Pleasant Grove, Oregon.

A foreword by Clifford M. Drury provides a biography of Janette Lewis Young, who accompanied her husband, the Rev. William Stewart Young, a Presbyterian minister, from Pennsylvania to Oregon in 1883. They lived in Oregon for a year and a half before she got sick, sought treatment in California, and returned to Oregon to die at the age of twenty-nine in 1887. Her account details the financial success of the Literary and Basket Sociable, musical and literary programs, housework, visiting and preaching with her husband, and provides observations on her spouse's duties.

721. Zimmerman, Barbara B., and Vernon Carstensen, eds. "Pioneer Woman in Southwestern Washington Territory." *Pacific Northwest Quarterly* 67 (October 1976): 137-150. Notes. One drawing, three photographic portraits of McFarland family members.

When the United States entered World War II, Northwest women filled jobs vacated by the men who joined the service. This photograph was taken by Howard Clifford in 1941.
(#11475, Special Collections, University of Washington Libraries)

These are reminiscences of Susanna Maria Ede, pioneer woman in the Grays Harbor, Copalis Beach, and Chehalis River areas in the 1870s and early 1880s. A two-page summary and analysis by the editors is provided. The entries cover domestic economy, Native Americans, medicine, bear stories, and other aspects of pioneer life. The memoirs reflect Mrs. Ede's intelligence and resourcefulness.

722. Ziontz, Lenore. "George and Isabelle Bush: Washington's First Family." *Pacific Northwest Forum* 7 (Summer-Fall 1982): 39-56. Notes.

Here is a detailed description of the farm and family life in Washington Territory of Isabella James, a Tennessee Baptist of German American extraction, and her African American husband George Washington Bush. The work of all the family members and their neighbors is explored.

Well before the advent of the modern women's rights movement asserting the ability of women to accomplish all varieties of work, Northwest women performed any job that needed to be done.
(#2328, Special Collections, University of Washington Libraries)

Northwest women have played an important part in organizing laborers into unions. This story is documented by historians Dana Frank and Maureen Greenwald.
(#17204, Special Collections, University of Washington Libraries)

ACKNOWLEDGMENTS

I owe considerable thanks to numerous University of Washington and Central Washington University undergraduate and graduate students who assisted me in the retrieval of this material, most notably Robert Topmiller. The interlibrary loan staffs at both institutions performed valiant service, with special vigor from Becky Smith at Central Washington University. The Ford Foundation, through the Northwest Center for Research on Women, provided early funding for typing, and Faculty Research Development Funds at Central Washington University facilitated the completion of this project.

The task of canning food has been performed by women at home, preserving their garden produce, and women in industry, preparing farm yields for market.
(#14738, Special Collections, University of Washington Libraries)

INDEX

Note: The numbers cited refer to bibliography entries.

Fullerton, Fay, 400
funerals, 433
Funnemark, Birgitte, 10
Funnemark, Christine, 10
fur traders, 359, 429, 441, 447, 544, 570, 583, 595, 615, 683, 684
fur trappers, 49, 62, 199, 201, 224, 238, 547, 602, 622, 684

Gabriela Silang Lodge, 167
Gaines, Margaret B. Wands, 401
Gale, Elizabeth Maria, 43
Gallagher, Sarah Jane, 96
Gallina Club, 415
Gamelin, Emily Tavernier, 372
Garden Club, Burlington, WA, 335
Garden Clubs, 373, 415
Gardener Garden Club, 373
Garfield County, WA, 458
garment workers, 23, 264
gas station attendants, 437
Gavin, Jessie M., M.D., 425
Gay, Theresa, 77
Gayton, Louise, 507
Gayton, Willetta Riddle, 508
Geer, Elizabeth Dixon Smith, 535, 562
Genealogical Society, Ellensburg, WA, 415
genealogists, 429
ghosts, 429
Gifford, Mae E., 88
Gil, Carlos B., 700
Gilbert, Adelaide Sutton, 284, 311, 315
Gilbreath, Margaret, 458
Gill, Frances, 562
Gill, Laura Francis, 339
Gillespie, Emma Wilson, 204
Gilliam, Martha, 446
Gilman, Charlotte Perkins, 398
Gingrich Family, 132
Girl Scouts, 22, 23, 282, 536, 718
Girls Rodeo Association, 390
Girls' Day, 664
girls, 9, 55, 79, 100, 111, 120, 132, 150, 163, 164, 223, 241, 233, 254, 325, 387, 391, 414, 437, 440, 446, 526, 536, 576, 595, 629, 638, 646, 664, 672, 718
Glantz, Annutta, 2
Glass, Cheryl, 507
Gleason, Caroline. *See* Sister Miriam Theresa Gleason
Glenn, Nancy Cordelia, 343
Goddell, Anna Maria, 343
Goffin, Marie, 339
Gold, Patricia Courtney, 605
Goldendale, WA, 363
Goldman, Emma, 276, 436
Goldmark, Josephine C., 270
Goltra, Elizabaeth, 58
Goodman, Rose Loewenberg, 671
Goodwill Industries, Tacoma, WA, 95
Goodwillie, Jeannie, 461
Goodwin, Alice K., 592
Goose-Dance, 433
Gordon, Mrs. Burgess Lee, 274
Gotcher, Emma, 270
Gotshell, Frances E., 562
Gottstein, Rose Morganstern, 462
government, 25, 427, 507, 544, 583, 588, 596, 648, 660, 664
Grace Presbyterian Church, 189
Grace Seminary, Centralia, WA, 40

Grady, Irene J., 373
Graham, Elizabaeth, 131
Graham, Florence, 665
Graham, Martha, 166
Graham, Susie Mercer, 35
Grand Army of the Republic, Auxiliary of, 592
Grand Laundry, 270
Grand Mound, Washington Territory, 343
Granges, 202, 285, 342, 369, 445, 568, 697
Grant County, OR, 229, 269
Grant County, WA, 678
Grant, Margaret N., 592
Grants Pass, OR, 88, 702
Gray, Clara Smiley, 252
Gray, Katherine, 184
Gray, Mary Augusta Dix, 77, 155, 204, 208, 211
Gray, Mary, 560
Gray, Mrs. George H., 365
Gray, Mrs. J. H. D., 131
Gray, Mrs. William H., 444, 489
Gray, Mrs.W. H., 210, 277
Gray, Sara Ann Moore, 43
Gray, Virginia, 444
Grays Harbor, WA, 721
Great Depression, 80, 552
Great Northern Railroad, 255, 256
Green Valley, WA, 316
Green, Congresswoman Edith, 100, 165, 201
Green, Laura, 437
Green, Mrs. B. Vonder, 203
Greene, Mabel, 678
Greenwich Village, NY, 187, 276
Greve, Alice Wheeler, 339
Griswold, Zula, 599
grocers, 21
Grose, Sarah, 509
Grumbach, Doris, 471
Guerin, Charlotte, 203
Gunther, Erna, 335, 437
Guthridge, Nelle E., 95
Guttenberg, Emma, 54
gymnastics, 696

Haber, Sybil, 21
Hadeson, Sarah Fisher, 562
Hadley, Amelia Hammond, 343
Hahn, Anna, 369
Haight, Mary B., 67, 121
Haines, Letitia, 633
Haines, Susan, 340
hairdressers, 21, 174
Hall, Eudora, 154
Hall, Evelyn H., 312
Hall, Hazel, 676
Hall, Isaac, 154
Hall, Jessie, 665
Hall, Martha, 203
Hall, Mary Virginia Bell, 195
Hall, Theo, 224
Halstead, Sadie, 665
Hamm, Mrs., 519
Hampton, Mrs., 343
handicaps, 177
Hanford, Abbie J., 292
Hanford, Mrs. A.J., 40
Hanna, Esther Belle, 14
Hansberry, Anna, 343
Hansee, Martha L., 278, 337

Mormons, 70, 78, 341
Morris, Catherine ("Kate") Thomas, 445
Morris, Clara, 244
Morris, Clydene Lauretta, 558
Morris, Kate, 444
Morris, Mrs. Enoch P., 365
Morrison, Catherine, 363
Morse, Maryette, 547
morticians, 429
Moses, Agnes, 629
Mother Coron, 372
Mother Johanna Zumstein, 610
Mother Joseph (Esther Pariseau), 22, 72, 85, 107, 111,
    324, 372, 399, 424, 437, 455, 464, 527, 544, 606, 610,
    644, 699, 693
Mother Joseph of the Sacred Heart, 372
Mother Katherine Drexel, 610
Mother M. de Chantal, 109
Mother M. Thomasina, 109
Mother of Lynden, 592
Mother Ryther Home, 22
Mother Ryther, 133, 488, 575. *See also* Ryther
Mother's Club of Ellensburg, WA, 415
Mother's Club, 592
Mother's Congress, 457
Mother's Magazine, 208
Mount Adams, WA, 422
Mount Angel, OR, 335
Mount Baker, OR, 646
Mount Emily, OR, 459
Mount Fanny, OR, 459
Mount Hood, WA, 343, 571
Mount Rainier, WA, 80, 422, 512
mountain climbers, 80, 159, 453
mountain guides, 705
Mourning Dove, 491, 692
mourning, 174
Mowell, Mrs., 519
Moynihan, Ruth Barnes, 656
Mozart Club, 227
Mt. Zion Baptist Church, 189
Muir, Mary L., 599
Mull, Mrs. S. J., 337
Muller v. Oregon, 271
Muller, Curt, 270, 714
Multnomah County, OR, 201
Multnomah Falls, OR, 599
Mumford, Esther Hall, 700
Mumford, Mrs. C.W., 277
Munsell, Patrice, 437
Munson, Sarah Kimball, 118
Murchard, Kate Hottois, 151
murders, 600
Murphy, Sona, 84
muscular dystrophy, 177
Museum of History and Industry, Seattle, WA, 22, 320, 512
Music Clubs, Washington State Federation of, 488
music, 21, 76, 116, 166, 174, 188, 227, 233, 243, 264,
    278, 312, 335, 390, 453, 483, 488, 509, 530, 538, 547,
    562, 592, 599, 619, 625, 650, 713, 720
Musical Club of Portland, OR, 170
Myers, Annice Jeffreys, M.D., 232
Myers, Barbara, 190
Myong-Soon, 659

NAACP (National Association for the Advancement of
    Colored People), 599
Naches Pass, 272

National Afro-American Council, 509
National American Woman Suffrage Association, 232,
    661, 663
National Apple Show, 224
National Association of Colored Women's Clubs, 184
National Consumer's League, 270, 271, 514, 599
National Council of Jewish Women, 149, 197, 204, 452, 673
National Defense Education Act, 201
National Education Association for Women, 551
National League for Woman's Service, 149
National League of American Pen Women, 497
National Organization of Women, 335
National Youth Administration, 172
Native Americans
    Athapascan, 602; Blackfoot, 150, 602; Cayuse,
    174, 222, 290, 356, 374, 378, 576, 595; Chehalis,
    174, 595, 618, 700, 717; Cherokee, 259; Chilkat,
    61; Chimakum, 174; Chinook, 33, 89, 148, 145,
    174, 219, 222, 331, 370, 534, 549, 559, 562, 570,
    603, 618, 681, 717; Chitko, 595; Clackamas, 370;
    Clallam, 174; Clatsop, 62, 89, 289, 618, 717; Coeur
    d'Alene, 91, 433, 576, 666; Columbia Plateau, 595;
    Colville, 4, 174, 210, 254, 437, 491, 574;
    Comanche, 130; Coos, 62, 370; Cowlitz, 174, 289,
    437, 577, 605, 681; Cree, 359; Dakota, 622;
    Digger, 43; Duwamish, 681; Flathead, 50, 91, 237,
    602, 618, 622, 666; Gros Ventres, 433; Iowa, 50,
    238, 441, 543; Kalapuya, 62; Kalispel, 174;
    Kittitas, 576; Klamath, 43, 174, 595, 599; Klickitat,
    43, 174, 289, 323, 422, 565, 576, 605, 681;
    Kutenai, 595; Lake, 174; Lower Chinook, 577;
    Lummi, 174, 646; Makah, 437, 595, 681, 700;
    Malheur, 260, 346; Methow, 174, 595; Modoc,
    259, 298, 485, 622; Molale, 576; Nehalem, 595;
    Nespilim, 174; Nez Perce, 174, 212, 437, 460, 576,
    603, 618, 628, 655; Nisqually, 307; Nooksack, 174;
    Nootka, 303; Northwest Coast, 218, 300, 303, 370,
    696; Okanagan, 218; Okanogan, 150, 174, 219,
    365, 437, 491, 576, 618, 666; Osage, 259; Palus,
    576; Paiute, 98, 117, 159, 222, 260, 346, 441, 585,
    586, 595, 622; Plateau, 3, 4, 174, 290; Puget
    Sound, 174; Puyallup, 254; Quilliute, 174, 533;
    Quinault, 174, 533, 681; Rogue River, 203, 595,
    601; Sahaptin, 603; Salishan, 89, 174; Samish,
    174; Sanetch, 174; Sanpoel, 174, 576; Semiahoo,
    174; Shasta, 174; Shoshone, 174, 326, 352, 580;
    Sinkaietk, 153; Sioux, 50; Sitetz, 62; Skagit, 595;
    Skokomish, 240; Snohomish, 307; Snoqualmie,
    307; Songish, 174; South Okanogan, 153; Spo-
    kane, 174, 215, 216, 224, 234, 348, 576, 618, 666;
    Suquamish, 493; Tenino, 576; Tillamook, 90, 370;
    Tlingit, 301, 305; Tolowa, 62, 174; Tututni, 62,
    174; Twana, 174; Umatilla, 174, 204, 289, 290,
    392, 576, 603; Upper Chinook, 289; Upper Rogue
    River, 601; Walla Walla, 174; Warm Springs, 159;
    Wasco, 159, 289, 604, 605; Wenatchee, 174;
    Willapa, 174; Wishram, 174, 289, 437, 604;
    Yakama, 174, 219, 260, 283, 323, 381, 392, 432,
    457, 484, 576, 603, 605, 620
Native Americans, 3, 9, 12, 23, 27, 31, 34, 35, 41, 43, 49,
    54, 55, 61, 77, 173, 174, 175, 178, 181, 190, 200, 201,
    204, 207, 211, 215, 216, 223, 226, 228, 246, 259, 260,
    269, 274, 286, 289, 292, 302, 303, 307, 308, 317, 318,
    331, 336, 337, 341, 346, 357, 366, 367, 373, 375, 387,
    417, 422, 429, 433, 446, 447, 448, 453, 468, 470, 491,
    493, 504, 511, 512, 534, 537, 540, 541, 544, 547, 562,
    564, 574
Native Daughters of Oregon, 361

Reese, William F., 595
Reeves, Secretary of State Belle, 488
Reinstedt, Mathilda, 701
religion, 35, 107, 215, 239, 292, 434
Republican Party, 497
Rescue Home, 234
reservations, 62, 484, 491, 565, 574, 610, 620
rest homes, 464
restaurants, 508, 509, 633
Revels, Senator Hiram, 21
Reynolds, Annie F., M.D., 705
Reynolds, Mabel M., 513
Rhinehart Theater, 244
Rho Chapter, Alpha Chi Omega, 176
Richard, Maria E.A., 592
Richard, Mary, 470
Richards, Rev., 691
Richmond, America, 500
Richmond, Georgia, 547
Richmond, Rev. John P., 500
Riddle, Frank, 485
Riddle, Mary, 343
Ridgeway, Ruth
Ripley, Frances B., M.D., 592
Risegari, Mrs. Silvio, 488
Rivers, Louisa Margaret, 525
Robert Newell House, 637
Roberts, Charlotte, 31
Roberts, Judge Betty Cantrell, 521
Roberts, Maria, 230
Roberts, Mrs. Charles E., 47, 592
Roberts, Mrs. E.P., 31
Roberts, Mrs. Joseph, 365
Robinson, Mrs. William J., 444
Rock, Annie, 595
Rock Creek, WA, 379
Rock Woman, 174
Rockwell, Kathleen Eloisa, 454
Rodeo City Grandmother's Club, 415
rodeos, 15, 390, 430, 654
Rodney, Mary B., 204
Roeder, Elizabeth Austin, 67, 121, 230, 592
Rogers, Bess Conn, 225
Rollins, Josephine, 459
Roman Catholicism, 23, 34, 120, 219, 222, 238, 277,
    324, 361, 372, 467, 529, 574, 591, 595, 610, 612, 622,
    627, 683
Ronald, WA, 468
Roos, Helen, 665
Roosevelt, Eleanor, 678
Roosevelt, Franklin Delano, 271, 309
Roper Survey, 115
Rose Festival, Portland, OR, 21, 719
Rose, Patty, 369
Rosebud Study Club, 21
Roseburg, OR, 335
Rosie the Riveter, 403, 437
Roslyn, WA, 363, 468, 510
Ross, Mrs. A. J., 170
Ross Park, Spokane, WA, 711
Ross Park Twentieth Century Club, 234
Ross, Zola Helen, 465
Rotary Anns, 282
Roth, Lottie Roedy, 121
Royal, Mary Ann, 632
Royal Neighbors of America, 282
Ruddell, M.M. White, 668
Rudnas, Ellen, 547

Rudy, Ann B., 312
Rugg, Mary S., 363
Russell, Annie, 488
Russell, Bess, 195
Russell, Mary J., 195
Russian Revolution, 187, 205, 276
Russians, 2, 166
Ruth School for Girls, 696
Ryan, Ella, 21, 705
Ryan, Katherine M., 67, 121, 592
Rygg, Ida, 246
Ryther Child Center, 133
Ryther Foundling Home, 133
Ryther, Mae Bird, 133
Ryther, Olive H.S, 133

Sacajawea (Bird Woman), 19, 111, 120, 130, 135, 140,
    165, 169, 186, 190, 232, 274, 294, 298, 326, 351, 352,
    437, 371, 391, 408, 413, 441, 560, 562, 579, 582, 589,
    591, 622, 634, 661, 663, 669
Sacajawea State Park and Museum, Pasco, WA, 669
Sacred Heart Academy, Salem, OR, 472, 473
Sager, Catherine, 77, 118, 150, 213, 366, 564, 584, 598
Sager, Elizabeth, 213, 598
Sager family, 227
Sager, Henrietta, 598
Sager, Mathilda, 213, 598
sailors, 10
Salem, OR, 335, 353, 399, 465, 483, 560, 702
Salita, 318
Salomonsky, Verna Cook, 558
saloons, 572
Sam, Annie, 307
San Francisco Chronicle, 322
San Juan Islands, WA, 108, 162
Sanger, Margaret, 617
Sanitary Aid Society, 483
Sanitary Commission, Astoria, OR, 106
Sapotiwell, 31
Sasse, Mamie, 97
Sas-we-As, 363
Saunders, Emma Hunter, 508
sawmills, 547
Saxon, Elizabeth Lyle, 47
Saxon, WA, 47
Scandinavians, 84, 122, 327, 581
Scannell, Agnes V., 571
Schenck, Mrs. J.S., 444
Scheuerman, Richard D., 700
Schminck Memorial Museum, OR, 637
Schnebly, Mrs. Philip Henry, 558
school bus drivers, 429
schools, 7, 13, 21, 22, 23, 34, 43, 54, 60, 92, 94, 96, 97,
    100, 148, 151, 155, 159, 182, 183, 207, 220, 223, 227,
    230, 234, 240, 246, 256, 277, 278, 283, 287, 309, 324,
    328, 333, 342, 354, 363, 366, 372, 380, 383, 414, 424,
    434, 438, 451, 457, 458, 460, 464, 467, 468, 478, 487,
    498, 525, 540, 547, 553, 554, 606, 610, 644, 671, 701,
    703, 707, 718. *See also* names of particular schools
Schultz, Cecilia Augsburger, 116, 696
science, 87, 599
scientists, 429
Scott, Catherine, 343
Scott, Harriet, 343
Scott, Harvey Whitefield, 408
Scott, Madge, 665
Scott, Margaret, 343
sculptors, 172, 187, 488

Snell, Margaret Comstock, M.D., 425
Snelling, Helen Crowe, 488
Snohomish County, WA, 701
Snohomish (WA) General Hospital, 358
Snoqualmie (WA) Mill, 23
Snowden, WA, 572
Snyder, Anna M., 440
Snyder, Mrs. M.A., 696
social services, 22, 25, 100, 124, 529, 599, 613, 627, 671, 672, 673, 688, 711, 718
Socialism, 56, 114, 623
societies. *See* women's clubs and fraternal organizations
Society of Literary Explorers, Port Angeles, WA, 170
Sohappy, Julia Pimms, 603
Sojourner Truth Home, 189
Somerset, Susan Margaret, 77
songs, 8
Soon-Hi, 659
Soroptimist, 282
sororities, 176, 653
Sorosis, Spokane, WA, 170, 227, 234
Soule, Elizabeth, 278
South Kitsap, WA, 414
Southern Oregon College of Education, Ashland, OR, 245
Southwest Oregon General Hospital, 547
Soviet Union, 220, 657, 658
Spalding, Alice, 236
Spalding, Eliza Hart (Mrs. Henry Harmon), 33, 49, 102, 120, 155, 165, 208, 213, 226, 236, 237, 341, 371, 378, 428, 437, 463, 544, 560, 584, 615, 632, 634, 694
Spalding, Helen F., 204, 337
Spalding, Rev. H.H., 694, 704
Spanish-American War, 52
Sparks, Mrs. John G., 86
Spastic Aid Council, 561
Spector, Marion, M.D., 249
spirit dances, 646
spirit quests, 578
spiritualism, 154
Splawn, Margaret Cenia, 558
Spokane Art League, 227, 234
Spokane County, WA, 163, 678
Spokane Fair, 655
Spokane Falls, 454
Spokane Federated Art Center, 201
Spokane Kindergarten Association, 234
Spokane Sorosis, 227
Spokane, WA, 194, 227, 252, 284, 315, 324, 335, 350, 368, 416, 568, 572, 711
sports, 100
Springer, Viola, 343
Sprinn, 357
Sprouse, Barbara Barker, 521
Spurgeon, Elizabeth Sarah, 494
Squiemphen, C.R., 654
St. Andrew's Episcopal Church, 568
St. Cecilia Chorus, 488
St. Elizabeth Cathedral, 610
St. Elizabeth Hospital, 610
St. Frances Academy for Orphan Girls, 627
St. Francis Academy, OR, 361
St. Francis Cabrini, 610
St. Germain, Mary Ann Plomodon, 358
St. Helena Club of Chehalis, WA, 170
St. Helens, OR, 399
St. Louis, OR, 238

St. Mary's Academy in Portland, OR, 627
St. Mary's Home for Boys, 612
St. Mary's mission, 574
St. Mary's School for Girls of Portland, OR, 277
St. Peters Hospital, 519
St. Rose's Academy of Seattle, WA, 627
St. Urban (WA) Grange, 697
St. Xavier Episcopal Mission, Seattle, WA, 85
Stacy, Amy P.S., 357
Stanley, Mary E., 444
Stanton, Elizabeth Cady, 64
Stanton, Phoebe, 343
Stanway, Mabel M., 21
Stanwood, WA, 246
Stanwood (WA) Lumber Company, 246
Starcher, Mayor Laura J., 689
Stasek, Marguerite Tilden, 599
State Normal School at Ellensburg, WA, 363
statues, 72, 111, 135, 140, 169, 186, 190, 232, 244, 294, 298, 317, 324, 408, 414, 424, 560, 562, 579, 584, 606, 663, 669, 696
Stauff, Clara, 547
Stearns, Olive J. Bell, 195
Steele, Elizabeth, 633
Steele, Fannie Sperry, 430
Steele, Janet Elder, 357, 500
Steele, Mrs. H.N., 705
Steeves, Sarah Hunt, 77, 141
Steilacoom, WA, 17, 644
Steinem, Pauline, 85
Steinhoff, Anna, 13
Steinhoff, Mildred, 13
stenographers, 623
Stephens, Phoebe A., 337
Sterling, Dorothy, 335
Sterling, Elizabeth, 478
Sterling, Henrietta Sager. *See* Sager, Henrietta
Stevens County, WA, 94, 365
Stevens, Harriet F., 38
Stevenson, Delia, 488
Stewart, Agnes, 58, 649
Stewart, Helen Marnie, 251
Stewart, Helen, 450, 544
Stewart, Mary, 444
Stillaquamish River, WA, 246
Stimson, Emma, 172
Stimson, Mrs. Charles D., 116
Stine, Emma, 233
Stone, Anna, 488
store managers, 436
Storey, Mrs. M. E. (Bonney), 95
Storie, Anna, 554
Story, Amy P., 170
Stovel, Jean, 264
Stowe, Harriet D., 678
Strahorn, Carrie Adell, 77
Strait of Juan de Fuca, WA, 423
Strang, Zenie, 547
Strayer, Eleanor, 665
Strickland, Mabel Delong, 15, 430
string calendars, 432
strippers, 172
Strong, Anna Louise, 73, 194, 201, 220, 225, 264, 388, 431, 437, 469, 475, 522, 626, 636, 657, 658
Strong, Florence B., 225
Stryker, Mrs. H.M., 116
Stuart, Abbie H.H., 170
Stuart, Mrs. A.H.H., 59

unionization, 1
unions, 262, 263, 264, 265, 297, 437, 526
United Daughters of the Confederacy, 149
United States Army, 102, 117
United States Department of Indian Affairs, 130
United States Forest Service, 571
United States House of Representatives, 613
United States Maritime Commission, 403
United States War Veterans, 23
United States Women's Bureau, 287
University of Oregon, 148, 187, 244, 480, 497, 560, 625, 707
University of Oregon Board of Regents, 625
University of Oregon Medical School, 451
University of Puget Sound, Tacoma, WA, 255
University of Washington, 22, 23, 81, 82, 107, 152, 176, 249, 355, 531, 550, 596, 667, 680, 711
Upson Ranger Station, 552
Urban League, 93
Ursuli, Madame, 243
USSR, 522. *See also* Soviet Union

Van Amburg, Jessamine, 369
Van Bevers, Myrtle, 705
Van Fleet, Eliza Farnham, 558
Van Ogle, Louise, 116
Van Volkenberg, Ellen, 166, 245, 488
Vancouver, British Columbia, 368
Vancouver, WA, 72, 111, 335, 353, 403, 404, 406, 464, 478, 605, 609
Vasa Sewing Club, 23
Vassar College, 299
venereal diseases, 534
Venier, Louis, 543
Venture Club, 282
Veterans of Foreign Wars Ladies Auxiliary, 167
Victor, Frances Fuller, 119, 144, 145, 201, 204, 475, 481, 562, 695
Vigilant, 48
Vincent, Mary Ann Lambert, 373
Vinland Schoolhouse, 125
Viola Allen, 488
violence, domestic, 192, 545, 546
voluntary organizations. *See* clubs
Volunteer Park, Seattle, WA, 36
volunteers, 182. *See also* women's clubs
Voss, Aline, 438
vote. *See* woman suffrage

Wade, Adeliea, D., 170
Wagen, Alma, 705
wages, 20
Wahkiakum County, WA, 678
Waiilatpu, Washington Territory, 150, 208, 377, 564, 703
Waitress Union, Seattle, WA, 264
waitresses, 1, 246, 264, 265, 525
Waitresses Union, 1, 23, 297
Waitsburg, WA, 322, 676
Waldo, Anna Lee, 582
Walker, Abigail, 210
Walker, Mary Richardson (Mrs. Elkanah), 33, 94, 120, 148, 155, 156, 208, 209, 210, 211, 215, 216, 252, 335, 341, 348, 375, 387, 437, 453, 463, 544, 591
Walker, Rev. Elkanah, 356
Walla Walla County, WA, 285, 364, 458
Walla Walla, WA, 111, 118, 227, 335, 377, 511, 560, 669, 695, 698
Walla Walla (WA) Women's Reading Club, 335

Wallace, Luzana Brazelton, 644, 668
Waller, Rev., 691
Wallis, Ellen Jane Mark, 668
Walters, Mrs. Dennis A., 444
Walton, Ellen Pauline, 335
Walton, Mrs. Joshua S., 148
Wanamaker, Pearl, 383, 437
war brides, 167
War on Poverty, 201
Ward, Jean M., 253
Ward, Nancy, 259
Warhanik, Elizabeth, 488
Warm Springs Indian Reservation, OR, 654
Warm Springs, Miss 654
Warren, Eliza Spalding (Mrs. Henry), 40, 118, 212
Warren, Emma C., 277
Warren, Mary, 58
Warren, Minnie, 243
Wasco County, OR, 229
Washington Children's Home, Seattle, 36
Washington Commission for the Humanities, 80
Washington County, OR, 343
Washington Equal Suffrage Association, 22, 349, 705
Washington Library Association, 333
Washington, Olivia, 509
Washington Park, Portland, OR, 111, 560
Washington State Art Association, 113
Washington State Bar, 705
Washington State Federation of Women's Clubs Forest, 669
Washington State Theater, 74
Washington Territory, 382
Washington Woman Suffrage Association, 519
Washington Women's Heritage Project, 80, 112, 624
Washingtonians, 566
Wash-us-etan-way, 605
Watkinson, Maria Childs, 558
Watson, Mrs. James, 41
Watson, Nellie, 400
Watt, Roberta Frye, 520
Watts, Caroline E., 277
Watts, Elizabeth, 277
Waud, A.B., 499
Waul, Alfred R., 101
WCTU (Women's Christian Temperance Union), 7, 8, 21, 22, 36, 107, 127, 146, 201, 225, 267, 282, 335, 507, 509, 554, 555, 563, 575, 592, 632, 693, 711, 713. *See also* temperance
WCTU Farm Home, 693
Weathermen, Seattle, WA, 647
Weatherwax, Clara, 339
Weaver, Mrs. William, 46
weaving, 240, 577, 603, 618, 646, 666, 681
Web, Katie, 619
Webb, Maggie, 696
Webfoot Saloon, 144, 713
Webster, Mrs. John, 36
weddings, 148, 196, 437, 548, 629, 681
Wednesday Afternoon Literary Club, 234
Weed, Ada, hydropathic physician, 231
Weichman, Orrel, 84
Welfare League, 497
welfare. *See* social services
Well Baby Clinic, 671
Wells, Mary Ann, 35
Wells, Merle W., 371
Welty, Emma J., M.D., 425
Wenatchee, WA, 510

Women's Committee of the Council of National Defense, 149
Women's Cooperative Clubs, 264
Women's Defense League, 563
Women's Democratic Club, 282
Women's Exchange, 252
Women's Exponent, 70
Women's Fortnightly Club, 625
Women's Inn, Tacoma, WA, 357
Women's International League for Peace and Freedom, 335, 521, 563
Women's League of University of Washington, 278
Women's Legislative League of Washington, 563
Women's Mission Society of the Baptist Convention of the North Pacific Coast, 693
Women's Organization for National Prohibition Reform, 146
Women's Refugee Home for Fallen Women, 711
Women's Relief Corps, 340
women's rights, 104, 148, 201, 231, 268, 287, 350, 482, 541, 631
Women's Temperance Prayer League, 145
Women's Thursday Club, 415
Women's Trade Union League, 264, 270
Women's Union Label League, 526
Wood, Elizabeth, 343, 715
Wood, Marion A., 48
Wood, Nora F., 701
Woodcock, Gertrude, 249
Woodruff, Mary A., 322
Woodson, Irene, 507
Works Progress Administration. *See* WPA
World War I, 21, 51, 81, 82, 85, 122, 123, 149, 201, 205, 220, 262, 264, 309, 329, 342, 411, 412, 499, 593, 615, 623, 650, 682, 711
World War II, 20, 23, 45, 59, 84, 122, 182, 192, 220, 342, 403, 404, 406, 437, 440, 484, 493, 552, 615, 628, 638, 664
woven bags, 290
WPA (Works Progress Administration), 59, 74, 172, 510, 696
Wright, Annie, 500
Wright, Dolly, 400
Wright, Ellen M., 592
Wright, Elsia, 337
Wright, Frances V., 492
Wright, Jennie E., 170
Wright, Laura, 343
Wright, Lavina, 21
Wright, Lily, 400
Wright, Nettie, 595
writers. *See* authors
Wurdemann, Audrey May, 431, 488
Wyckoff, Ursula, 195

x-ray operators, 444

Yakama Indian Reservation, 620
Yakama Indian Tribal Council, 484
Yakima County, WA, 363, 457, 633, 678
Yakima Herald Republic, 369
Yakima Hotel, WA, 369
Yakima Valley Museum, WA, 369
Yakima, WA, 201, 227, 335, 369, 380, 432, 488, 510, 572, 696
Yallup, Martha Beulah Mann, 620
Yamhill County, OR, 155
Yasui, Masuo, 410

Yates, Alice Elizabeth, 552
Yates, Minnie H., 592
Yesler, Sarah (Mrs. Henry), 22, 61
Yes-to-Lah-Lemy, 457
Yoshida, Mrs., 493
Young Ladies Seminary, 227
Young, Janette Lewis, 720
Young, Margaret C., 592
Young People's Bible Institute, 592
Younger, Mary Meany, 105
YWCA (Young Women's Christian Association), 22, 23, 36, 79, 85, 100, 107, 149, 282, 329, 335, 357, 369, 484, 536, 571, 592, 711, 718
YWCA, Phyllis Wheatley Branch, 22

Zieber, Eugenia Shunk, 343
Zion Sewing Circle, 440
Zonta, 497